Influence is the only way to manage, lead, and get things done in today's organizations. *Influence Without Authority* is a hard-nosed, realistic, and, above all, practical guide to the new world of work.

Michael Silva
Coauthor of Creating Excellence

A great read from two very wise authors. The examples are bright, moving, and *real*. I cannot think of anyone in an organization from the CEO to the freshest management trainee who will not warm to *Influence Without Authority*. Most important, it makes the reader want to practice its wise advice. It is in the spur to action that the book most excels.

Allen Kluchman
CEO, Access Technology

In an era when speed and flexibility are critical, organizational members must learn how to manage beyond the bounds of their formal authority. With *Influence Without Authority*, we finally have a package of useful insights and action steps that help in making it happen. Without question, the book is needed; without a doubt, the book delivers on its promises!

Leonard Schlesinger
Harvard Business School

A readable and immensely useful book on how to create change and partnerships in contemporary organizations. This book will help any manager who wants to achieve his purposes in the "white knuckle decade" ahead.

Warren Bennis
Distinguished Professor of Business Administration
University of Southern California
Author of On Becoming a Leader

Through their widely read, influential books and articles, as well as superb hands-on consulting, the Cohen and Bradford team has helped countless managers improve their effectiveness by becoming better leaders. This dynamic duo combines insight about real world managers' everyday lives with intelligent, research-based advice to produce winning performance guides.

Rosabeth Moss Kanter
Professor, Harvard Business School
Author of When Giants Learn to Dance

This book deserves to be widely read and will certainly be useful to people at all levels in today's increasingly complex business organizations. Particularly helpful are the many case studies that provide valuable insights into the skillful use of influence, clearly demonstrating "the subtle art of getting things done."

Richard W. Kazmaier, Jr.
President, Kazmaier Associates, Inc.

This is a book whose time has come. *Influence Without Authority* is the name-of-the-game in this age of collegial organizations, joint-ventures, partnerships, and alliances. Bradford and Cohen understand this and offer practical, common-sense advice to those who would lead when they cannot command.

James P. Baughman
Manager—Corporate Management Development
GE Management Development Institute

Bradford and Cohen have done it again. In their last book, they argued convincingly for better leadership models. In this fine book, they recognize that anyone's responsibility always exceeds authority. They teach us how to cope effectively with that reality.

Robert H. Waterman, Jr.
Waterman & Company
Coauthor of In Search of Excellence
Author of The Renewal Factor

This book, like Machiavelli's *The Prince,* is an analytical and descriptive study of the various workings of power within the corporate managerial environment. Where others look at the functions and titles, these authors pursue their search for the behind-the-scene means of propulsion of events. Anyone with corporate experience or ambition will learn something from reading it.

Jean Montagu
Chairman of the Board
General Scanning Inc.

A complete training package on *Influence Without Authority* will be available from Organizational Dynamics, Inc., located in Burlington, Massachusetts (617) 272-8040.

INFLUENCE
WITHOUT
AUTHORITY

Allan R. Cohen

David L. Bradford

JOHN WILEY & SONS, INC.

New York • Chichester • Brisbane • Toronto • Singapore

ISBN   0-471-62268-0 (cloth)
ISBN   0-471-54894-4 (paper)

Printed in the United States of America
18 17 16 15

To our wives,

Joyce and Eva,

who, as our toughest and most supportive colleagues,
have taught us the essence of mutual influence
in strategic alliances.

Preface

Everyone wants to be more influential at work. There aren't many situations left where issuing orders gets desired results, especially with bosses and colleagues, but even with so-called subordinates. Most people wouldn't mind more influence at home either, with spouses, friends, siblings, parents, or children (especially teenagers!). Thus, we welcome you to the results of the longest-running "research project" in the work world. We have each been trying to understand influence for all of our lives—a combined total of over 100 years—and we suspect that you too have been a life-long student of this vital subject.

Much of what we have found has grown out of our work with managers and organizations who wanted to become more effective. The workshops and consultations that led to writing our previous book, *Managing for Excellence,* and developing a leadership training package from it, confronted us time and again with influence as an issue. We were teaching managers to be less heroic by sharing responsibility with subordinates, yet the more they liked our ideas, the more they worried about how to get their bosses and associates to accept and support a new way of leading.

In response, we created a seminar called "Managing Superiors and Peers," which we ran through National Training Laboratories (NTL). There we began to draw on the social science literature, our own observations, and a variety of life experiences that shaped our thinking. This book shares what we learned about how to achieve your goals while helping others achieve theirs. In a book on influence, it seems only fair that we mention some of what has personally influenced our thinking at earlier stages of our lives.

Allan Cohen, grew up in a family business where his parents, aunt and uncle, brothers, and cousins all worked at times. His father's brother, Uncle Harry, had a hot temper and often responded to Allan's suggestions or demands by "firing" him or screaming at him to "get out." This proved a wonderful crucible for practicing standing one's ground while seeking ways to be heard.

One day, Allan's father—with a brother's instinct for how to nudge his brother off-balance—provided a lasting lesson on the expectation of reciprocity in relationships. He proposed "a little joke" on Uncle Harry, who had invited the family to a special pre-work pancake breakfast at his house. The proposal was that after eating, they all withhold comments of any kind about the food—positive or negative. When the feast ended, there was dead silence. Uncle Harry began to make excuses about his cooking. Long after he had been told that the absence of compliments and appreciation was just a joke, he kept muttering about the "lousy eggs that spoiled the pancakes." Only years later did Allan discover that social scientists had studied reciprocity and exchange, and could account for Uncle Harry's confusion when the expected gratitude for his (truly delicious) pancakes did not materialize.

David Bradford grew up in another kind of "family business." His father was a founder and the first president of NTL. David, as a teenager, helped in the logistics of running training groups. As the son of a prominent father, he had to learn to deal with older professionals who had agendas with his father. Later, as an emerging professional in applied social science, David carved out his own reputation and expertise. This gave him the chance to practice upward influence with powerful people who did not especially want to listen to "Lee's kid."

As an only child, David was already practiced in upward influence, with all the natural struggles to induce two adults to give room to a much younger and inexperienced person with ideas of his own.

Living abroad has also pushed us to learn to influence people who march to a different drummer. For example, as a doctoral student, Allan was a consultant to the Indian Institute of Management in Ahmedabad and, in order to make contributions, he had to overcome considerable skepticism from senior Indian faculty members.

On sabbatical in London in 1973, Allan worked with a creative organizational consultant, David Moscow, who had developed a seminar on "Influencing Skills." Although that approach to influence was somewhat different from the one in this book, many of the ideas stimulated Allan's subsequent inquiries, and implicitly shaped his thinking about the influence process.

In addition, both of the authors have been in academic leadership roles that were loaded with responsibility but virtually devoid of authority. David was the first director of the Organizational

Behavior Teaching Society, one of the most egalitarian institutions in the history of collective effort. Faculty members from universities around the country, who were not exactly noted for their willingness to take direction even in their home institutions, had to be lured into cooperation and voluntary commitment. Allan's terms as MBA program director at University of New Hampshire (a job equivalent to product manager) and Management Division Chairman at Babson, provided lessons in coaxing collaboration out of professional mavericks.

Finally, our work as organizational consultants has provided ample opportunity to discover the difficulties of inducing change in those who have a lot to lose if the advice is wrong—and perhaps even if it is right!

These are just some examples of the kind of forced research ("learn or be trampled") we have done in addition to our formal academic studies. Perhaps they help explain why we believe there is a universal need to learn to influence others without the use of formal authority; and, as we will show, why the need is growing in importance with the increasing complexities and rate of change in organizations.

THE DANGERS OF MANIPULATION: DO NOT TRY THIS TRICK WITHOUT ADULT SUPERVISION!

As we have tested the ideas you are about to encounter, we discovered that plain talk about influence makes some people very uncomfortable. Explicit descriptions of how the process of influence actually works, accompanied by our advice on how to use the process, raises the spectre of manipulation to those who fear that our insights will be abused. We want to tackle this issue head on before launching into Chapter 1.

The way of thinking and the techniques we explain are potent tools for acquiring influence. Like any tools, they may be used to make work proceed with less effort and wasted motion, or they may be abused. Just as explosives can be used to move earth for constructing valuable buildings or slipped into a suitcase by a terrorist intent on killing, the tools of exchange and reciprocity can be used for good or ill.

As we see it, manipulation consists of actions to achieve influence that would be rendered less effective if the target knew your actual intentions. Direct attempts to discover what another wants in order to cooperate, so that you can respond appropriately by making a fair exchange, is not manipulation. It can be done without hiding or distorting your intentions, and should result in both parties gaining from the transaction.

There is often temptation, however, to seek a "good deal," by exaggerating your requests so you can settle for less, by promising more than you know you will deliver, or by pretending to like someone you can't abide. Artfulness in concealing your intentions may yield short-term gains. We would be hard-pressed to deny that there are times when temporary advantage can be won by deceit. Nor would we argue that in discussions with colleagues it is necessary to immediately reveal everything you know or want, since that isn't expected in the natural give and take of work relationships.

We concede, then, that a clever manipulator might be able to capitalize on the ideas in this book to achieve personal gain at the expense of others, rather than to find ways of accomplishing important organizational goals. That kind of self-seeking already goes on in organizations, with or without conscious awareness of our approach to influence, and very skilled game-players sometimes get away with outrageous abuses of their positions—at least for a while.

Nevertheless, we have found that sooner or later—and mostly sooner—manipulation, deceit, and cynicism catch up with almost everyone. When people are interdependent with so many others, and can only get work done with the help of many colleagues, they can run for a while, but they can seldom hide for long.

Fooling some of the people some of the time is not enough for sustained success in today's interdependent organizations. Those who lie to get their way are almost inevitably found out, and then frozen out of the action by peers and bosses who do not trust them. Repeatedly, we have found that authenticity works, not only because it gets on the table the most data to work with, but because it helps to build trust. A reputation for shady practices, or even for constant self-interest at the expense of others, is corrosive; colleagues and bosses resist the influence attempts of those they don't trust.

Why be authentic when that might hurt the particular case you are making? Not only is it ethically right, but it enhances your reputation—your most valuable asset—and it helps you and the person you want to influence arrive at the best decision for the organization. Winning for its own sake may feel good and give you an ego-boost, but the organization does best when the right decisions are made, and, over time, being a party to creating those decisions is more important than getting everything you want. Besides, who wants to work in an organization where you can't trust anything your colleagues say? Why contribute to such an atmosphere?

Thus, this is a book that can help you achieve potent results, but only when you look out for the interests of the colleagues with whom you work and whose cooperation you need. Cross them and it will come back to explode in your face—or behind your back. Pay attention to their needs, and give back something valuable for whatever you get, and you will not only be more powerful in achieving results, but live to join them for many more days.

ALLAN R. COHEN
DAVID L. BRADFORD

Lexington, Massachusetts
Berkeley, California
August 1989

Acknowledgments

Many people have influenced us in positive ways, and we are deeply indebted to them. A number of colleagues read portions of the manuscript in draft form and made helpful suggestions, including J.B. Kassarjian, Lynne Rosansky, Les Livingstone, Jan Jaferian, Farshad Rafii, and Roy Lewicki. Rosabeth Kanter, Barry Stein, Richard Pascale, Jerry Porras, and Jean Kirsch provided useful stimulation over many years. National Training Laboratories gave us the opportunity to develop and test our ideas in a series of workshops for managers. Many wonderful friends and clients provided the rich examples we have used, but regrettably, most must remain anonymous to preserve confidentiality. We thank former students Tom Greenfield, Marianne McLaughlin, Spencer Lovette, and James Wiegel, and good friend Leslie Charm, for their contributions. In addition, our students and clients have been a continuous source of learning. Our editor, John Mahaney, went far beyond the call of duty in helping to shape this book, and we're almost sorry for all the grief we give him. We very much appreciate the perspective he brought. Sydney Craft Rozen and Louann Werksma buffed our prose, and Nancy Marcus Land's cheerful wisdom made the production process more than bearable. Tom Hart gave us valuable advice on contract issues. We want to thank Sydney Cohen for preparing the index.

We are very grateful to Babson's Vice-President for Academic Affairs, Gordon Prichett, the faculty nominating committee, and Ex-President Bill Dill, for choosing Allan to be the first occupant of the Walter H. Carpenter Chair. The selection was perfectly timed to permit concentrated writing effort just when the book needed it, and we literally couldn't have finished without this opportunity. Although the miracles of word processors let us do most of the typing ourselves, several people at Babson were incredibly helpful in producing draft after draft of the manuscript; for their support we thank Margie Kurtzman, Jim Murphy, Sheila Faherty, as well as George Recck and his angels of computer mercy, Ara Heghinian,

Scott Andersen, and especially John Walker, who promptly and patiently rescued lost files and answered countless questions. The Graduate School of Business at Stanford also provided valuable support.

Our extended families have also played an important part in helping us, not only by their encouragement but also by the lessons on influence they teach as we interact with them. For their contributions to our ongoing education, we are forever grateful to our wives, children, parents, brothers, in-laws, aunts, uncles, and cousins—a veritable army of informal instructors.

Alas, despite our profound gratitude to a lengthy list of helpful influencers, we can not escape final accountability for the results of their splendid efforts. Only we had the authority to complete this book, and we are responsible for its contents.

A.R.C.
D.L.B.

Contents

1

Influence and the
New World of Work

Every enterprise is composed of people with different skills
and knowledge doing many different kinds of work. For
that reason, it must be built on communication and
individual responsibility. Each member has to think through
what he or she aims to accomplish—and make sure that
associates know and understand that aim. Each has to think
through what he or she owes to others—and make sure that
others understand and approve. Each has to think through
what is needed from others—and make sure others know
what is expected from them.

Peter Drucker
"Management and the World's Work"
Harvard Business Review, September–October, 1988

This new kind of business hero . . . must learn to operate
without the might of the hierarchy behind them. The crutch
of authority must be thrown away and replaced by their
own ability to make relationships, use influence, and work
with others to achieve results.

Rosabeth Moss Kanter
*When Giants Learn to Dance; Mastering the Challenges
of Strategy, Management, and Careers in the 1990s*

Whether you work in an organization of three or
300,000, you probably already know that it is not
an exaggeration to speak of *heroism* in connection with the growing problem of how to accomplish work when you cannot order
people around. The workplace has become excruciatingly challenging. Today's organizations expect employees to make things
happen without giving them the tools to insure results. Hard-
working managers and specialists can feel as if they have been
asked to move mountains using nothing more than elbow grease
and faith. Small wonder that some people throw up their hands
and shout in frustration, "The hell with faith; pass the dynamite!"

Following are several "snapshots" of organizational life. This collection reveals a variety of organizational members struggling to find organizational dynamite—the leverage they need to dislodge what appear to be mountainous obstacles. Like the mythical Sisyphus, eternally condemned to roll a large rock up a steep cliff, they are in an uphill battle to move fellow organizational members in desired directions.

□ Anne Austin is a sales forecaster in a consumer goods company. She has spotted an opportunity for a new shampoo with excellent potential, but company policies prevent her from trying to bring it to market. Because she is only a sales forecaster and not in the high-status marketing department, she has no official way to get the idea considered and implemented. How should she proceed?

□ Bill Heatton is director of research at the telecommunications component division of a large company. He is convinced that Roland, the recently appointed marketing program manager for an important new contract, is incompetent. Bill's repeated efforts to convince Roland's boss to remove Roland so far have been completely unsuccessful. Bill is extremely frustrated, because he is sure that Roland will screw up; but Roland's boss won't respond. What can Bill do?

□ Chris Hammond is a sales trainee whose boss is giving her grief. Ambitious and talented, she is striving to win a sales award so that she can be promoted to sales representative. Her boss, however, wants to allow his favorite sales rep to receive credit for some of Chris' sales efforts so that he, rather than Chris, will win the company award. Can Chris do anything to insure fair treatment from her boss?

□ Leslie Charm arrived at his first post-MBA job, as a private loan placement analyst, full of ambition and plans. But Prudential Insurance was then a conservative, traditional company. Leslie felt confined by the paperwork and bureaucracy, as well as the narrowness of the job. He was eager to get out and find loan deals. What could he do to convince the department head to let him forget the rules and scout for business?

□ Warren Peters is desperately trying to fill a newly created unit manager position that has been vacant too long. He has tried to hire several people from within the company; but, for various reasons, none of them accepted the job. Now he has selected Debbie Casey, but Chuck Stevens, her boss, flatly refuses to let her go.

Stevens outranks Warren and has strong feelings about the qualifications required for a unit manager, but still Warren is very reluctant to give up and start his search all over. How can he persuade Stevens to release Casey?

□ As the head of a project to create a major new product at a medical equipment company, Monica Ashley needs the cooperation of a senior engineering manager who is blocking a crucial decision. He announced that it would only be "over my dead body" that the company would go outside to purchase a key component that supersedes his original design. Although the company president has been supportive of Monica in the past, he has warned her not to fight with the engineering manager on this one. How can Monica get the project completed without engaging in warfare that she has been advised to avoid?

□ Ellen Battles has been plagued by Bill Barker since she began work at Midwest Technologies as a quality control assistant. He tried to get her fired, insulted her by getting drunk at a conference and making a pass, and in general made her life miserable. Now they are in a new job relationship that requires they work closely together. Can Ellen alter Bill's behavior to make work less stressful and accomplish their goals?

□ Mark Buckley, the new president of the financial services subsidiary of a large company, found that the joys of being president were seriously undermined by the behavior of his boss, the group vice president at the parent company. Mark's boss frequently talks with people lower in Mark's organization, then bugs Mark with questions about the scraps of often inaccurate information he picks up in the conversations. Mark has concluded that his boss is an interfering meddler who just wants to look smart at Mark's expense. What can Mark do to get his boss to stop interfering?

What's missing from these pictures? The "crutch of authority!" All of these people have important work to do. They want results, or the freedom to do their jobs in the most productive way, but they are not authorized to give orders to the colleagues or managers whose cooperation they need. They must find a way to overcome whatever reasons these associates—bosses and peers—have for not going along and persuade them to respond. Somehow they have to find the influence to get what they want.

Even a company president like Mark Buckley or a senior executive like Bill Heatton has no guarantee that people will automatically fall into line—not in today's corporate world. It is no longer a sure thing that even directly reporting subordinates will do what the boss demands, since many subordinates no longer are willing to blindly follow orders. Whether they have high or low rank, these managers and professionals have to use whatever influence they can muster to get things done.

The problem worsens when someone needs cooperation from peers or those higher in the organization. These people don't have to listen; and on difficult issues that require new behavior, altered priorities, or annoying inconvenience, they often don't. What can a conscientious employee—one looking to make a difference—do?

This book will help you answer that question. You will meet all the people whose problems were captured in the snapshots you just viewed, as well as others like them who are struggling to get things done when they lack the formal authority. Some have been successful; others spectacularly unsuccessful. Their experiences can help you become more effective as you learn to use the process of influence.

We will offer a great deal of advice, based on our own organizational explorations and on social science discoveries about acquiring influence. Most importantly perhaps, we will challenge and encourage you to use this book as a tool for building solid, mutually beneficial relationships to accomplish vital organizational goals, rather than as a manipulative "technique" for acquiring power for its own sake.

IT'S A NEW WORLD, AFTER ALL

Why are the people in our photo album having so much trouble getting their way? Are they just poor specimens, picked to demonstrate the decline of the best? Is there something about their personalities that prevents them from taking charge—or from taking no prisoners?

We don't think so. All are bright, industrious managers and professionals working in a world that makes the acquisition and use of influence necessary. The organizational world is undergoing fundamental change, and each of these people is either in a rapidly changing organization, or is trying to help a sluggish organization become more adaptive to the accelerating changes around it.

□ For Anne Austin, the issue is dealing with changing consumer tastes in an organization that clings to old bureaucratic policies about where product ideas can originate.

□ Bill Heatton works in a complex matrix organization designed to be responsive to multiple new projects, but the "lines of command" can't handle horizontal management problems.

□ In Chris Hammond's case, can super-competent people move up rapidly, or do they have to walk lock-step through long apprenticeships?

□ Leslie Charm wants to use his new approaches to go after new kinds of business, but he works for a cautious, rule-bound company.

□ Warren Peters wants more "cross-fertilization" and risk-taking around promotions, but his organization is governed by hierarchy and is possessive about talent.

□ Monica Ashley has to influence way up the organization against a very powerful opponent stuck in a "not-invented-here" posture.

□ Ellen Battles is in a new position designed to meet competition by improving the quality of the company's products, but that will require working closely with a former enemy.

Although each of these people must summon considerable individual strength and skill to perform effectively, the work day situations that demand such feats are becoming more common. Organizations are being buffeted by external changes that force them to make internal changes in an attempt to survive. We will review these forces of change so that the growing need for more capacity to influence others can be seen in proper context.

WHAT NEXT? THE END OF PREDICTABILITY

Influence has been a fundamental skill at least since the snake in the Garden of Eden convinced Eve, who then persuaded Adam, to go against direct orders and eat the apple. With the passing of the fig leaf as the official corporate uniform, however, life at work has become ever more complex. The old rules and regulations have been replaced by the challenging but vague appeal to "do the right thing." Modern organizations literally depend for their survival on people at all levels being able to exercise responsible influence—even when they don't really have clear marching orders.

Business life is no longer as predictable as it was a generation ago. Changes in economic forces, employee expectations, domestic and global competition, financial markets, technology, government regulation, and information availability all have combined to create the sensation of careening at a furious pace through the twists and turns of the economy without roadmaps, steering wheels, or brakes.

Economic gale forces now make organizations less certain about what direction to lean in. Despite the inevitable business cycles to contend with, economic conditions in the 1950s and 1960s tended to remain stable from year to year. In many industries, competition was sluggish at best. Major competitors were known and unchanging; foreign products were inferior or too expensive, and America was considered the pacesetter for product innovations and management techniques.

The workforce is different from yesterday, too. In the "good old days," employees who had never gone to college were grateful to have steady work and a gradually rising standard of living. As a result, most were relatively compliant and willing to take direction. Conventional wisdom called for multilayered bureaucracies that made jobs as simple and clearly defined as possible so that ordinary people following directions could do the work—and leave the decision making to the boss.

Within a relatively stable world, this clear chain of command made a great deal of sense. Those at the top had usually worked their way up the ladder, learned from experience, were expert in the necessary technologies, and had seen what had worked in the past. Although there were exceptions, of course, and stability may have been in part an illusion, in comparison to present conditions organizational life proceeded like a 78 rpm record played at 33 rpm. Many companies felt little need for rapid adaptation, constant innovation, or skilled improvisation. Routinized mass production was how businesses made money.

Hurry Up, Please; It's Time: The Forces Demanding Faster Organizational Response

A reader would have to have been in Rip Van Winkle-like hibernation for the past 10 years not to have noticed that times not only are a-changing, but have changed dramatically. Despite a relatively prosperous economy during most of the 1980s, fears about government deficits, inflation, savings rates, and recession reflect an uncertain future.

At the same time, competition is rising in many industries, spurred by faster technological change, more foreign players, deregulation, and a wave of mergers and acquisitions, including leveraged buyouts, all of which force companies to carry greater debt and to be hungrier for opportunities. These forces drive businesses to be much faster on their feet, quicker to come up with new products and new ways of serving customers, better at seeking market opportunities and at taking advantage of company skills to find niches that can be attacked or defended.

Jack Welch, chairman and CEO of the corporate giant General Electric, now talks about the need to have both size and responsiveness: "In addition to the strength, resources, and reach of a big company (which we have already built), we are committed to developing the sensitivity, the leanness, the simplicity, and the agility of a small company. We want the best of both . . . our strategy [is to] create a company . . . of world-class global businesses that can compete and win in the 1990s and beyond . . . [and to] make this $50-billion enterprise as lean, as agile, and as light on its feet as a small company—a big company with the heart and hunger of a small company." Welch has articulated what many companies must do to cope with the accelerating rate of change.

If we look closely at these forces for change, we can begin to see why it is no longer possible for a few smart people at the top to have all the answers, and why it is so important that employees at all levels be able to take initiative and to influence their bosses and colleagues without having the responsibility and authority all spelled out in advance.

Now You See It, Now You Don't: Technological Speed-Up

The impact of technological change, for example, is mind-boggling. When there was only one national telephone company, AT&T, telephone equipment was depreciated over 40 years, its predicted lifetime. Now the obsolescence rate for telecommunications equipment, not to mention other electronic equipment, can be as little as two to three years. In some areas, products take as long to develop as they last, so that they are already obsolete by the time they come to market. The more innovative companies, such as 3M, expect up to half of total sales to come from products introduced in the past five years, which shows the speed at which good products now move through their life cycles.

As technologies churn, new players can enter markets because they see opportunities and can move faster than established companies that have huge economic and emotional investments in the old technology. Most computer companies, for example, have been started by people who had worked at other computer companies that could not respond to their ideas. The proliferation of computer companies attacking the marketplace with products from mainframes to microcomputers to personal computers to work stations to laptops to interconnection devices—all within the last 25 years—is a good example. No wonder Jack Welch is concerned about making GE agile!

In response to these pressures, more organizations are trying to dramatically reduce the time-to-market. Hewlett-Packard, for example, has decreed that the time span for product development, from conception to breakeven on sales, must be halved. Companies such as Northrop, Westinghouse, Lockheed, Xerox, and Digital Equipment are using computer-aided design and manufacturing systems to dramatically cut product development time by as much as 96 percent. These computer systems are supported by bringing together manufacturing people and design engineers from the beginning so that manufacturing can influence designs for "manufacturability." This reduces later engineering changes, which are very expensive and time-consuming.

At Northrop, for example, computer simulation paid off handsomely in designing their latest aircraft. Ninety-seven percent of the parts fit perfectly the first time; the best previous performance was 50 percent. Engineering changes were reduced to one-sixth of their previous numbers, and were implemented five times faster.

Involving manufacturing people at early stages and giving them veto power over designs they believed to be too slow at first caused resentment by the design engineers who were used to dictating to the factory. "But when the designers saw the types of changes that the downstream folks brought in, they realized it really avoided a lot of engineering change orders. Now it's the accepted practice." So, at Northrop and companies like it, technological change has forced mutual influence to replace the crutch of authority.

Who Left the Door Unlocked?
Other Forms of Competition

Not all organizations are faced with such lightning-fast technological change, but nearly all feel pressure from other external forces. Banks and insurance companies, for example, once were insulated from competitive pressures and could afford to be sluggish. But, as regulations have been reduced, the walls protecting these financial institutions have become far more penetrable. Because today they compete with each other and with brokerage houses for savings and investment dollars, they quickly must come up with new forms of products; and that requires departments to work together in new ways and at greater speed.

As the number and complexity of financial services increase, employees must learn to influence each other, or to "cross-sell," informing customers about products and services that formerly were someone else's specialty. "Nothing is more important now than influencing peers in our organization," a training manager at a major New York bank told us. His counterpart in a competing bank explained how hard it was for salespeople to get the attention of their product specialists, who are "bombarded with requests." If they can't gain the help of these specialists, their salespeople can't provide what customers want.

In many organizations, staff specialists must increasingly interact with line managers to obtain critical information, determine important needs, and design and implement new systems to make the organization more efficient or better able to serve customers. New staff jobs are created to address important issues such as productivity, quality, equal opportunity, or cost reduction; the people who fill the positions must then find ways to be heard by already busy line managers.

Professional firms in accounting, law, consulting, medicine, and engineering also are being shaken by the winds of change. Barriers to advertising have been blasted away, bringing out-and-out competition to professions that once held themselves "above all that." Customers are "shopping around" and raising questions about fees, so that billings are not protected by the old client-expert relationship. And new services, such as information-system consulting in accounting firms, often have outpaced the original functions, causing tension among competing professionals as well as strategic confusion. The threat or reality of dissatisfied partners spinning off, as at Arthur Anderson or First Boston, has also forced organizations to direct their attention to increasing their adaptability and response times.

As management consultant Barry Stein put it, only partially tongue-in-cheek, the "mean time between surprises" is becoming less than the time it takes to make decisions, so "long-range" planning is futile! An oil company strategic planner confessed that his company's planning now extends only six months. A recent *Fortune* survey of 200 top company CEOs reported that, "Most agree that so many external and unforeseen factors bombard CEOs today that long-term planning can quickly give way to crisis planning." Organizations are and will be asking more of members, who in turn will ask more of each other as opportunities and crises arise.

ORGANIZATIONS NEED TO "F" THEMSELVES

The forces of change are driving all kinds of organizations to the new corporate "F words": *fast, flexible, focused,* and *fit* to the environment.

Today's company must be able to:

- □ Be *fast* at realigning products and services to stay competitive;
- □ Be *flexible* enough to change gears when necessary;
- □ *Focus* on what it does best so that everyone is working toward the same goals and developing skills that differentiate the firm from its competitors; and
- □ *Fit* its structure and practices to the changes it faces.

These are not just nice things to do if there is some spare time for corporate experimenting; they are necessary for survival. The need to be *fast* and *flexible* in order to respond to the new competitive forces we have outlined, and the need to *focus* on the particular skills that will allow a firm to develop special competence compared to its competitors, have driven considerable experimentation with organizational structure. Organizations have tried to *fit* themselves to their churning environments.

Keep It Simple:
A Stupid Idea

The simple fact is that the world is too complex now for simple organization. No matter how smart top management is, it cannot have all the answers in advance. It no longer can organize in simple hierarchies with old rules. Managers at all levels can no longer expect to be the dispensers of tasks, the dividers of work, the solitary expert problem solvers, and the final arbiters. They have to depend on those below to take the initiative, deal directly with one another, and inform, stimulate, and challenge the managers who are nominally "in charge."

As we demonstrated in *Managing for Excellence,* managers can *no longer be effective by heroically trying to be responsible for everything; they must make heroes out of their subordinates* by sharing responsibility. Things are moving too fast in today's world of work to rely on the "wise men" at the top to know all the technological possibilities and nuances, understand in detail the shifts in competitors' strategies, invent all the product ideas, and manage assets to fight off potential raiders or sharks who are only too willing to relieve present management of its burdens. But the sharing of responsibility is possible only if the sharers are competent and know how to influence one another effectively.

Flatten or Fight Me:
New Organizational Forms

To compete successfully, many organizations have literally had to change their shapes, from the towering bureaucracies of the past to the horizontal designs of the 1990s. Sometimes this is done by creating smaller divisions to focus on one product line, geographic area, or technology, and bringing into the unit all the expertise that will be needed. The lines of communication are thus shortened, and colleagues who share a common purpose presumably can find each other more easily.

IBM, for example, was recently broken into six groups, each similar to an independent company. Chairman John Akers wanted to eliminate overlapping jobs and bureaucratic layers of people checking up on others. Customers had been complaining that they couldn't find the right person to get answers to their questions, and that whoever they reached had to talk to "4673 other people" first. Other companies, like Nucor and Walmart, have slashed their organizations to only three layers, placing more responsibility on all employees and trying to make communication rapid, or unnecessary.

Another structural approach is the matrix, in which two or more differing units are forced to make decisions together. Matrices are designed to manage conflict by bringing together people with relevant expertise, but differing viewpoints, at the lowest possible level where the differences can be resolved.

Organizations where equally powerful sides must resolve conflicts by influence and negotiation often have a similar, though less formal, arrangement. A decision maker may have authority formally assigned but is expected to listen seriously to and reach agreement with a variety of staff experts, task forces, committees, and other managers who have interests in the issues supposedly under the command of the decision maker.

Even apparently traditionally structured organizations now display much more "ad-hocracy," with special task forces or temporary one-issue committees formed to deal with a problem and then disband. There just isn't time today for disagreements to be sent up the chain of command to the highest levels, then for a resolution to slowly trickle its way down. Conflicts must be resolved—*fast*—and close to the action.

Still more streamlined forms of organization are springing up. Many internal functions that once were sacred possessions are being farmed out to specialist firms, creating the network-as-organization. Manufacturing, sales, distribution, purchasing, warehousing, payroll—all the way down to keeping the building beautiful through art acquisition and plant watering—are being subcontracted. The core can be a few executives, with telephones, computers, and fax machines, who act as coordinators of a network of specialists, each ready to respond rapidly to changes in demand because they are focused on one function and do it superbly.

Who Knows?
The Power of Information

Another factor that affects influence is the dramatically increased demand for and availability of information. The number of people with direct access to computers is increasing at a rate of 30 percent a year. As more computers are linked by network within the company, those who need information can get it themselves. They no longer wait for permission to "speak" directly with peers who have the expertise they need to get their jobs done.

Since titles are seldom used in electronic mail messages, status among communicators becomes less important. Ideas and knowledge circulate freely and rapidly, without the delays of official reports. Managers who sought power by hoarding data now have less control. They must use persuasion to get cooperation, since others are less dependent on them as sources of knowledge.

I Don't Wanna Hold Your Hand:
The Desire for Challenge

Another force pushing organizations toward greater use of influence, instead of authority, is the changing character of the workforce: Educated modern employees have changed expectations about work. They are less interested in safe but dull careers, doing any boring tasks assigned, in hopes of slowly climbing the corporate ladder or finding a comfortable niche.

Successful factory floor experiments with unsupervised work teams have demonstrated that the desire for challenge and responsibility is not confined to the executive suite. The pressure to give more employees a say has reduced management's ability just to give orders from above and assume they will be followed. And greater emphasis on quality, productivity, service, and use of advanced technology has made organizations far more dependent on the commitment of their employees.

Who Will Buy?
Tougher Customers

It is not only employees who are more educated and demanding; consumers, too, offer a new challenge to today's organization. They expect high quality, convenience, safety, customization, value pricing, and good service; and they are more willing than ever before to actively protest when they don't get them. Brand loyalty has diminished. Just as TV viewers zap programs, commercials, and networks they don't like, customers now switch brands, switch stores, buy by mail, buy foreign, or stop buying altogether. It is harder and harder to sell junk, unless it comes in the form of bonds with extraordinary interest rates attached, or can be called "collectibles" and put into permanent rotation at flea markets and yard sales.

Corporate customers are also becoming more demanding, looking for perfect quality to allow inspection-free delivery to support just-in-time manufacturing. Suppliers unable to meet quality and delivery standards are being cut out as the old model of preserving several sources of supply is giving way to favored status for the few that reliably meet standards. Xerox, for example, has cut its number of suppliers from some 5000 to about 350.

Managerial Diet:
The Shrinking Middle

The competitive forces propelling speed and flexibility also are having a dramatic impact on middle management. As organizations flatten, fewer jobs and promotions are available for middle managers or those who hope to become supervisors. De-layering increases managerial span of control, forcing middle managers to let go and pass work down. Yet they want challenging work, as do their subordinates. They want to contribute and be able to take initiative.

With fewer layers of management, there will be less deadwood, and fewer people to back up bosses. Because there won't be so many bodies to throw at problems, every decision will be more critical. Managers more than ever will need to be supported from below and helped by their peers.

The kinds of dilemmas we described in the snapshots at the beginning of this chapter will become increasingly common. Because managers and a wide variety of other professionals—engineers, scientists, designers, architects, physicians, market researchers, actuaries, nurses, lawyers, and accountants, among others—are interdependent for information and support, they need to know how to build influential relationships.

Whatever your job, you will be expected to join your colleagues in doing important work, which will lead you to influence and be influenced. You will need to know how to sell important projects, persuade colleagues to provide needed resources, create satisfactory working relationships with them and your managers, insist that your boss respond to issues that may not appear important to him or her, and, in turn, give thoughtful responses to requests associates make of *you*. The person asking something of you today may be the very one you'll need next week.

THREE FACES OF ORGANIZATIONAL INFLUENCE

Look Up, to the Right and Left, and (If You're a Manager) Down Before Crossing Others

Along with death and taxes, an inevitable reality of organizational life is that everyone has a boss. In a flat organization, the boss may be a distant and benevolent resource and, in a more hierarchical one, the boss may be breathing down your neck; but no one escapes having a person officially responsible for him or her. Even the company president has a board that demands accountability, so there is no rest for the wary subordinate.

Similarly, virtually everyone in organizations has peers to deal with. There are very few jobs where a person works completely solo; perhaps a few technical specialists and the president do not have to deal with others at their level in order to do their jobs. But most members are dependent upon, and in turn important to, a variety of colleagues.

Finally, some people also have responsibility as supervisors of others—the bosses to all those subordinates just mentioned. These managers are expected to see that the work their area is assigned gets done, and they are supposed to utilize the talents of their subordinates in doing it.

The cyclone of changes we described earlier has altered the relative importance of these three aspects of organizational responsibility. In the past, the managerial role was most prominent, as managers were the decision makers for and initiators of the work done by those they managed. Even today, when we ask managers to say what managing is, they often mention only the downward aspect of the role, even though they will acknowledge when questioned that far more of their time is spent managing upwards and sideways.

But the flattened, more responsive, and flexible organizations required to meet current and future conditions demand that more initiative, judgment, and self-direction be expected from people in their roles as subordinates and peers—whether or not they also have formal supervisory responsibilities.

Your colleagues and superiors are now as much a part of your job as your own activities, and they have to be considered as part of your responsibilities. You have an obligation to keep them informed, push them to do what is needed for the organization to be successful, anticipate their needs, and respond sensibly to their requests.

Even if you don't supervise anyone else, you still are as obligated as a manager is to be a good subordinate and colleague; and you must be able to draw on the skills and knowledge of people over whom you have no authority.

In the Same Boat:
The Case for Sharing Responsibility

In our previous book, *Managing for Excellence*, we developed a new model of leadership that made it possible for managers to free themselves from some of the ineffective aspects of supervision so that they could spend more time dealing with the lateral and upward aspects of their role. We explained the fundamental shift that managers need to make in dealing with employees if they are to achieve high performance. We showed how traditional approaches to leadership block excellence because they have embedded within them the heroic assumption that it is the leader who has the responsibility for departmental success.

When this heroic manager feels sole responsibility for the department's performance and for managing subordinates, those below feel less responsibility for initiating ideas. They focus only on their own unit's success and let the boss worry about the larger picture. Rather than looking for ways to initiate and take reasonable risks, they tend to "delegate upward." They let the boss have the responsibility for all important decisions. As a result, the manager has to devote even more time checking up, keeping up, and sweeping up.

Today, however, it is only possible to achieve outstanding results when all employees feel a sense of responsibility for success. Heroism doesn't have to die; rather, it should flourish among all employees, especially when they deal sideways and upward, where they do not have the crutch of authority to demand what they need. The leader's task is to build conditions in which all directly reporting subordinates feel responsibility for success. That makes the concept of "participation" far richer and more extensive then ever, and frees the boss from the constant need to push subordinates to do more than follow directions.

Letting go of such tight heroic control is not easy. It takes courage to build a strong team of competent subordinates and to allow (let alone encourage) them to act heroically. That will be much easier, however, if the manager has subordinates who are not only technically competent but also good at influencing their peers—and the manager.

We are asking you to think about your role in a new way. As a subordinate, you need to learn the influence skills that will allow you to responsibly handle the increased responsibility from your superior. As a colleague, you need to be effective at influencing and being influenced, shaping the behavior of your colleagues, and learning from and supporting them.

If you are a manager, you not only need to exercise influence skills with your peers and your own boss, but also to help the people who work for you learn to be effective influencers—even of you—since that will free you to spend more of your time seeking new opportunities and working the organization above and around you.

MAKING IT HAPPEN: THE WAY TO INFLUENCE

With so much interdependence required, wielding influence becomes a test of skill—skill in interpersonal communications. Going hat in hand to throw yourself at a colleague's mercy with a request is not a powerful or very effective option. Of course, trying to bull your way through by sheer nerve and aggressiveness can be costly as well. Antagonizing crucial peers or superiors is a dangerous strategy, since they can so easily come back to haunt you.

We have developed an approach that allows you to be influential without being antagonistic. We will describe a way of thinking that shifts the focus from preoccupation with your own goals and frustrations, to understanding and satisfying the world of the other. This will help you achieve win-win outcomes as you influence those around you.

FINDING COMMON GROUND: THE MODEL OF STRATEGIC ALLIANCES AND PARTNERSHIPS

Effective influence begins with the way you *think* about those you want to influence. You have already won half the battle when you can see each person, no matter how stubborn and prickly he or she seems to be, as a potential *strategic ally* or *partner.* You increase the number of your potential allies by seeing who has a stake in your area and working at building mutual trust. The time will most assuredly come when your well-cultivated network will serve you; and you, in turn, will help others gain influence.

Just as companies have responded to the changing conditions described earlier in this chapter, multiplying their resources and increasing their agility through strategic alliances with unusual partners, you can extend your influence capacities. Because no one company is big enough to go it alone anymore, strategic alliances, joint ventures, and partnerships *between* companies are growing at a rate of 20 percent a year. For example, over 300 joint deals, crossing national boundaries and fierce rivalries, have been struck among auto makers. The lessons from this dramatic increase in alliances between companies and their competitors, suppliers, or customers, provide a model for influence *within* organizations.

According to a study reported in *The Harvard Business Review,* successful alliances adhere to these principles:

☐ Collaboration is competition in a different form.

☐ Harmony is not the most important measure of success.

☐ Cooperation has limits. Companies must defend against competitive compromise.

☐ Learning from partners is paramount.

These principles illustrate the harsh reality that alliances across company boundaries may open the door wider than is appropriate, since allies have their own interests as well as common ones. This can also hold true among individuals in the *same* organization. At once competitors for resources, reputation, and future promotions, your colleagues are also your potential and often necessary collaborators toward goals you can establish as mutual. Skillful people recognize that dilemma and manage it.

Listen, for example, to Mike Pittino, director of corporate operations and systems at a major bank, advising his subordinates after a reorganization:

> I don't want to see any ass-grabbing for turf and power. You can't win when you do that; everyone you deal with can recognize it! . . . Of course, we all want more turf, but some of us are more skilled at getting it by seeming not to try for it.

Pittino, street wise and hard-nosed, understood the tension between competition and collaboration. He wanted to resolve it by building a collaborative team, but his own competitive instincts crept in. Only when teams are united by a common vision do members get past their own self-interest.

Unfortunately, peers in most organizations are not welded into collaborative teams and still tend to be too narrowly focused on their own department's needs. Bounded by the pressures from their boss, department, and job assignments, they tend to see reality from only their own viewpoints. Going along with a request to accommodate a colleague is considered "giving way," and tantamount to a loss of face or lowering of standards.

Because of this inward focus, many employees want to be as independent of their colleagues as possible. They consider it a pain when others make demands that appear to arise only from their own self-interests. That perception easily degenerates into win-lose fights and a division of the workaday world into good guys, who are supportive and usually agree, and bad guys, who won't cooperate or who see issues from very different perspectives.

Viewing peers as strategic allies, on the other hand, leads to a more positive focus. You begin to recognize that everyone has legitimate stakes; therefore, you all will have to seek areas of mutual interest. You can't expect to agree about *everything* with an ally, but that is no reason to be nasty or disparaging. You just have to work harder to find some common ground.

Good strategic allies recognize the importance of long-term alliances. They interact not just to resolve particular differences, but also to build even more trust and give-and-take into the future relationship. Although there are no guarantees that the alliance will always continue, each partner has a commitment to keep the relationship going as long as there are mutual interests and mutual trust.

Come Out from Under: Your Boss as a Partner

Even so-called *sub*ordinates can treat their bosses as partners— senior partners, if the boss is concerned with hierarchy—and contribute as true (even if junior) partners would. Indeed, the modern "subordinate" is very likely to know a great deal that the designated "superior" does not. Thinking like a partner means sharing that knowledge, even when the boss *doesn't know* what he or she doesn't know and therefore can't ask for it.

Already some companies, such as Marriott and Lechmere Stores, have dropped the word "subordinate" in favor of "associate," "stakeholder," or "team member." The issue here is not semantics alone. New names will be nothing more than hype unless they reflect a change in the way people do—and think about— their work and relationships.

No self-respecting partner could stand silently by when other partners, no matter how senior, are about to make a huge mistake, overlook important opportunities, or miss vital information that could affect success. It is the *obligation* of a partner to be as responsible as possible, even at the risk of personal discomfort or embarrassment.

Although this can lead to a great deal of conflict, it is tempered by the recognition that the dissenters care, are trying to do their best for the firm, and are basically intelligent and competent or they wouldn't have been admitted to partnership in the first place. As long as there are processes for separation or removal of a partner if necessary, all can act as if competence can be taken for granted. (As our colleague J. B. Kassarjian has shrewdly noted, provisions for obtaining a graceful divorce are often just what prevent it!)

To illustrate some of the difference between the traditional superior–subordinate relationship and a more partnerlike arrangement, let's eavesdrop on a typical meeting between a traditional pair: David Byer is a newly appointed purchasing manager at a very large division of an industrial company; his boss, Mike McGowan, is the manufacturing manager.

Mike: David, I want to hear about your efforts to straighten out our purchasing problems.

David: [Thinks to himself, *I wonder why he's asking. I hope he's not expecting too much yet. Let's see.*] I've determined that 40 percent of our purchases are not made under contract, and I will start to address that. Also, we are too often paying different prices to the same supplier, because the purchasing agents at our plants don't follow procedures.

Mike: We've probably got too many suppliers. You could probably reduce the number by 50 to 80 percent and get much better control and reliability.

David: [*Here we go. He thinks I don't know about reducing suppliers. But if I start there, I'll never show early results. Can I directly disagree with him? Better be careful . . . I'll try to gently move him off it.*] Yes, that's a good idea, although I was thinking that it might be useful to get some discipline into the purchasing organization first.

Mike: If there are fewer suppliers, discipline will be a lot easier, and we can control all purchases through headquarters.

David: [*Well, I guess that's how it's going to be; he acts nice, but will insist on having things his way. I've survived that kind of boss before; I know enough not to get him mad by pushing too hard. I'll go along, and throw in a goody to make him happy.*] So speed up the supplier reduction program? OK. And I'll look at consolidating our travel through one travel agent, which will save us at least half a million a year.

Consider how differently this meeting might proceed if David thought of himself as his boss' partner:

Mike: David, I want to hear about your efforts to straighten out our purchasing problem.

David: [*Here's a chance to get some good ideas and get his help with the guy in Singapore who doesn't want to deal with anyone from the home office.*] Good. And I need your help in dealing with one of our plant managers. Can we talk about both?

Mike: Sure.

David: I've determined that 40 percent of our purchases are not made under contract, and I will start to address that. Also, we are too often paying different prices to the same supplier, because the purchasing agents at our plants don't follow procedures.

Mike: We've probably got too many suppliers. You could reduce the number by 50 to 80 percent and get much better control and reliability.

David: You're right in the long run, but you probably don't realize the best sequencing. I don't see that as producing the same kind of short-term results. We first have to qualify the vendors, renegotiate contracts, and get our factories geared up.

Mike: Yes, but I want this to happen fast. There's a lot of potential savings.

David: Mike, hang on a minute. You're too quickly jumping to conclusions. We have the same interest in cleaning up the purchasing mess, but I want to be sure we do it in a way that will get us there. I agree it's a priority, but in sequence.

Mike: I just don't want us to lose the momentum.

David: [*He doesn't quite see this yet, so I've got to make it clearer.*] I know you need results, but I'm also sure you don't want our efforts to fragment. We need to keep our primary goal in focus. Maybe I can do an analysis of one of our main purchased parts and use that as a pilot while we try to get the plant purchasing people to use more discipline. I've got to be sure they have the information they need, so they have no excuses for ignoring contracts.

Mike: Good, a pilot might show us what's necessary to reduce the numbers. Now which plant manager did you want to talk about?

As a partner, David helps set the agenda, can challenge the boss's assumptions and push back, learns from and teaches him, jointly makes the decision with his boss, and they both give the company's needs precedence over rank or self-interest.

Not with My Reputation, You Don't: Four Fears That Prevent Building Alliances

Unfortunately, many people can acknowledge that they should take the initiative to create alliances with colleagues and partnerships with their bosses, but at the same time they deeply fear they will be seen in one of four negative ways by those important people:

□ *Uncontrollable.* Will my manager fear a loss of control if he or she builds a partnership with me and encourages me to form strategic alliances with others in the organization? Could this push my boss' control buttons: Will he fear I'll go charging off on my own and do something dumb? Will he worry there won't be a reasonable limit to how much I will push back as a partner? Will these concerns be so great that "partnership" is a sham and, in the last analysis, I will be forced to do what the boss insists has to be done?

□ *Disloyal and insubordinate.* Some managers are very concerned with their version of loyalty. Will mine worry about whether I'll know the difference between healthy disagreement and disrespect? Will I cross the line in his mind between "arguing for what I think is right" and "not being a team player?" My goal of expressing loyal disagreement might be seen as being insubordinate.

□ *Being political.* If I need to be highly influential with colleagues and negotiate agreements, will they see me as the proverbial "organizational politician," forever cutting deals to get myself ahead? Will I be perceived as always looking out for what I can get and not interested in doing the right things for the organization's sake? Will I be seen as changing my position with whichever way the wind blows?

□ *Empire builder.* If I act as if I'm not limited by my formal job description, will I be perceived as building an empire and trying to grab additional areas? What is the difference between "taking initiative" and "grabbing turf?" Will my attempts to get things done be threatening to colleagues' territory?

Give and Take: The Process of Exchange

In developing the new kind of alliance, how can you overcome these fears? What's in it for the boss or peer whom you want to influence? Why should they respond to your new found method of approaching them?

We have discovered that it is the process of give and take that governs influence. Making *exchanges* is the way to gain *influence;* and that process leads to *cooperation* rather than retaliation or refusal to engage. People cooperate because they see something of value that they will gain in return.

The valuable item may be as concrete as a budget transfer, as intangible as a heartfelt "thank you," or as self-generated by the recipient as a warm glow from believing that cooperating was the right thing to do for the organization. But, whenever associates help one another, some kind of exchange always takes place.

To be successful in making exchanges, you must first determine what the potential ally's interests are, assess your own resources, and find something you can give that will be valuable enough to produce what you want from the ally. When you are able to give something desirable, you can press hard for your interests, since the ally's cooperation is much more likely if he or she wants what you are offering. This is a tough but nonexploitive way to build mutual interests. Each of you wins.

We will make clear how this universal mechanism works, how you can use it to determine what the other person wants, and how you can engage in mutually satisfying transactions that let you get things done when you can't force cooperation. For now, however, it is important to get into the right frame of mind about the people you will be trying to influence.

Making Alliances Work

The exchange techniques we describe in this book will work best if you approach their use as a partner in a strategic alliance. Although it's undoubtedly true that not everyone in your organization is as competent as you would expect your partners to be, nor as dedicated to the firm's success, assuming that they *are* is the best way to increase the likelihood that they *will be.*

The operating rules for treating those you wish to influence, whether peers or superiors, as if they are potential allies are easy to specify but tough to carry out:

□ *Mutual respect.*   Assume they are competent and smart.

□ *Openness.*   Talk straight to them. It isn't possible for any one person to know everything, so give them the information they need to know to help you better.

□ *Trust.* Assume that no one will take any action that is purposely intended to hurt another, so hold back no information that the other could use, even if it doesn't help your immediate position.

□ *Mutual benefit.* Plan every strategy so that both parties win. If that doesn't happen over time, the alliance will break up. When dissolving a partnership becomes necessary as a last resort, try to do it in a clean way that minimizes residual anger. Some day, you may want a new alliance with that person.

Of course, when you have overwhelming evidence that the potential ally you are trying to influence is competent and of good will, it is much easier to act accordingly; but that's also true for the ally's view of you. If you start with the opposite set of assumptions, however, openness and trust cannot develop.

How do you establish such respect? Someone has to take the first risks, since it is almost impossible to prove ahead of time that a potential ally will act honorably. If you already have an established and trusting relationship, you're in luck; you know how much easier it is to influence under those conditions. It is obviously a good idea to build as many trusting relationships as possible. Because that isn't always feasible, the problem of how to create a partnership remains.

If each side waits for the other to prove his or her trustworthiness, a standoff results. When you are suspicious of the ally's intentions, display a bit more openness and trust than the ally shows. Although of course it is not really quantifiable, we suggest staying about 15 percent ahead of what is being returned to you. That helps you pull the ally along without being too threatening or taking inordinate risks.

We will also show you how to use the ideas in this book when relationships are not good or well-established. You will learn how to accomplish the influence act while simultaneously building or improving the relationship. To start, you must take the initiative and consider each transaction as the beginning of a potentially profitable alliance.

When the existing relationship is characterized by openness and trust, you can take the initiative without being seen as out of control, insubordinate, over-political, or empire-building. When the relationship is poor or questionable, however, it is hard to know how the other person will interpret new forms of initiative. You may be in danger of creating suspicion, which will reduce your effectiveness, or increasing mistrust and jeopardizing the future of the relationship.

In Chapters 2 through 11, we will demonstrate that the skills for attaining influence are within your grasp, even when your relationship is not a good one. In fact, we will show that the exchange principles for influence work even when the relationship is not open and trusting—and are themselves a way to improve the relationship while you are gaining influence.

2

The Law of Reciprocity: Exchange as the Basis for Influence

> I have done enough for you, Apollo; now it's your turn to do something for me.
>
> Rough translation of inscription on a
> Greek statue of the god Apollo, 700–675 B.C.

> Both a borrower and lender be . . .
>
> Contemporary folk wisdom
> for gaining influence in organizations

The breakneck pace of the new world of work we described in Chapter 1 requires a view of fellow employees who can't be controlled as partners in strategic alliances, and forces renewed attention to the give-and-take of relationships. If a follower of Apollo 2700 years ago could invoke the principles of reciprocity and exchange, maybe there is something universal in these ideas that could make organizational life better and more productive.

We will look closely at two people, Bill Heatton and Anne Austin, laboring mightily to influence colleagues they don't control. Their experiences—one frustratingly unsuccessful and the other improbably triumphant—will help illustrate the advantages of making mutually satisfying exchanges.

WHY WON'T HE LISTEN? AN ALL-TOO-FREQUENT EXAMPLE OF FAILED INFLUENCE

Bill Heatton is the director of research at a $250-million division of a large West Coast company. The division, which makes exotic telecommunications components, has many technical advancements to its credit. In the past several years, however, the division's performance has been spotty at best. Despite many efforts to become more profitable, it has racked up multimillion-dollar losses in some years. Several large contracts have been big money-losers, causing each part of the division to blame the others for the problems.

Note Bill's frustrations as he talks about his efforts to influence Ted Lowry, his peer and the division's director of marketing. Ted is the direct supervisor of Roland, the program manager for an important new contract that marketing and research (along with production) will work on together:

Bill: Another program's about to come through. Roland, the program manager, is a nice guy, but he doesn't know squat and never will. He was responsible for our last big loss, and now he's going to be in charge again. I keep fighting with his boss, Ted Lowry, to move Roland off the program, but I'm getting nowhere. Ted doesn't argue that Roland is capable, but he sure as hell isn't trying to find someone else. Instead, he comes to me with worries about *my* area.

I'm being a team player here. I responded to their requests by changing my staffing plan, assigning the people they wanted to do the research on Roland's program. I even overruled my own staff's best judgment about who we should assign to the program. But I'm still not getting the progress reports I need from Roland, and he's never "available" for planning. I'm not hearing a lot of argument, but there's no action to correct the problems, either. That's bad, because I'm responding but not getting any response from *them.*

There's no way to resolve this. If they disagree, that's it. I could go for a tit-for-tat strategy. I could tell them that if they don't do what I want, we'll screw them next time. But I don't know how to do that without hurting the organization. That would feel worse than the satisfaction I'd get from sticking it to Roland!

Ted, Roland's boss, is so much better than the guy he replaced that I hate to ask that he be removed as director of marketing. We could go together to our mutual boss, the general manager, but I'd really hate to do that. You've failed in a matrix organization if you have to go to your boss. I have to try hard before I throw it in his lap.

Meanwhile, I'm being forced into insisting that Ted get rid of Roland, but I'm afraid it's in a destructive way. All I want to do is yell. I don't want to wait until the program has failed to be told *I've* blown it!

Bill is clearly angry about the situation and frustrated about his inability to influence Ted Lowry. He finds himself behaving in ways he doesn't feel good about. Like other managers who very much want to influence someone who is not cooperating, Bill has begun to perceive Ted, his potential ally, as an intractable enemy. In his frustration, Bill is starting to attribute negative motives to Ted. Because he doesn't know how to get what he needs from Ted, nor does he understand Ted's behavior, Bill is beginning to leap to dangerous conclusions about why Ted is ignoring his efforts.

In turn, Bill's anger and assumptions about Ted are narrowing his sense of what is possible. Although he fantasizes revenge, Bill is too dedicated to the organization to cause it harm. He is genuinely stuck.

The Problem: Ignore the Law of Reciprocity at Your Peril

Bill's failure to use fully the *law of reciprocity* lies at the heart of his inability to influence Ted. Reciprocity is the almost universal belief that people should be paid back for what they do—that one good (or bad) turn deserves another. This belief about behavior, evident in primitive and not-so-primitive societies all around the world, carries over into organizational life. This book is based upon the fundamental truth that everyone who does anything for anyone else expects to be paid back eventually in one form or another.

Because Bill believes he has gone out of his way to help Ted, he expects Ted to reciprocate automatically and remove Roland from the project. When Ted does not act, Bill's anger reflects his belief that, by changing his own staffing patterns, he has created an obligation in Ted. He has established a "credit" with Ted, and Ted should honor that credit and agree to replace Roland.

Bill is also worried about a *negative exchange*—being blamed unfairly for project failures when he has done his part. He has strong feelings about what credit he should deserve for his efforts; to be judged harshly after extra effort would violate his sense of justice.

People generally expect that, over time, others will roughly balance the ledger and repay costly acts with equally valuable ones. This underlying belief in how things are supposed to work allows people in difficult organizational situations to gain cooperation. A classic study of prison guards found that the guards could not control prisoners, who greatly outnumbered them, by threats and punishments alone. The guards did many favors for the prisoners, such as overlooking small rules infractions, providing cigarettes, and the like, in return for cooperation from prisoners in keeping the lid on. All the formal authority in the world can't keep rebellious prisoners in line; they exchange their cooperation for favors that make their confinement more pleasant, not out of respect for "the rules."

Similarly, a much higher status group, the general managers of various divisions of a large company, have learned to "help each other out" by absorbing each other's excess costs or profits each quarter. They are judged by headquarters on how well they meet quarterly budgeted targets but results are dependent on economic events outside their control. By using cross-charges to smooth results, they can work together and more readily meet their individual goals. The overall impact on corporate profits is nil, but this kind of horsetrading allows them to save for a rainy day or borrow when in need. A general manager who refuses to cooperate in this way soon finds himself frozen out of the other forms of cooperation among the group.

EXCHANGES: THE ART OF GIVE AND TAKE

We can consider all transactions in organizations as exchanges between people. The exchanges can support the organization's goals, or undermine them. They can be overt ("I'll support your proposal if you'll go to bat with your boss for mine"), or implicit ("It's good to have the data early; it sure is nice to work in a place with such great people"). They can occur between peers, between boss and subordinates, or between managers on different levels in different parts of the organization. An exchange can be of *tangible goods*, such as budget dollars, equipment, or personnel; of *tangible services*, such as faster response, information, or public support; or of *sentiments*, a special kind of service, which includes gratitude, appreciation, or praise. Whatever form the exchange takes, without rough equivalence over time, hard feelings will result.

Jobs in organizations are a straightforward example of exchanges. The organization hires and agrees to pay employees—in money as well as in prestige, security, or interesting work—and, in return, employees carry out their tasks and support the organization's objectives.

In a typical week, you probably respond to many requests from fellow employees without expecting direct or immediate "payment." You comply because your larger contract with the organization is reasonable compensation, and you accept as part of your job the expectation that you will routinely carry out requests related to your job. Also, if you respond willingly to what someone else asks, you know you have created the expectation that the person will come through for you when you make a reasonably similar request. In this way, work goes on without extra effort needed to get cooperation.

Often it becomes necessary in organizational life, however, to make a request that exceeds routine expectations. Then people expect that one way or another, sooner or later, they will be compensated fairly for the acts they do above and beyond the obligations of their job. This requires that some form of "currency" equivalent be worked out, implicitly at least, to maintain balance and good feelings between those involved.

Expectations of reciprocity and equity usually are quietly understood. They become noticeable when they are violated. Think of the irritation you would feel if your boss asked you to work through several weekends, never so much as thanked you, and then claimed credit for the extra work you had done. You might not say anything the first time this happened (expecting or hoping that the boss would make it up to you); but if your efforts were never acknowledged, you would believe that an important trust had been violated.

That is similar to what people feel when they realize that frequent dinner guests have never extended a reciprocal invitation. With friends, it is inappropriate to keep very close track of who owes whom what, but when one party consistently fails to reciprocate, the other will eventually notice and feel let down.

One of the authors always buys the milk for tea in his office; his closest colleague, the other tea drinker in the office, never does. When their secretary asked if this bothered the supplier, he explained that his colleague is a generous person who periodically makes an extravagant gesture in return. Even if the return favor didn't come for a year or two, no sense of injustice would be perceived; the relationship is too good and long-established for that.

In a very different situation in the same office, a certain ex-colleague was famous for asking inconvenient favors, which he never repaid. He got each newcomer in turn to "cover a couple of

classes for him while he was at a conference"; but as his coworkers came to recognize the one-sidedness of his game, they slowly
froze him out of all important interactions and decisions.

If milk for tea and covering a few classes create the expectation of eventual reciprocal actions of some kind, then the unusual,
beyond-the-routine requests that are increasingly needed in today's organizations will inevitably require appropriate exchanges.

THE THREE FUNDAMENTAL FORMS OF EXCHANGE

When it is necessary to ask for more than the routine, to request
new goods or services, or even changed behavior, there are three
ways to go about it. An exchange can take one or all of the following forms, depending on what each side wants and has to offer:

1. *Compliance for mutual benefit.* This form of exchange is
least costly to the person making the request. Because the action
requested is also in the potential ally's own interest, the benefits
of going along are at least as great as the cost of complying. If, for
example, Ted Lowry had been looking for a reason to get rid of
Roland, then he would have welcomed Bill's request, and both
would have benefited.

This form of exchange happens all the time. For example,
Julie has a brainstorm about how to provide faster turnaround on
the work for Jim's department; but, for Julie's system to work, Jim
will have to put the information into a new form. Because Jim sees
that the new form would actually be easier to complete, he gladly
agrees.

Jim's ready cooperation allows Julie to provide her service
better than Jim thought possible. When the situation allows that
kind of fit, the exchange is essentially *compliance for mutual per-
sonal/departmental benefit.*

This is the most preferable kind of exchange, since you don't
need extra resources to use it. If you can show the potential ally
the benefit to be gained from meeting your request, or the inevitable costs of not meeting it, you can be resource-poor and still
get what you need. Because this set of conditions does not always
exist, you'll need another form of exchange.

2. *Compensation for costs.* This form of exchange, identified by social scientist David Berlew, requires the asking party to
cover the costs incurred for compliance with the request. For example, Bill Heatton might have offered Ted the name of a very

good program manager as a replacement for Roland and expressed willingness to help recruit this person. Assuming that it is the difficulty of finding someone good that has been keeping Ted from going along, Bill's action would cover Ted's cost of replacing Roland.

This kind of exchange works when the person making the request has specific resources that can directly compensate for the costs. If these resources are not available or applicable, a third, very common, form of exchange can be tried.

3. *Equivalent payment.* A classic form of barter, this method offers something to your potential ally at least as valuable as what you request. Whether it is made on the spot or in the future, or even made in advance, your payment must be perceived by the recipient as equivalent in value to that which you request. For example, Bill might have arranged to provide Ted with better staff and information from his research group if Ted replaced Roland with another program manager. As long as the person making the request and the potential ally can agree on equivalent value for the goods and services being considered, an exchange can take place.

One of the advantages of this form of exchange is that, when mutual trust exists, payment does not have to be made immediately. The possibility of extending the terms of an exchange allows more leeway to find or generate desirable resources—as all credit card holders know!

May the Force Be with You: Negative Exchange Variations

All three forms of exchange contain an unspoken message about the negative consequences to the potential ally that will result from not cooperating. Instead of demonstrating how compliance will result in mutual benefit, you can show how *not* complying will lead to negative results for both parties. Where compliance will earn compensation, refusal will incur future costs. Instead of paying in kind, you make clear how you will repay refusal with a comparable future refusal to cooperate.

While the threat of negative consequences is a less friendly way to make exchanges, it may be necessary in difficult situations. If Ted, for example, were deliberately ignoring Bill's requests about Roland and could not see any positive benefits to him or his area from removing Roland, Bill might show how bad Ted's marketing department would look if the new project failed (negative mutual benefit); or Bill might warn Ted that failure to respond would lead Bill to protest to the general manager, causing considerable discomfort to Ted (negative compensated costs); or Bill might even threaten to assign the project low research priority (negative payment in kind). Sometimes the mule needs a whack with a two-by-four to get its attention when no amount of coaxing will move it.

Keep Your Sunny Side Up

Although negative exchanges can be powerful influencers, we will stress the positive side of exchange for several reasons. All too often, frustrated influencers like Bill Heatton move rapidly to negative ways of operating; they rely on threats as a first resort rather than a distant last one. Although there are some people who find it more difficult to get tough than seek mutual gains, we believe that a positive emphasis will expand the influence repertoires of more people because so many find it too easy to be hard.

Another reason for accentuating the positive is that peers and superiors may well have at least as many resources available to retaliate as you do, which heightens the potential dangers from getting into a spitting contest. The powerful potential ally may salivate at the chance to show who is tougher, and you may find that you are in for an unpleasant experience.

Further, taking a negative approach may create its own form of reciprocity, one in which the potential ally feels compelled to oppose you. Many people will automatically start to fight fire with fire, increasing their resistance if they feel threatened. Even worse, if you gain a reputation for the negative, some potential allies will take a negative posture toward you *before* you do anything to them. The potential threat of your setting fires causes them to burn you first.

Positive expectations, on the other hand, create an atmosphere that makes positive outcomes more likely. Much of what transpires after a request is made relies on how much the potential ally trusts you; your assumption that the ally is a good corporate citizen makes you automatically more trustworthy! This is more evident in reverse: When you treat someone as difficult, uncooperative, or untrustworthy, you create a self-fulfilling prophecy. The potential ally becomes more difficult, reinforcing your assumption, which induces you to be tougher. The negativism escalates until each of you is irritated and unlikely to bend.

Looking for the positive opportunity is important for another reason: The pace of change in modern organizations makes it hard to know what your future relationship to the potential ally will be. You may one day find yourself in the position of the other person's subordinate, boss, or dependent peer. If it is likely you will have to deal with the ally again, act as if you probably can find mutual objectives and outcomes. By doing that, you give your potential ally credit for being as interested in good results as you are. Should the assumption later prove to be untrue, you can fall back on other strategies and assumptions.

Although the three forms of exchange (with positive and negative variations) may seem straightforward, many questions remain to be answered in order to make successful exchanges with potential allies who may not be eager to cooperate. For example:

- □ Am I clear on what I really want?
- □ Do I know what the ally needs; and, if not, how do I find out?
- □ What resources do I have, and would any of them equate to the interests of the ally?
- □ Is our relationship positive enough to make transactions possible and relatively easy?
- □ If not, how do I create sufficient trust to allow exchanges to take place?
- □ Does my interaction style fit with the preferred style of the potential ally? How much can I change my style and still be true to myself?

These are the kinds of questions that you will learn to answer as you read this book. Like the person who discovered that after all these years he was unknowingly speaking "prose," you probably already are instinctively doing much of what we describe here. Close attention to the subtleties of exchange, however, should yield enhanced influence.

SUCCESSFUL EXCHANGE: THE CASE OF ANNE AUSTIN

With these fundamental ideas about exchange and reciprocity in mind, we can now look in detail at the experience of a young, ambitious manager who used many forms of exchange to accomplish her organizational and personal goals. We will then use her experiences to extend the concepts presented in the rest of this book.

When Anne Austin joined Cosmarket Corporation as a sales forecast associate, she was excited about using what she had learned as an undergraduate business major to create and market quality consumer products. She knew that Cosmarket's tough requirements would make it extraordinarily difficult to work her way over to a brand manager's job in marketing where she would have the leverage to achieve her goals, but she was determined to find a way to do it. The competition for marketing jobs at Cosmarket was intense, and only a very few had ever made it from within other functions at the company. Furthermore, Anne's undergraduate degree was from a good but lesser known college, which put her behind the eight ball for entry into a marketing organization dominated by MBAs from Harvard, Wharton, and Northwestern. Despite the odds, however, she was determined to make it.

Anne's strong analytical skills had boosted her up the market research department's ladder twice in three years, to her present position of senior forecast analyst; and she had been rated in the top performance category two years running, a rare occurrence. Along the way, she had befriended two other managers who had managed to cross functions into marketing. These colleagues advised her to do two things to increase her chances of getting a marketing job: obtain an MBA and get experience with consumer goods.

Anne entered an evening MBA program that allowed her to continue working at Cosmarket while pursuing her degree. To acquire consumer goods experience, she took advantage of a course requirement to conduct a consumer study of an about-to-be launched Cosmarket Corporation laundry product. Anne's research findings had the potential to make a real contribution; she discovered that the product's package design did not communicate clearly to consumers the main feature of the product. When she realized this, Anne wanted to go immediately to the product's brand manager with her findings; but she was told by the vice-president of market research that, since hers was only a pilot project and she was not a professional researcher, she should keep quiet about her findings. Ignoring the warnings, Anne went informally to the product brand manager with her findings and concerns. The product manager listened, agreed, and implemented a last-minute change that overcame the problem. Not only did the product make a successful launch, but Anne made a good friend and future ally in the grateful brand manager.

In order to do her project using actual Cosmarket data and customers, Anne had obtained permission from Henry Logan, vice-president of market research. In granting permission, Henry told Anne that her "school project" could only be pursued after office hours; and, although the project's outcome was beneficial to the company, Henry barely acknowledged her efforts. (See Figure 2–1 for a partial organization chart.)

The last course Anne took as part of her MBA program was on "intrapreneurship," which also required a project within an organization. Students were expected to find an activity that would generate at least $1 million in sales or $50,000 in savings, develop it, prepare a business plan, and present the idea to the relevant executives.

An Opportunity

Timing and opportunity were on Anne's side; just as she began the course, she hit upon an idea that seemed to have great potential. As part of her job, Anne had been conducting a market segmentation study of shampoos, digging through a newly acquired research study for what she needed. In the process, she discovered that 10 percent of the shampoo sold had wheat germ added, yet Cosmarket had no wheat germ in its lines. She was shocked to find a "natural" product, one with sales as large as the dandruff or baby shampoo segments, sold by competitors but ignored by her company. The opportunity for a wheat germ-added shampoo in the price–value (inexpensive) end of the market seemed great; Cosmarket's "Dew Drop" brand line of products was a likely candidate for addition of this popular ingredient.

This seemed like a wonderful opportunity to do a good course project and at the same time make a significant contribution to the company while demonstrating her marketing skills. Because the company was very strict about allowing new product ideas to come only from marketing, or from chemists who somehow discovered a new formulation, Anne knew she had to proceed cautiously. She could not even use the company suggestion system, since it expressly ruled out new product ideas. Furthermore, as a forecast analyst working for market research, Anne had no formal channel for initiating product ideas to marketing, the high status group in the company. And she correctly anticipated that Henry Logan once again would provide no support and restrict her to pursuing her idea only as a school project on her own time. Because he was a very thorough market researcher who operated

Figure 2-1

PARTIAL ORGANIZATION CHART—COSMARKET CORPORATION

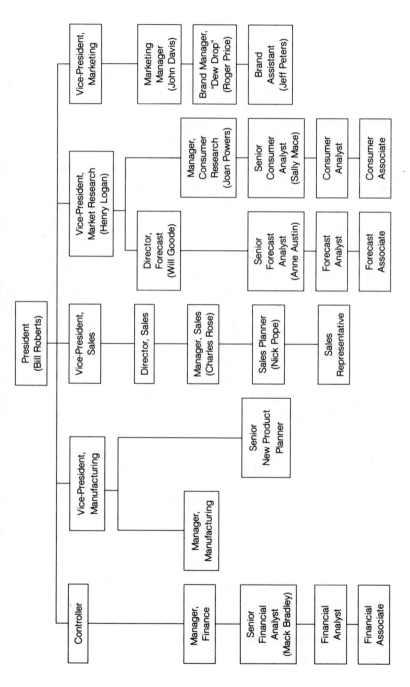

cautiously and by the book, Henry didn't get excited about a project developed in an unorthodox and informal way.

First Move:
Test Her Idea

Anne decided that her first move would be to test her idea on someone from the sales side. She approached Nick in sales planning, a peer with whom she was friendly. Nick had just returned from a field visit where he had seen the competitors' products on the shelves, and he reacted positively to Anne's idea.

After she spoke with Nick, Anne recalled that during her training period she had spent a week in the field with a sales manager who had pumped her for information about company plans. The sales force was informed about new product launches only after everything was in place. As a result, sales personnel often felt uninformed and sought every scrap of information they could glean. If they got wind of a possible new product, they could become useful allies in encouraging Cosmarket to develop it. In addition, Charles Rose, Nick's boss and the sales manager, was too busy to get involved in exploring new product ideas. Having heard from Henry that Anne's efforts were merely a "school project," Rose was not likely to be much help.

Accordingly, Anne suggested to Nick that he run her idea by some district sales managers. As she anticipated, the seed she planted took root with the sales force, which subsequently began to ask for the product.

Overcoming Consumer Research Objections

Anne's next step was to approach Joan Powers, manager of consumer research, to get confirmation that wheat germ was an attractive additive and to determine who was buying the competitors' shampoos. To her surprise, Joan was very negative. She declared that wheat germ was a 1960s product for "hippies" and totally inconsistent with the Dew Drop efforts to keep its image up-to-date. When Anne argued that the market was big and that significant segments of it were buying wheat germ shampoos, Joan's curt response was that it was a bad idea to go back to a product that had been dropped 10 years earlier. Anne retreated.

But she didn't surrender. She went to Sally Mace, senior consumer analyst under Joan, who had traded information with Anne in the past, and requested results from a national consumer survey of personal care products, along with any available focus group data. Although Sally asked Anne what she was working on, she supplied the data and didn't express disapproval of the idea.

Still unsettled by Joan's reaction, Anne dug into the data. When she finally went to the marketing managers with her idea, she didn't want them to throw it out because she hadn't done her homework. Careful reading of the studies led her to the belief that wheat germ product purchases were made by athletic consumers who liked the "back-to-nature" aspect of natural ingredients. In fact, the majority of the purchases were of products that had protein additives along with the wheat germ. Her conclusion: The combination of both wheat germ and protein appealed to the athletic-minded consumer. This was good news; she now had a better story to tell, one that was more consistent with the new, updated image of Dew Drop. Joan's negative reaction, and Anne's homework in response, had probably saved her neck!

Approaching the Brand Manager

Using what she had learned, Anne prepared a sales forecast for a Dew Drop Wheat Germ and Protein Shampoo. She took it to Roger Price, brand manager for the Dew Drop line. Anne knew that Roger, who was young and well-respected, had a reputation for getting things done in far less time than other brand managers. Part of the secret of his success was that he gave his assistants great latitude to work on a variety of projects instead of having them all work on the same project under very close supervision. He apparently was more willing to take risks than most brand managers. On the wall of his office was a sign that read:

> The brand manager's job:
> To inspire creativity and entrepreneurship
> among the group working
> with me and around me.

Anne also knew that Roger was highly respected by his boss, John Davis, the marketing manager. It was John who would make the decision about Anne's product idea, and who also held the key to her eventual entry into the marketing division. He was responsible for hiring new assistant brand managers.

Anne decided that a direct approach to Roger would work best; she marched into his office and said, "I have an idea for a wheat germ and protein addition to the Dew Drop line; I think it will make you an incremental $4.4 million a year in sales. Are you interested?"

"Of course," he replied.

Anne told Roger what she knew so far: the forecast, size of market, competitors' wheat germ products, and the interest in sports among consumers. Although Roger liked the idea, he told her that she had a long way to go if she wanted to sell it to John. He mentioned a number of questions for which she would need answers, including many she had not considered, such as color of the shampoo, color of the bottle, sales dollars lost from existing products, purchaser consistency (repeat sales) in relation to wheat germ products, and so on. When Anne responded that she estimated the wheat germ addition would draw away approximately 10 percent of existing Dew Drop sales, comparable to a line extension the previous year, Roger explained that John would want to see in far more detail the impact on each existing product, on the competitors' products, and so on.

Finally, however, Roger called Jeff Peters, his new assistant, into the room, asked him to help Anne, and told him "to make sure she gets everything she needs." This gave Anne the impression that Roger saw this as a chance to get an extra person working on his line. In addition, Roger enthusiastically remarked, "This is a great new product idea with a proven formula; I won't have to spend anything on market research."

Roger then contacted Anne's boss, Will Goode, and cleared the way for her to work on the idea. Since Anne had been a standout performer for him and could get her regular work done in far less time than the other forecasters, Will agreed, even though his boss, Henry, had said that Anne should work on the project only on her own time.

Informing Her Boss' Boss

Anne knew that Henry sat on the operating committee, which had final sign-off on new products, and she didn't want to alienate him; so she made it a point to keep him informed by memo at every stage of what to him was still her school project. She wanted him to be able to say, "That's one of my people," if the product actually made it into production. She thought that Henry would be won over if other people, specifically people from marketing, showed interest. He had to maintain his position with the marketing people, after all, and wouldn't resist their interest.

Nevertheless, Anne was concerned about how Henry would react to the absence of any budget for market research. His departmental budget had recently been cut, and she thought that he might be unhappy that marketing would develop a new product, with the help of someone from his organization, without spending money on research. Anne decided to turn again to Roger, in an attempt to head off any problems down the line with Henry.

Obtaining Research Funds from the Project Manager

"Roger, remember how you asked me about whether wheat germ buyers always buy wheat germ or whether they switch around to other shampoos?" she asked at her first opportunity. "Well, there are no data on that now. You asked me, and so you *know* John will ask. It's probably a good idea to spend some money on research so that we're ready for John," she concluded.

Although he had not planned on any research expenditures, Roger was persuaded. He approached Joan to negotiate for a research project. The request piqued Joan's interest; she began to wonder if something interesting was going on, and she got Henry involved. A research contract was established. Anne's behind-the-scenes strategy had worked beautifully.

Gathering More Data

Meanwhile, Anne gathered other information she needed. Having been introduced by Roger's assistant, Jeff, to people whose cooperation she needed, Anne secured cost data from the chemist and manufacturing data from the plant where Dew Drop was made. She found that the plant was not producing at capacity, which helped her arguments. Some of Anne's interactions were with people who often requested sales data from her; she knew that their cooperation created an obligation, and she thanked them vigorously for their help. When subsequently she received requests from them, she got them answers in less time than usual.

Anne found that if she told people she was working on a project for Roger, and that *he* wanted the data, she usually got cooperation. For example, she realized that she would need profit-and-loss statements; if she herself prepared them, even though she knew how, John might not trust her numbers. So Anne went to Mack Bradley, a senior financial analyst, and said, "Roger has me working on this project. He wants you to run P&Ls on it. I'll give you all the information; when you're done, please give copies to Roger and me." This request created an obligation to Mack; later, she invited him to attend the presentation to John, to help defend the numbers if necessary. Mack was delighted to have the opportunity "to hear what's going on."

Preparing to Approach the Key Player: The Product Manager's Boss

During the research stage of this project, Anne had decided to allow Roger to be the one to keep John apprised of what was going on. She assumed that Roger would have the most credibility with John and would have the best chance of selling him on the merits of the idea. But now Anne, having assembled her data into a huge report complete with statistical back-up, was ready for her presentation to John. Roger didn't make it easy, however. He wasn't offering to set up the presentation, so the next time he asked Anne to do some marketing paperwork needed to get the ball rolling, she replied, "Be glad to, Roger. By the way, when can you set up the meeting with John?"

When Roger finally agreed to arrange the meeting, Anne made another request: "Roger, if we both want to look good at this presentation, I'd better know what John will ask. Can you show the report to him and get me an early read?" Anne had correctly assumed that Roger had been building her up to John; and if Anne came across as unprepared, Roger would look bad. To avert such danger, Roger granted Anne's request. John's preview questions caused Anne to scramble for answers. Her boss, Will, helped her with some of the questions; and she convinced Roger to have the chemist run a product cost analysis. Although the chemist was reluctant to work on a product that he believed would be killed, Roger convinced him that the product was likely to see the light of day. As it turned out, wheat germ was actually cheaper to add than any existing ingredients; that fact made Anne's analysis of sales lost from existing products look even better. Replacement sales would boost gross margin, and additional sales would increase total revenue.

Making Her Pitch

The presentation meeting included John, Roger and all his staff, plus Anne's invitees: Mack Bradley, the financial analyst; Joan and her senior analyst, Sally Mace; and Anne's boss, Will Goode. Anne worked long and hard on the presentation, especially the ending. As one not from the marketing "inner sanctum," Anne knew she had to be thoroughly prepared. On the other hand, she realized the marketers in attendance had special expertise to offer; and she knew that leaving them room to create the final product would help avoid not-invented-here feelings.

Anne summed up her presentation in this way: "I'm an analyst. I specialize in forecasting. My business is to analyze whether something can sell. I've shown that a wheat germ–protein shampoo should sell, and that Cosmarket can and should compete in this area. But there are decisions I can't make because I'm not a marketing person. One of these decisions involves packaging; we think we know from our research that people who buy price-value brands like certain colors, but we're thrown off by the fact that our competition has gone with other colors. Second, Dew Drop traditionally has used a transparent bottle, but our competition is using an opaque, cloudy bottle. It's up to the marketing group to decide whether a clear bottle is an important part of the image. Only marketing has the knowledge and expertise to address the packaging situation."

At the meeting, John made a tentative decision to proceed; and he assigned the remaining issues to Roger's group for resolution. He concluded with high praise for Anne, Will, and Roger; and he voiced special appreciation that such good, detailed work and a terrific idea had come out of the market research area.

Campaigning for an
Assistant Brand Manager's Position

In a fairy tale, Anne immediately would have been swooped up by marketing and put in charge of something important. But that didn't happen. She continued in her forecasting job, pleased that the shampoo was being added to the line. A few months passed, and Jeff Peters, the assistant brand manager who had helped her out, asked her if she knew that John was about to interview for a new assistant brand manager. In working with Jeff, Anne had learned a great deal about the actual tasks in his job, and she had helped him by introducing him to her contacts. They maintained their friendly relationship, and he tipped her off to the opportunity.

Anne believed she was ready to make her move. She consulted Will about a course of action, and he recommended that she talk to the personnel department. She made an appointment with a recruiting interviewer, during which meeting she was stunned to learn that there was "no way" she could be considered for a marketing job because marketing had a policy that mandated new staff be hired only from the outside. The recruiter explained that Anne could quit her current position and then apply for the new job; but, since she did not have an MBA from Harvard, Northwestern, or Wharton, she wouldn't even be invited for an interview! Incredulous, Anne went to the head of personnel, cornered him in his office at the end of a day, and expressed her outrage. He tried to calm her down by promising to talk to John.

Certain that nothing would be done on her behalf by personnel, Anne mobilized her network of company friends and associates. She sought help from a brand manager whom she had once helped overcome salesforce resistance to a new product, asking him how to get to John, how to present herself, and what marketing would look for. The brand manager not only offered to talk to John, but he also gave her the evaluation sheet used for recruitment interviews and coached her on how to meet the criteria. Roger also agreed to help her; he talked to John on Anne's behalf and gave Anne valuable advice on how to sell herself to John. A few days later, Anne got her chance. Jeff Peters arrived in Anne's office bearing a request from John for certain data he needed for a project. Anne smiled and said, "Tell John he can have what he needs by Monday morning if he'll give me five minutes to talk with him." John met with Anne.

Anne stated her case assertively and with confidence. She told John that she wanted to join marketing, and that she knew she was damn good and could be successful. If he wouldn't consider her, she would respond to the inquiries she had been receiving from a major competitor and leave the company. John agreed to include Anne in the formal search process. A few days later, Anne was notified of the time and date of her interview.

More conversations with colleagues about how to play it in her interview helped Anne prepare both the content John might ask about, and an appropriate interview style. As a result, she arrived armed with a list of five examples of things she had accomplished for *each* of the major qualities John required in potential hires, and she was ready for the particular questions John asked that had not been spelled out in the interview guide. At the end of the interview, John admitted that he had been impressed by Anne's performance on the wheat germ project but hadn't realized the range and depth of her experiences. She was offered the job.

3

The Power of Mutual Exchange: Getting What You Want and Giving Others What They Need

A penny for your thoughts.

Pre-inflation folk wisdom on how
to make a profitable exchange

Trades would not take place unless it were advantageous to
the parties concerned. Of course, it is better to strike as
good a bargain as one's bargaining position permits. The
worst outcome is when, by overreaching greed, no bargain
is struck, and a trade that could have been advantageous to
both parties does not come off at all.

Benjamin Franklin

A nne Austin successfully used a variety of exchanges to wield organizational and personal influence in a difficult situation. Bill Heatton, however, did not have the influence he wanted because he could not figure out the appropriate exchanges. This is typical of organizational life. Without exchanges, it is hard to imagine how people could achieve anything important. In this chapter, we will look closely at how to use exchanges to get things done. We begin by drawing your attention to Figure 3–1 on the following page.

SUMMARY OF THE EXCHANGE MODEL

ASSUME OTHER IS A POTENTIAL ALLY

When you need something from someone who has no formal obligation to cooperate, begin by assuming that the person is a potential ally. Failure to do so can easily wreck an influence attempt.

Figure 3–1

THE COHEN-BRADFORD MODEL OF INFLUENCE
THROUGH EXCHANGE

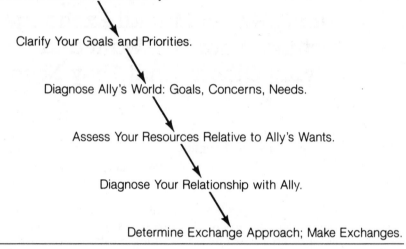

Assume Other Is a Potential Ally.

Clarify Your Goals and Priorities.

Diagnose Ally's World: Goals, Concerns, Needs.

Assess Your Resources Relative to Ally's Wants.

Diagnose Your Relationship with Ally.

Determine Exchange Approach; Make Exchanges.

Assuming the other person will be an adversary rather than an ally prevents accurate understanding and leads to misperceptions, stereotypes, and miscommunication. The right mindset is the basis of a mutually rewarding relationship, but you have to know yourself as well.

Clarify Your Goals and Priorities

It may seem obvious that you need to know what you want from the potential ally in order to achieve influence, but this isn't always so easy. You have to be clear about just what you require, your priorities among several possibilities, what you are willing to trade off in order to get the minimum you need, and whether you want a particular form of cooperation on a specific item or would settle for a better relationship in the future. Would a short-term victory be worth the creation of hard feelings, or is the ability to come back to the person in the future more important? You need to think hard about your core objectives, so you won't get sidetracked into pursuing secondary goals.

Diagnose Ally's World:
Goals, Concerns, Needs

Make every effort to diagnose what is important to the potential ally so that you can determine in advance something he or she wants. For example, it is helpful to know enough about the potential ally's job situation so that you can tell what might be valued in terms of job and personal interests. What costs would be incurred if the ally were to comply with your request? It is important also to determine the potential ally's preferred style of interaction; with this knowledge, you can plan a strategy that has the best chance of acceptance on its merits rather than risk rejection of your *style*.

Assess Your Resources Relative to Ally's Wants

Know what resources you command or have access to, so that you can use whatever "legal tender" you may need. Because many people underestimate the resources they can muster, they jump to the conclusion that they have nothing to offer. But a careful look at the many things you can do without a budget or formal permission—the alternative currencies you command—can reveal potential bargaining chips.

Diagnose Your Relationship with Ally

Do you have a prior relationship, and is it positive or negative? If you know the potential ally already and have a good relationship, it is easier to ask for what you want without having to prove your good intentions. If, however, the relationship has a history of mistrust—whether for personal reasons or because you represent departments in conflict—or there has been no prior contact, proceed with caution. You will need to pay attention to building the requisite trust and credibility.

Determine Exchange Approach;
Make Exchanges

Once you have determined what goods or services can be exchanged, which of the three types of exchange to use, and whether to use a positive or negative variation, then you are ready to offer what you *have* in return for what you *want*. Your approach will be shaped by how attractive your resources are, how badly the ally needs what you have, how badly you need what the ally has, the organization's unwritten rules about how explicit people are allowed to be in expressing what they want, the prior relationship you have with the potential ally, and your own willingness to stick your neck out. We will discuss all of these issues in more detail later in this book, but for now it is important to understand that expectations of reciprocity are vital in gaining influence.

Let's look at how the influence exchange process worked for both Anne Austin and Bill Heatton. First, how did they *think about* the people they wanted to influence—as obstacles to progress or potential allies?

Moving Targets: The Potential Allies of Anne and Bill

There were numerous people for Anne to influence, and she couldn't easily tackle all of them. John, the marketing manager, was the person she cared most about, because he would not only make the decision about the new shampoo, but could open the door to a marketing job. Roger, John's subordinate, was also critical, since he was the brand manager. She regarded both of them as potential allies, and devoted considerable energy to thinking about how to get what she needed from them by connecting to their interests. She wanted to create alliances with them that would benefit all parties to the transaction.

To a lesser extent, Anne perceived many other people as potential allies, including members of the salesforce, the assistant brand manager, the financial analyst, her friend in market research, and so on. Because she had built prior relationships, some of these people were already strategic allies even though she had not yet called on them; she considered others as potential allies and approached them accordingly.

Yet, Joan Powers, the manager of consumer research, and Henry Logan, vice-president of market research, were kept at a distance. Whether Anne could have directly persuaded them to help her isn't clear, but instead of trying to engage their support, she worked around them. At the same time, she did not think of them as enemies; rather, she anticipated their concerns and avoided antagonizing them. She kept Henry informed in a general way so that he would not be surprised and sabotage her efforts. While this doesn't exactly constitute an intimate strategic alliance, she did think about his interests and accommodate them. It must have been very tempting to write Henry off as an old fogey, or to treat Joan as a closed-minded blocker; but, because Anne wanted to keep later alliance possibilities alive, she maintained her civility—and even acquired valuable ammunition as a result of Joan's resistance.

Thus, Anne did not actively pursue every potential alliance, but she did consider many as potential allies at one time or another and always kept her options open. The person she made the least effort to influence was the personnel manager, partly out of her frustration at the rigid, depersonalizing response he gave, and partly because she knew that the power to select her resided in marketing, not personnel. Since she expected nothing from the personnel manager, she was willing to risk alienating him in an attempt to make him uncomfortable enough to act. It isn't easy to embarrass a colleague into becoming an ally (a negative exchange), but sometimes even that may produce cooperation.

Because Bill Heatton, on the other hand, never once regarded Ted, his counterpart in the telecommunications division, as a potential ally, he quickly got angry and frustrated when Ted failed to respond. Also, he had already written off Roland as a worthwhile ally; his boss, the general manager, he saw only as a court of last resort rather than as a possible resource for problem solving. Thus, Bill isolated himself from potential allies, and felt incapable of effecting any mutually satisfying solution. Bill learned a painful lesson: Perceiving those you want to influence as enemies does not lead to productive interactions.

Anne's World, Bill's World: Goals and Priorities

Anne had two goals: to get wheat germ shampoo accepted and to land a marketing job. Although she wanted to build good relationships for the future, first she had to determine her priorities as they changed from moment to moment. In pursuit of her primary goals, Anne was very focused; and she was able simultaneously to affect the welfare of Cosmarket and her own career. As a result, she had a sense of when to push and when to back off.

For example, when preparing her presentation to John, Anne knew that John would expect every "i" dotted and every "t" crossed. On the other hand, Anne knew that marketing would want some ownership of this new product, and that the in-depth marketing expertise of John and his staff would certainly help determine the best way to package the product. If she were pursuing a singular goal of landing a job in marketing, Anne might have had trouble deferring to their expertise; she would have felt compelled to show off her preparation and knowledge. Instead, she was able to take the long view that a successful product introduction would be best for the company and eventually boost her reputation, and she made space for the brand management group to decide issues she knew less about.

Unlike Anne, Bill had a lot of trouble sorting out his goals and priorities. He wanted to get rid of Roland, but that was actually a means to a more important end: improving the project management process and reversing the division's current slump. Bill wanted Ted to acknowledge his needs; but he wanted only a particular response, not joint problem solving. He wanted revenge, but he didn't want to harm the organization. He wanted the problem resolved, but he didn't want to involve the general manager because that would look weak. No wonder Bill was unable to muster influence; he had not figured out exactly what mattered most to him. As a result, he was unable to develop a plan of action.

MATCHING THE WORLDS OF POTENTIAL ALLIES WITH ANNE'S AND BILL'S RESOURCES

Although it is conceptually elegant to separate the diagnosis of what matters to potential allies from the resources available to give them what they want, it is easier to discuss the experiences of Anne and Bill by linking these steps. In this way, we can keep track of the players without an elaborate scorecard. For added convenience, we have included a table, Figure 3–2, which shows what was important to (the currencies of) each of the key potential allies we introduced.

Anne had to figure out what was important to Roger and John, what in their work lives might be keys to understanding what mattered to them, what she could then pull together for resources to offer in exchange for their cooperation, and what interaction styles in her repertoire might match theirs.

Anne discovered a market opportunity for shampoo with wheat germ, but she was blocked because there was no formal organizational channel through which to introduce her idea. She needed to get Roger, the relevant brand manager, on her side. Her first step was to act upon Roger's interest in the views of the salesforce. Remembering also from her earlier experience the salesforce's hunger for any scraps of information about company plans, and wanting a constituency for her idea, she tested their reactions and determined the likelihood of their receptivity. The salesforce was an important part of Roger Price's world, constituents on whom he depended for sales of his existing products.

Figure 3-2

IMPORTANT INTERESTS OF ANNE'S ALLIES—ROGER PRICE AND JOHN DAVIS; AND BILL'S ALLY—TED LOWRY

Roger Price

- Sales force views and support
- Increased sales
- Extra resources for researching product-line extensions
- People who work directly and fast

John Davis

- Thorough proposals with all angles covered, all details thought through. Probably does not want to invest in losing products or his judgment would be questioned.
- People who can be bold

Ted Lowry

- Minimize project management costs
- Utilize existing talent
- Keep his department from feeling that he doesn't protect them from outside attacks

---

Their questions about when they could expect a wheat germ product inspired Roger's interest.

Next, Anne looked for other ways to gain Roger's support. She realized that his goals for brand sales might make him receptive to a product that (almost) *guaranteed* a sales increase. The possibility of "free" help researching the idea was also likely to be attractive to him; and Anne could increase her visibility with marketing if she were the one doing the legwork for the new product. Both would benefit.

As for the *style* of interaction she should use, Anne banked on her knowledge that Roger was a fast worker and likely to respond to a concise approach. Thus, her direct appeal to him on the basis of a $4.4 million addition to sales, without undue warm up, was tuned to the things that mattered to Roger as well as to his preferred work style. Anne both judged accurately and acted upon the things Roger valued and the way he preferred to interact, important parts of the potential ally's world.

Similarly, Anne wanted to sell John Davis, the marketing manager, on her worthiness as a potential brand manager. She correctly surmised that, as someone who heard many proposals for new products in an industry where most new products fail,

John valued extraordinary thoroughness. She also learned that, in terms of interactive style, he responded best to detailed proposals that had been fully researched. Furthermore, she picked up on his preference for boldness, which told her to be assertive in insisting on his attention. Once again, Anne first determined what was important to a person she wanted to influence and the style he preferred, and tailored her approach accordingly.

Other Resources Anne Mobilized

As a sales analyst in a company dominated by marketing, Anne was a lesser player and could easily have given up when she learned it was "impossible" even to make her product idea suggestion, let alone sell it to the marketing organization. She found, however, that despite her lack of formal power, she could muster some valuable resources to trade. Earlier favors had given her friends who were glad to help her even though they were under no obligation to do so.

For example, she could create a win-win exchange by inviting to the presentation meeting the financial analyst who helped her. His presence was useful as a backup for Anne. But even more importantly, for him it was a chance to be visible and to observe how his work was utilized. In this way, Anne repaid his assistance with the opportunity to be seen. With Roger, Anne could trade her time and research skills for his influence and support. That she was an excellent performer in her job gave her leverage with her boss, whose willingness to allow her to work on the new shampoo was crucial. And for Henry, the skeptical head of marketing research, Anne created something he would value—supplementary research funds—when he was treating her work as merely a "school project." For an apparently powerless person, Anne managed to muster quite an arsenal of valuable resources.

Finally, Anne practiced versatility matching her style of interaction to the person she was dealing with. She was deferential to Joan and Henry, who let her know they did not regard her as either powerful or knowledgeable about marketing, and she retreated without stirring their anger. Yet with Roger she was direct and challenging; with John she was bold, but thoroughly prepared. With the bureaucratic personnel manager who was trying to dismiss her, she was demanding and expressive, which made it hard for him to ignore her. And with peers she was casual and friendly.

In all her costume changes, Anne was never phony; she just called upon different aspects of her own personality, responding instinctively whenever she could to the preferred style of others. Indeed, she may have been too deferential to Henry, who was rather patronizing to her, which may have prolonged his treatment of her as a harmless student. When she persuaded Roger to provide funds for Henry's research area, she never went back to Henry to mention her part. She guessed that Henry knew, but she wasn't certain. Anne's reticence with Henry was an indication that she should develop her rapport with conservative elders to expand the range of styles available to her.

Bill's Failed Diagnosis

In contrast to Anne, who demonstrated the ability to anticipate the interests of those she wanted to influence and then figure out how to offer them something they valued, Bill Heatton was frustrated at his inability to influence Ted Lowry. As a result of the very human tendency to focus on self-interests, Bill missed seeing the issue from his potential ally's point of view. When he stopped thinking of Ted as a potential ally, Bill became blind to Ted's world.

For example, Bill did not think about what costs Ted would incur if he were to remove Roland from the project. Bill should have first asked himself the following questions:

□ Does Ted have anyone better?
□ Does Ted believe that he can coach Roland into a better performance on this project?
□ Does Ted even agree that Roland did a poor job on the last project, or does he blame the project's failure on other departments' shortcomings?
□ Is Ted trying to save face with his other subordinates?
□ Does Ted fear he will set a precedent by allowing R&D to determine his staffing?

Bill was so intent on telling Ted that he should get rid of Roland that he never bothered to assess what Ted's perceptions might be or to consider how it would affect Ted to go along.

Finally, Bill never even asked Ted why he had not responded. Perhaps Ted was being measured by different criteria or pressured by the general manager in some way that made it impossible to respond to Bill's request. Instead of fuming and dreaming of revenge, Bill might have set out on a fact-finding mission to learn what he could do to fashion an exchange worthwhile from Ted's point of view as well as from his own.

Bill might have approached Ted in a friendly, nonthreatening manner and said, "Ted, I'm really baffled. It seems to me that you are reluctant to address my concerns about Roland. Obviously, my view of him is different from yours, so help me understand where you are on this." Such a first move might have at least broken the ice. Without knowledge of the potential ally's world, it is difficult to pinpoint what would produce the desired response.

While Bill's values prevented him from striking out in a way that would hurt the organization, he seemed completely unaware of the resources he could muster for a positive exchange. His relationship to the general manager was a card he hated to play, but there might have been ways to do it without appearing weak and unmanagerial. Could he have used the general manager as a sounding board on how to approach Ted? Could he have suggested that the general manager meet with him and Ted, not as the final arbiter but as a problem-solving consultant?

Furthermore, Bill appeared to have only two styles of interaction: nice or nasty. When nice did not work, he turned to nasty. More moderate styles—inquisitive, calmly insistent, or speculative—did not seem to occur to him. With a scientific background, Bill probably was capable of calling on such alternative styles, but he did not look carefully enough at his behavioral options to get any use from them. Thus, he had far less impact than he could have had.

THE RELATIONSHIPS OF ANNE AND BILL WITH THEIR POTENTIAL ALLIES

The way you can attempt exchanges is shaped both by the history of the relationship, and the degree to which you care about preserving or enhancing the relationship after you make an overture. Anne barely knew Roger and John, her two most important allies, so she did not have to overcome a bad history with them. But because she came from the wrong side of the organizational tracks, she correctly anticipated that they might not take her as seriously as they would a marketing person with the same idea. She knew she would have to move quickly to position herself as a force to be reckoned with, a competent professional with marketing savvy even though she did not hail from marketing. She accomplished that goal by doing her homework and making a direct and confident approach.

She had, however, fostered many other relationships with potential and existing allies. For example, a brand manager she had once helped proved to be a vital source of information about how to impress John. An alliance with Sally Mace in consumer research kept her in the game after Joan virtually shut the door in her face. Because Anne's boss liked and respected her, he agreed to release her part time. A tradition of linking and building—rather than burning—her organizational bridges—made it easier for Anne to get help without undue effort. This freed her to focus her energy in areas where she had less of a history and needed to build relationships.

We know less about Bill's history with Ted, although it appears to have been neither unpleasant nor extensive. The possibility that interdepartmental rivalry was shaping Ted's reactions, however, should have been something Bill considered before he approached Ted. Even if marketing wasn't blaming Bill personally for the problems in the past, as a representative of research he probably entered the transaction with some tar sticking to him. He should have allowed for that possibility and determined how to neutralize it, perhaps by a candid admission that research had undoubtedly contributed to past problems.

ANNE'S EXCHANGES VERSUS BILL'S UNRECIPROCATED ATTEMPTS

There are many varieties of exchange; Anne used several. She made exchanges that gained compliance for mutual benefit, such as when she asked the financial analyst for help and, in return, invited him to the meeting at which his data would be presented. In exchange for data he had no *obligation* to provide and his voluntary support at the meeting, the analyst received visibility and a sense of how his work was utilized.

Anne compensated others for their costs in responding to her requests, such as when she scrounged for research funds to be used in her division as a way of paying Henry for allowing her to use Cosmarket data in her course projects (and to compensate for the time she spent on marketing instead of sales analysis against Henry's instructions). In an interesting twist on using a compensate-for-costs strategy, she also created a self-generated kind of exchange. She first raised the costs to the other side for not complying, by shouting at the personnel officer to increase his discomfort, then lowered the costs by backing off. That is, she created the very cost that she could reduce by calming down when he agreed to help.

Anne proved herself a skilled horse trader in other, more straightforward, swaps of services, such as when she sent the message to John that she would deliver his information early in exchange for five minutes of his time. Some of her exchanges allowed her to "save for a rainy day," such as when she helped a brand manager by pointing out a package design flaw, then at a much later date secured the same manager's help in anticipating what John would ask her in an interview.

Bill, on the other hand, failed to make the most of exchange possibilities. Although he believed that he acted in good faith by juggling assignments in his own area, thereby creating an obligation in Ted, it isn't clear that Ted realized that Bill was reacting to his requests, or that Ted got something he wanted. It isn't even clear that Ted knew that Bill expected anything in return. Although Bill altered his own organization in anticipation of a comparable response from Ted, he did not make it clear to Ted how inconvenienced he was by this accommodation. As a result, Bill gave but he didn't get. What is the sound of one side exchanging? Resentment.

GENERAL LESSONS FROM ANNE'S EXPERIENCES

What broad conclusions about influence and exchange can we glean from Anne Austin's successes (and Bill Heatton's failures)? We will use their examples at many points throughout this book, but for now we will highlight a few general guidelines that apply to making the exchange process work.

An important lesson is that skillful use of exchange leads to effective influence and mutual advantage, while failure to use it makes it very difficult to achieve your goals or help allies achieve theirs. Influence involves exchange and reciprocity whether they are explicitly acknowledged or not; assuming that what you want is worthy, you might as well learn to use them.

No Wasted Motion: Attention to Exchange Helps You Focus Your Work

Anne devoted a considerable amount of time to diagnosing John, Roger, Joan, and others; but, because she was doing it to figure out currencies for exchange, it saved effort by letting her focus only on useful data. She didn't sit around spinning theories, getting angry, or reinforcing stereotypes with scraps of evidence; rather, she was able to determine who the key players were, what they wanted, what style they preferred for interactions, and what she could offer them. Although Anne rarely had to say in so many words, "You scratch my back and I'll scratch yours," she had a clear, intuitive sense of how exchange works, and it served to direct her attention.

Bill also recognized some aspects of exchange as integral to influence, prompted by the lack of reciprocity he felt from Ted; but Bill didn't have Anne's natural ability to use exchange. Because he had no frame for diagnosis, he could only stew in his own frustration. He didn't know what to ask Ted or how to initiate a dialogue about Roland that could guide him to a workable strategy. This is an apt illustration of social psychologist Kurt Lewin's maxim, that "There is nothing so practical as a good theory"—or, we might add, so impractical as the lack of a good one.

For example, think of how Anne reacted to Joan Powers' disparagement of wheat germ as a hippy product of the 1960s. Rather than get discouraged or furious, she treated it as a spur to investigation. She saw Joan's resistance as useful, not just as a nuisance, and took it as a stimulus to further analysis. If everyone is a potential ally with legitimate interests and viewpoints, opposition is a source of information about what matters to others and helps determine how to address their concerns. It doesn't guarantee that you can overcome all opposition—and if your opposer is right it shouldn't—but it gets you into the right frame of mind to learn from resistance and to do the homework necessary to overcome it.

Nose to the Grindstone: No Substitute for Hard Work

Although Anne had many interpersonal skills and intuitive understanding of influence techniques, her success was based on doing her homework. She devoted enormous energy to researching the key questions that would lead to a good decision, and her ability to influence some tough customers was very much a function of her preparation. Wheeling and dealing are no substitutes for having the right data.

Hard work itself is not always enough. (After all, Bill Heatton worked hard too.) However, hard work *is* a prerequisite for sustained influence in organizations. And using exchange as a model helps focus and guide the hard work toward the appropriate discoveries about both the problem and the person you want to deal with.

In the remainder of the book, we concentrate on the concepts and techniques for developing influence. We do so assuming that you have completed the appropriate spade work at each stage.

All-Star Team: Exchange Makes Everyone a Winner

We further assume that what you want is some kind of cooperation that will benefit the organization as you see it; and that you are not trying to gain influence for its own sake, or for pure ego gratification. Even then, however, there is no guarantee that the potential ally will see the merits of your request, will want to respond, or will be able to. As suggested in the first chapter, in a fast-moving, complex organization, the number of requests that members face will make tough choices necessary.

Anne certainly had her own ambitions, but in every transaction she took care to see that the organization would benefit and that the person she was trying to influence would get something valuable in return. Indeed, the way she gained influence was to first determine what would help the potential ally and then offer something to further the ally's goals as well as her own. Roger, for example, smoothed Anne's way into the shampoo line extension project and into the relationship to John, partly because Anne's efforts would add to his resources and to his ability to deliver for John.

It is important, then, to think about how to *join* the person whose cooperation you want and how to create conditions that make it most likely that each of you will come out a winner. Whenever possible, win-win outcomes are best; and you should approach each situation thinking about how to make that happen. Although it will not always be possible, the general mindset of "I want to help you accomplish your goals while accomplishing mine" is the best approach.

Remember: *Listen* to each key person and *take resistance seriously.* These steps not only reduce future negativity but let you learn what is important to others so that you can use it to shape your strategy.

Keeping Push from Coming to Shove: Exchange Lets You Be Assertive, Not Antagonistic

Anne Austin was in an environment that did not make it easy for her to accomplish her goals. She could have become discouraged or nasty; in one instance, she did. When she ran up against arbitrary personnel policies, she let her anger show. For the most part, however, she was persistent rather than offensive.

When Anne was trying to figure out how she was going to get marketing to listen to her product idea, she sought advice from friends outside of work. One friend listened to her description of the rules and norms at Cosmarket and advised Anne to go on a kamikaze mission to the president's office and demand that he listen to her idea. Anne was savvy enough to realize that there was virtually no way that the president was going to see her, let alone listen to her arguments for a product line extension. That would be blindly suicidal on her part.

Another friend advised her to quit and go get a marketing job at a more receptive, less rigid company. That was always an option, but Anne was wise and determined enough to make a serious effort before giving up. She knew that careful planning could make the odds of success much better, and she had confidence in her ability to figure out who the key players were, what they cared about, and what she could offer them for their cooperation.

For example, when she had done her homework about the brand manager job and was still waiting for an appointment with John, she used his request for information on another topic to apply just the right amount of pressure. Her readiness to speed up the answer to his request if he would meet with her for five minutes was impossible to refuse gracefully, yet it was not an ultimatum that might have blown up in her face if he declined to talk with her. Because her willingness to be a bit nervy on her own behalf fit with John's appreciation of confident, energetic brand managers, she was not taking a gigantic risk of being offensive.

Anne's diagnosis was obviously good, and she also was good at expanding her own repertoire of approaches. She got clarity about just what she wanted from each key figure, so that her interactions were focused. She used everything from friendly inquiry to threats, instead of relying on just one approach. She often used currencies accessible to her without permission of anyone, and once or twice she even went against what she had been told in order to deliver information that she was certain would be valued, thereby creating allies for future requests. She did not directly try to alter anyone's behavioral style, probably because she did not need to. If she were interested in changing the individual behavior of those around her, she would have needed to give them feedback connected to their goals, but she was more interested in using the existing system than changing it.

In part, Anne gained power because she was flexible and persistent. Although she assumed only one person was immovable, the vice-president of market research, Anne even found a way to get resources for him, which aroused his interest and made him more responsive. Interestingly, she never directly told Henry that she was responsible for prying research funds from the product manager, perhaps because he was much older than she, was her boss' boss, and was therefore an intimidating figure. With others she was not shy about reminding them what she had done for them, or about asking for reciprocal help.

The dilemma for hopeful influencers often is that they cannot find any ground between antagonistic domination and passive niceness. The exchange process allows you to exercise influence by using hard-headed toughness without being abrasive.

The process is powerful precisely because the nature of exchange gives the recipient something he or she values. The assertive pushing is directed at helping the potential ally also achieve desired objectives, not just at helping you achieve your goals. When you are aligned with an ally's goals—even if the ally is your boss—you can push very hard on almost anything, including behavior you'd like to change. "If that's what you want, I'll be glad to support you, but you're shooting yourself in the foot by the way you're behaving," is tough talk; but when it is linked to the ally's goals, it can be heard without offense. If you focus on helping your partner win, you can disagree even with a resistant boss.

OVERDOING EXCHANGE? WHAT HAPPENED TO PERSUASION, ALTRUISM, AND SPONTANEITY?

Making exchange explicit and advocating the conscious use of reciprocity can sound sufficiently narrow and self-serving to induce considerable discomfort in those not used to this way of thinking. Therefore, we want to address such concerns head on, demonstrating that persuasion is another form of exchange, altruism still involves a special kind of exchange, and that conscious use of these ideas, rather than purely spontaneous interaction, need not be manipulative.

Talk Me into It: Persuasion as a Form of Exchange

Often when people want to wield influence, they think first of being persuasive, of being able to speak in a way that convinces the other to go along. For example, the manager of a large group of engineers at Exotech Inc. claims, "Bullying is how researchers get their way in our company. They try to dominate each other with brilliance and look for weaknesses in the other's arguments. One of their best tricks is to ask a question that the person they're arguing with can't answer, which demonstrates that the questioner knows more!" Is there exchange in persuasive bullying, and if so, who gets what payoffs?

A closer look at this kind of persuasion reveals that it too is a subtle and usually implicit form of exchange. Arguments perceived as persuasive are those that help the listener achieve existing goals. Whether the goals are organizational or personal, successful arguments are those that help the potential ally achieve them. Thus the exchange is *compliance* for *progress toward a goal.*

It also helps when the source of an argument has credibility with his or her listener on that subject—such as the researcher who can dominate an argument because he or she is an acknowledged expert. It is easier to be persuasive if you really know what you are talking about and have a reputation for knowing. Technique becomes less important with genuine expertise. Nevertheless, compliance is exchanged for a perceived benefit. The benefit may only be known in the future, when results are in, so part of persuasion is the request for an act of faith that will only be proven later.

In the Exotech research lab where bullying prevails, for example, products that achieve intended functions are the ultimate goal. Although this goal *should* supersede the individual's desire to be "right," the desires do not vanish just because someone else's argument prevails. In fact, a bullying style proves to be short-sighted in this lab, because it produces unnecessary resentment that leads to retaliation attempts to one-up and embarrass the previous "winner." When that happens, serious examination of competing arguments is displaced by attempts to win at all costs, even when wrong.

Furthermore, because the technology Exotech deals with has become so complex that generalists have been replaced by specialists in each area of the business, bullying has been slowly eased out by more exploratory negotiations. Even former "know-it-alls" have had to concede to colleagues' greater expertise. Persuasion is still based on trying to show that one's arguments are correct, so that the product will be improved, but arrogance has decreased. When you pretend to be absolutely correct, but colleagues recognize the tenuousness of your knowledge on that subject, the credibility you need to be influential is diminished.

Although the parties involved may fail to recognize it, any attempt at persuasion can be seen as an effort to complete an exchange. They may not think about it in this way, preferring to perceive their actions as "just explaining why what I want is a good thing," or conceiving of the other's compliance as "just doing what makes sense," but there is implicit exchange going on.

Exchange can involve the subtle and intangible—nothing more than feelings and perceptions. For example, one member of an organization may secure another's agreement in exchange for confirmation that the potential ally is a "good corporate citizen." Cooperation is given for reinforcement of a certain self-image. While only words and perceptions have been exchanged, a form of influence has been executed. Each of the components of the influence process will be examined in more detail in succeeding chapters. There is, however, another aspect of the exchange process that tempers everything discussed so far.

When What You Know Can Hurt Me: The Fear of Manipulation

In some organizations where exchange is an accepted way of life, members talk freely about horse-trading and collecting chits. The phrase, "What's in it for me?" is frequently heard, and significant effort is devoted to determining colleagues' "hot buttons" to elicit the desired response. The practice of making exchanges is a comfortable one, and the only issue that remains is how the individual can sharpen his or her exchange skills.

We have encountered some people, however, who are very uncomfortable with the explicitness of what we propose. Something about deliberately reframing requests to fit the interests of the potential ally, or being nice now in order to create obligations for the future, raises their hackles. They see the conscious diagnosis of others' needs, the keeping score of who owes whom—indeed the very idea of doing anything to gain cooperation except for clearly stating what you want and why you want it—as manipulative.

Such people see themselves as sincere and generous, even altruistic. They are nice to others because they have friendly feelings toward them, not to get something in return. Most at ease when they function spontaneously in their work relationships, they want others to do the same. Planned interactions seem *calculated* and a denial of altruism; adjusting a request, language, or style to fit the audience seems *insincere*. They prefer to believe that the unvarnished truth (as they see it) will triumph—or should.

We wish that we could recommend just such a "damn-the-torpedoes; say-what-you-mean" approach. That would be a straightforward way to put the subject to rest. Unfortunately, the question of manipulation is complex. A number of considerations need to be weighed in order to develop a way of operating that is neither cynically self-defeating nor ineptly naïve.

First of all, it can be very difficult to distinguish genuine payment of intangible goods, such as appreciation or gratitude, from deliberately false compliments. When you show obvious pride in the way you have organized a report, is the colleague who wants you to make substantive changes sincere when he praises your organization before asking for those changes, or is he merely smart enough to recognize your investment and trying to soften you up? Is he calculating the effect of his very specific positive comments, or does he mean what he says? Worse, is he clever enough to do both: say only what he means, but select what to say to fit your obvious (or not so obvious) interests?

And, to make things even more complex, does it really matter? If he is telling the truth as he sees it, even as he chooses which aspect of the truth to convey, does it really matter if he is aware of the impact on you? No one likes a snow job, but when does careful selection of words cheapen the goods? Would any two readers of this book automatically have to distrust one another just because each knows the other understands the principles of exchange?

To argue that knowledge about influence automatically prevents authenticity, would render all learning useless—such an absurdity would make even the worst enemies of interpersonal training squirm. Yet, insincere use of knowledge can indeed turn its power to ashes.

The strategy is complicated by research which reveals that, in any negotiation situation, a number of less-than-totally-honest tactics can lead to a more favorable outcome for the negotiator who uses them well. You will gain more if you convincingly over-inflate your costs, the payoffs to your ally, and your exclusive command of valuable resources while at the same time you understate your own needs or the costs to the ally for cooperating with you. If you are skilled at this kind of word and number play and are in a situation in which the ally cannot easily check your claims, you can extend your influence. Conversely, the person who has mastered the same skills can gain influence with you.

In some organizations, exaggerating to sell your points is considered part of the game, and everyone understands that no harm is intended. Each side applies appropriate discount factors to what the other side claims, and no one objects to a bit of poetic license. There is grudging admiration for the person who has a way with words and can put the best face on any request or resistance.

Nevertheless, even in organizations where a bit of hyperbole is considered legitimate, deliberate lying is regarded as wrong. Although it might be okay to say, "You're going to love this new procedure once you're used to it," knowingly making a false claim ("This procedure will increase your bonus payments") would be unacceptable. To make exchanges work, you must build a track record of trust. The whole system breaks down when it becomes an endless hand of liars' poker.

Furthermore, in many organizations exaggeration is not considered acceptable. In some it is tantamount to deception. Thus, there is a good chance that even skillful bending of the truth will backfire. Facts have a way of emerging over time, and misstatements return to haunt the person who sacrifices the truth to get cooperation. Often your potential ally has ways of verifying what you are claiming about your costs, or the exclusivity of your resources, and can determine in advance if the benefits you promise will indeed materialize.

In addition, because organizations contain many informal networks of relationships, there is a high probability that no "secret" can be kept for long. As Ben Franklin observed over 200 years ago, "If you want three people to keep a secret, two have to be dead." (But we recommend you don't mention this to a soul.)

The likelihood of being able to be untruthful consistently and always get away with it is small; and the costs of developing a reputation for bending the truth are high. If you become known for being dishonest about what you want, have to offer, or will do in return for help, many of those you want to influence will shy away from dealing with you at all.

To understand fully the issues surrounding honesty and effectiveness, we will now discuss the aspects of relationships that affect what you can say or do in trying to get your way.

It's Not All Work: The Relationship with an Ally Before, During, and After Exchanges

As suggested in the discussions of Anne Austin and Bill Heatton, all exchanges between any two parties will be affected not only by the strategy of the person who wants influence, but also by the nature of the prior relationship between the two parties. Relationships loom large when it comes time to trade influence.

First, any prior transactions between you and a potential ally will affect each side's willingness to consider a deal, the extent of belief with which you listen to each other, and the degree of openness each of you feels in making interests and needs clear. It is easier to gain compliance if your relationship to that point is one of good will, and each person has confidence in the other's trustworthiness and commitment to fairness.

Second, the way in which you act *during* the discussions about the exchange can directly affect the outcome. If you seem to have a hidden agenda, if you talk but do not listen, or if you try to bully the wrong person, you can sour what might have been a sweet deal.

For example, one of our colleagues, Fred, tells a story about being approached by another associate, whom we'll call Wally. Wally was nicknamed "The Hustler," as a result of the deals he was always trying to pull off, usually at a colleague's expense. When Wally approached, everyone instinctively covered his wallet.

Wally came up to Fred, threw his arm around him, and said in a conspiratorial way, "Fred, old buddy, I want to help you along in your career. If you want to build your consulting practice, you need to socialize with the right people. I can get you in to the local country club, which is just what you need to make contacts."

The combination of Wally's reputation and too-familiar tone made Fred wary. He figured there had to be a catch, but he couldn't identify it. The high initiation fees were not as much of a deterrent as was the suspicion Wally aroused. Fred declined. It was much later when he quite by accident learned that Wally was trying to quit the country club and had to find a member to replace him in order not to forfeit his dues.

Third, the way you conduct the exchange discussions can also have a major effect on future dealings. This outcome is at least as important as whether you get the goods and services you wanted. Your future reputation is shaped by how you behave today. If you sow your seeds properly, you can reap many harvests.

Prior Relationship:
The Way We Were

In organizational life, reputation is a critical success factor. Two distinct perceptions shape your reputation and the way your requests will be received. The first is determined by your own prior behavior; the second part of your reputation is determined by factors you don't control, such as age, gender, department you work for, and the behavior of your predecessor.

For example, if you have become known as someone who puts self-interest first, like Wally did, people will respond to you with considerable caution. If you are in the accounting department and approach a member of the sales organization who accepts the sales stereotype of accountants as bean counters who care more for rules than results, you will find your requests met with something less than enthusiasm. In general, the greater the degree of trust you have established in a relationship:

□ The more readily your request will be taken at face value, and the less you will be required to prove your case
□ The less stringent will be the examination of whether you are paying back in kind, that is, the less your "quid" will be measured to confirm that it equals the potential ally's "quo"
□ The larger the line of credit that will be extended you; therefore, the more the potential ally is likely to be willing to do for you
□ The more liberal will be your repayment terms

Furthermore, the more time and effort you have devoted to finding common ground and a comfortable style of relating to the potential ally:

□ The less misunderstanding and frustration is likely to occur during the discussions and
□ The more rapidly the discussions will proceed to a favorable conclusion.

Of course, it is not always possible to have a prior relationship with everyone you want to influence. In such a case, the potential ally's attitude toward dealing with an unknown person will affect the outcome; but you can be sure someone who doesn't know you will pay attention to "the book" on you. Be sure you know what the book says before you make your move. Anne Austin, for example, had a generally positive reputation at Cosmarket, and it allowed her to work faster and more effectively than she could have otherwise.

Who's Counting?
Not Your Friends

In summary, the better the prior working relationship, the greater your latitude. With close colleagues or friends, it is usually considered bad form to look too closely at reciprocity and obligations, or even to talk about them directly. Going out of your way for a friend is just part of the relationship, and not done consciously to create obligations. The better the relationship, the longer people will go before even noticing they are supposed to be paid back, and the less likely that pressure will be put on the person who has acquired an obligation.

If with close colleagues the problem of paying back only arises in the breach, over a long period, it is easy to ignore reciprocity as a principle. It remains, however, especially important to know the score when dealing with those who know you less well, owe you no favors or allegiance, and have many competing claims on them. In such circumstances it is necessary to spend far more time diagnosing just what is needed to gain the cooperation you require to accomplish important work.

Relationship During Exchange Discussions:
Nothing Up My Sleeve

The second important aspect, beyond prior relationship, involves the manner in which both people conduct themselves during the discussions and negotiations. If you come across as open, fair, trustworthy, and sincere as discussions proceed, the results are likely to be different from those you get when you are seen as covert, underhanded, working a hidden agenda, or interested only in your own gain. Notice that the emphasis is on how you are *perceived* by the potential ally rather than on the true state of your intentions. Personal style plays an important role in making exchanges. With careful attention to the *content and style* of his or her communication, an unknown influencer can win the confidence of a suspicious ally. Conversely, even a trusted colleague can conduct an influence attempt in a way that makes the likely ally more cautious or suspicious.

There is no one correct way in which to attempt exchanges that increases likeliness of a favorable response. The issue is more one of fit between the styles of the two parties. Some peers or bosses will prefer straightforward demands made with confidence, as was true of Roger Price when he was approached by

Anne Austin. Others will be offended by anything but a friendly, indirect approach. Some will want hard data and numbers to support any request, while others recognize more intuitive or qualitative approaches. Some managers tune out lengthy, unfocused requests. (At Proctor & Gamble, legend has it that the one-page summary memo is an art form to be mastered before one can be taken seriously.) Other managers prefer more open-ended, exploratory approaches that allow them to get a hands-on "feel" for the issues. Keep in mind the cardinal rule of communication: Know your audience.

Not only must you consider your ally's style, but sometimes you might have to set aside the task considerations for a while and work directly on the relationship. If the discussions seem unusually strained, it may be impossible to make progress on exchanges until you address the reasons behind the strains. Smoothing communication problems will be discussed in more detail in Chapter 7, but for now we'll note that you and your potential ally may require a direct discussion of preferred style before you can get the exchange process on track.

As we have shown, there are few one-time-only exchanges in most modern companies. Today's peer is tomorrow's task force leader, next week's boss, or next month's peer with scarce, vital resources. *The outcome of any exchange, therefore, is important both for the goods and services you get, and for the impact on future ally relationships.* A short-term win can be very costly if it sours your trading partner for the next trade, or for the really big one down the road.

Burning your bridges is tantamount to organizational suicide. Survival is dependent on preserving open access in all directions. Anne Austin's gingerly treatment of Henry, the crusty old head of market research, reflected her genuine concern about future dealings with him. And Bill Heatton, the angry R&D manager, was wise not to behave in a way that would be seen as destructive toward the organization. Even if the people you are dealing with will never again be personally important to you, they still might spread your reputation in a way that later proves to be a handicap—even in another organization. It is very different from selling a used car to a stranger passing through town. Today, you never know when you might meet that stranger again. You might even be a passenger in that car someday!

Those who gain a reputation for being interested only in their own side of the bargain often are shunned, even when dealing with them might be in the organization's best interests. The same concept of reciprocity that makes it possible to gain influence—by finding a way to exchange something approximately equal in value to what you want—also governs the process of making exchanges over time. It is crucial to carry out exchanges in a way that both gets the tasks done and strengthens the relationship for known or potential future transactions.

Indeed, it is sometimes more important to strengthen the relationship than to get what you are asking for. Unless your request is absolutely critical to you and your organization, an unfulfilled exchange softened by an improved relationship has a double payoff: Future dealings will be easier, and the (still) potential ally might feel more obligated to cooperate in the future to compensate for his or her past refusal. Rarely will a potential ally keep saying no to someone he or she increasingly likes and trusts.

On the other hand, when you already have a strong relationship with the potential ally, you can push harder against the relationship's boundaries. If, for example, you have many resources to spend and a very good reputation for delivering on promises—or you are dealing with someone who does not comfortably resist an aggressive person—you can afford to make greater demands or pursue your own interests. It is unwise to hold back your interests unnecessarily, just as it is shortsightedly dangerous to push them so far that you create future resistance.

We believe it is possible to be tough in relationships without being seen as untrustworthy. If you are consistently reliable and honest, and always try to find ways to provide what allies want, then that will become part of the reputation you carry with you into influence transactions and which helps you push hard without seeming to be unduly self-interested. Again, we assume throughout this book that you want influence to do what you see as best for *both* yourself and your organization, rather than for you alone. You might not always be able to reach your goals *and* enhance your relationships; tradeoffs may be necessary, but you need to keep a careful eye on the tension. At the very least, be certain that you don't lose both the battle and the war!

The Road to Hell?
Or an Honest Map?

We hope this discussion of manipulation and its consequences on relationships has cleared up some of the complexities. Now we are in a position to say that *influence attempts are not manipulative if you can tell your potential ally your intentions with no loss of influence.* Following this rule does not require that you tell everything at once, nor does it prevent you from making your best arguments, but it does suggest that outright lies are beyond the pale.

There could be times, of course, when you would decide to be purposefully deceitful in the belief that the risk is worth the outcome and that truthfulness could not work; but that is the rare exception, and not the same thing as fitting your argument to what is important to your potential ally.

There are people who would prefer to make their case represent only their own concerns, who refuse to acknowledge that the ally has interests, too; but that amounts to moral righteousness, not influence. For example, an outraged woman who worked in the affirmative action department of a large company argued that it wasn't enough to persuade a key executive to advance women "as a cost-effective way of finding talented managers." She insisted that he be made to admit personal and corporate sexism in the past—even if that might cause him to back away from helping promote women. While such a strategy might make *her* feel better, it is not an effective way to enhance influence, and in our eyes is not less "manipulative." Unless the intention is about revenge rather than opportunities for women, this woman can achieve intended goals best by tapping into the executive's own goals.

A Rose by Any Other Name: Exchange Is Inescapable

Finally, despite the way we have described the *conscious diagnosis and use of exchange,* it is really a description of a fundamental and universal set of expectations. Overtly or not, everyone operates by the notion that, sooner or later, people should pay one another back, even if creating obligation was not the original intent. Violate those expectations for too long, and you will either earn wariness, retaliation, or, worst of all in interdependent organizations, isolation. Since reciprocity and exchange are what make the organizational world go 'round, you might as well consciously *recognize* and *use* them for sound personal and organizational ends.

Overdoers Syndrome

An overuse of exchange can be a barrier to influence. An engineering manager got himself into trouble when he got so carried away having fun with his new found exchange tools that he began turning every transaction into a negotiation. One of his colleagues finally yelled at him, "For Pete's sake, if you want to borrow my printer, just ask for it—and quit the fancy bargaining production number!" It is possible to trivialize any good idea by treating it as an elaborate game to play with people, rather than a useful tool to be brought to bear at appropriate times.

Your best protection against running away with your new found power, or being accused of harboring a secret agenda, is to work toward making your good intentions known. When it is apparent that your ultimate goal is to complete important work, you will be forgiven some awkwardness along the path. We trust that with this in mind, you will be able to invest wisely the portfolio of currencies that Chapter 4 will place at your disposal.

4

Goods and Services: The Currencies of Exchange

A horse! a horse! my kingdom for a horse . . .

> Shakespeare's Richard III, in the heat of battle,
> desperately seeking an attractive currency
> to exchange for immediate transportation.

Leonard Hirsch, vice-president of software development at a young software company, believed that all of the research activities in the company's recent acquisitions should report to him. Sheldon Marx, the company president and Leonard's boss, however, was inclined to create separate research departments reporting to separate divisions. Leonard believed strongly, and wanted to persuade his boss, that the programming knowledge needed for all the products, old and new, was comparable, and that programmers would make a greater contribution if they could work on many products rather than be confined to those in the division they would be assigned to. Leonard feared that the company's considerable expertise would be seriously diminished if all research wasn't coordinated across products.

Sheldon had been resistant to Leonard's arguments, in part because he thought that research would be less bottlenecked if it were in separate divisions, but mostly because Leonard had made his case in terms of *control* of product development; and Sheldon tended to be dismissive about concern for control. Because control wasn't something Sheldon valued, Leonard's apparent preoccupation with it created more resistance. Leonard was sure he was right, but he couldn't seem to get anywhere with Sheldon.

72

COIN OF THE REALM:
THE CONCEPT OF CURRENCIES

The metaphor of currencies can help you determine what you might offer a potential ally in exchange for cooperation. Because they represent resources that can be exchanged, currencies are the basis for acquiring influence. If you have no currencies in your treasury, you do not have anything to exchange for what you want.

All too often, people in organizations think too narrowly about the needs of potential allies, especially those they do not know well, and thus limit their own potential influence. They see only the ally's resistance in the immediate situation and fail to perceive the range of interests that might be satisfied in return for cooperation. Like Leonard Hirsch, they become preoccupied with their own needs and ignore the possibilities inherent in the ally's interests and values.

This chapter will offer ways of expanding your ability to tune in to the needs of others so that you can find currencies of your own to exchange. We will help you recognize the valuable resources you control, even if you're not a supervisor with formal currencies such as pay, promotion, status, and security in your war chest.

Although eventual trades will be of actual goods or services, knowing how to convert organizational resources into a common currency can be a great help when it is not obvious which of *your* available resources the ally wants. Whether explicitly discussed or implied, conversion always takes place. The key to a successful trade lies in figuring out which currency the potential ally prefers. Leonard Hirsch, for example, could get nowhere until he pondered his boss's currencies and realized that Sheldon Marx, an entrepreneur, most valued *innovation* and *excitement*.

Since the arrangements that Leonard wanted were actually quite consistent with these currencies, all he really needed to do was to reshape his arguments. He could work to show Sheldon that the synergy created when product developers for both old and new products were free to work side-by-side and share ideas, would allow many new features to be adopted across product lines. Leonard's plan would make the company *more* innovative, responsive, and creative, not less. But Leonard's approach to Sheldon was all wrong.

Although Leonard certainly wouldn't mind control over more people, he was not striving for control, but for serendipity and cross-fertilization. As programmers found new features, or better ways to reduce lines of code to speed up processing for the user, they could transmit those developments to the related products that colleagues in a united research department were working on. *That* was the message he had to get across in order to achieve his aims.

ESTABLISHING EXCHANGE RATES: HOW TO EQUATE APPLES AND ORANGES

If it is true that everyone expects to be paid back, in one form or another, then it is important to address the question of "one form or another." What will it require to make an offer in a currency that the other person considers equivalent?

In the economic marketplace, everything is translated into monetary equivalents, which makes it easier to say what a fair payment is. Does a ton of steel equal a case of golf clubs? By translating both commodities into dollars (or their equivalent in yen, pounds, or rubles), strangers can arrive at a fair deal, increasing the amount of one or the other to make things "even."

In the organizational marketplace, however, calculating the payback is more complicated than trading dollars for goods. How do I repay your willingness to help me finish my report? Is a simple "thank you" enough? Will it be sufficient for me to say something nice about you to your boss? And what if your idea of fair repayment is very different from mine? Absent an established "coin-of-the-realm," influence trading is a complicated process. That is why it is critically important to understand the world of the person you want to influence. Without a good understanding of what that potential ally experiences and values, it will be very difficult to create mutually satisfying exchanges—the basis for continuing influence.

WORKING THE INFLUENCE TRADE: GOODS, SERVICES, AND CURRENCIES

A useful way of conceptualizing what is important to the potential ally is to use what management educator Robert Kaplan refers to as trade metaphors—goods, services, and currencies—to identify interests. *Goods* are tangible items that may be exchanged, such as budget allocations or equipment. *Services* are intangible goods, such as when someone rushes a report in return for a tidbit of information; or sentiments, such as gratitude, respect, or liking, which are perfectly exchangeable, sometimes for concrete goods and sometimes for other services or sentiments. *Currencies* represent what is important to people, the general dimensions they value. We can say, for example, that a manager who will do anything to be liked by his subordinates trades in the currency of *affection*, while the boss who wants deference and admiration from her subordinates trades in the currency of *respect*.

Occasionally, members of organizations know exactly what they want in return for favors or help at work; but more often they will happily settle for very rough equivalents—provided there is reasonable good will. It may therefore be more important to identify the currency the potential ally likes to trade in, and offer to pay with goods that you have translated into that currency, than it is to determine the exact right amount. In other words, think about the nature (*quality*) of the currency in each transaction before you worry about the *quantity*.

YOU ARE MORE POWERFUL THAN YOU THINK

Later, we will devote an entire chapter to showing how to expand your ability to make things happen, but it is important to note here that most people are far more powerful—that is, have more capacity to influence—than they believe. The premise of exchange as the basis of influence is that you have something to exchange for what you want. If, indeed, you have nothing to offer, then you are in a low power position. The ability to say "yes," to give what another wants, is the basis for power.

Unfortunately, for many people the word "power" conjures up negative images. The stereotype of power is that powerful people say no to everything, and act like petty tyrants who have taken over a banana republic and go around shouting, "Off with their heads." But far more often in organizational life it is the ability to deliver, to provide what someone else needs, that makes one powerful.

Printing Money: Expanding the Currencies You Can Spend

Why is potential for power so often underestimated? As suggested earlier, sometimes people who appear to be impotent have been thinking too narrowly about what resources they command. They think only of budget dollars or promotions as relevant resources and, lacking these, assume they have nothing of value to trade. People also think they need permission to bestow valuable resources on others. But no supervisor or higher-up has to give permission for anyone to write a thank-you note, to publicly praise another, or to rush responses to a request. Often, valuable goods or services are at your disposal if you cast your net wide enough.

Similarly, many frustrated influencers have less clout than they could muster because they don't tune in to what potential allies really want or need. They are so caught up in their own concerns that they don't pay close attention to what is important to the person they want to influence. For example, we have seen many people, even at high levels, who are so certain that it would be impossible to influence their manager that they completely miss something as obvious as the manager's desire for proposals to be made in writing. The subordinate wants early feedback, but she is so sure that the boss won't like her idea that she doesn't bother to put it into a concise memo and send it ahead before the meeting. Creating a memo is within the subordinate's control, but she never sees how crucial that is to her reflective and busy boss, so she fails to take a simple but effective step to gain influence.

People also underestimate their own power because they aren't creative in seeing connections between what they have and what someone else wants.

For example: Nigel Howard was very frustrated at his inability to persuade a key colleague serving on the same compensation task force to come to grips with the implications of Nigel's proposal to adopt a "pay-for-knowledge" scheme for factory workers. Nigel was certain that this pay system was more consistent than the current one with the anticipated move to autonomous work groups and would boost performance; but he had encountered an apparent lack of interest from a key task force member. Although this colleague claimed she was too busy to master the thick pile of articles Nigel had given her, the reasons she gave for opposing the system showed that she did not understand it.

Despite Nigel's increasing frustration, he could not crack the apparent indifference of the task force member whose opinion most mattered. Finally, a colleague pointed out to Nigel that the apparently indifferent potential ally probably was too busy to master a scheme she didn't understand. Until she did, she could not get interested.

This perceptive colleague helped Nigel see that he had to find a way to save time for the overworked task force member.

"Why don't you write a two-to-three page summary that walks her through the ideas before trying to discuss the merits?" he suggested. "Then, if she agrees, you can show the others." It hadn't occurred to Nigel that his capacity (and available time) to do some homework and predigest the issues would be a valuable way to meet an important currency need of his colleague—*saved time.*

Helping you figure out how to utilize the resources you control or can access is one of the key aims of this book. You can learn to be as clever as Anne Austin in mobilizing currencies, even when you're not in an apparently high-power position. Anne (see Chapter 2) used the resources she had to create valuable currencies:

□ She always did her job well, which built her boss's confidence in her and, when the time came, made him willing to let her spend half her time on an out-of-department project.

□ She considered the information she collected and analyzed for her job as a way to develop new opportunities, and she traded that information for help from others.

□ She used her control of response-time priorities to offer a fast reply to the marketing manager with whom she wanted an audience.

□ From her genuine interest in people, she created friendships that later served her well when she needed help. The simple giving of time and attention to others was a powerful use of a resource that almost anyone can offer; and Anne did it freely, long before she knew how she would use the connections created. You can, too.

TOPS OF THE POPS:
FREQUENTLY VALUED CURRENCIES _____

If it is true that recognizing another's favorite currency is extremely important, both for choosing goods to offer and the language in which to offer them, then it is helpful to have in mind a variety of currencies that people in organizations find attractive. We have observed at least five types of currencies at work in a variety of settings:

□ Inspiration
□ Task
□ Position

□ Relationship-related
□ Personal.

Although the list is by no means comprehensive and is somewhat arbitrarily grouped for convenience, it does provide a broader view of possible currencies than many organizational members conventionally think about; and therefore it can be useful in alerting you to possible currencies valued by others or available to you to offer. In any particular instance, you may well find a group of currencies not covered in this rather general list. (Figure 4–1 summarizes our starter list.)

Inspiration-Related Currencies

These are currencies reflecting inspirational goals that provide meaning to the work a person does. They are increasingly valued by people at all levels of organizational life.

Vision

Vision is perhaps the grandest of currencies. Portraying an exciting vision of the company's or department's future, and imparting a sense of how the ally's cooperation will help reach it, can be highly motivating. You can help overcome personal objections and inconvenience if you can make the potential ally *believe in* what the organization is doing.

Stephen Jobs, for example, has been admired for his ability, first at Apple Computer and now at NeXT Computer, to inspire many employees with appeals to help transform the way people learn. This kind of broad, bold vision can move many people who want to feel they are doing significant work.

Sometimes the vision is about a department and how it should be run; at other times the vision is of an exciting project and its outcomes. In either case, there are people who only respond to doing work that they believe can make a big difference.

Excellence

The opportunity to do something really well, and pride in having the chance to accomplish important work with genuine excellence, can be highly motivating. In this sense, craftsmanship is not dead; it is only in hiding, waiting to be tapped. There are many people who want to do high-quality, polished work, and knowing how to make that happen can be a valuable currency.

Figure 4–1

CURRENCIES FREQUENTLY VALUED IN ORGANIZATIONS

Inspiration-Related Currencies

Vision	Being involved in a task that has larger significance for unit, organization, customers, or society.
Excellence	Having a chance to do important things really well.
Moral/Ethical Correctness	Doing what is "right" by a higher standard than efficiency.

Task-Related Currencies

New Resources	Obtaining money, budget increases, personnel, space, and so forth.
Challenge/Learning	Doing tasks that increase skills and abilities.
Assistance	Getting help with existing projects or unwanted tasks.
Task Support	Receiving overt or subtle backing or actual assistance with implementation.
Rapid Response	Quicker response time.
Information	Access to organizational as well as technical knowledge.

Position-Related Currencies

Recognition	Acknowledgment of effort, accomplishment, or abilities.
Visibility	The chance to be known by higher-ups or significant others in the organization.
Reputation	Being seen as competent, committed.
Insiderness/Importance	A sense of centrality, of "belonging."
Contacts	Opportunities for linking with others.

Relationship-Related Currencies

Understanding	Having concerns and issues listened to.
Acceptance/Inclusion	Closeness and friendship.
Personal Support	Personal and emotional backing.

Personal-Related Currencies

Gratitude	Appreciation or expression of indebtedness.
Ownership/Involvement	Ownership of and influence over important tasks.
Self-Concept	Affirmation of one's values, self-esteem, and identity.
Comfort	Avoidance of hassles.

Unfortunately, in the past several years the notion of excellence has been talked to death, often without much significance to the words. As the coauthors of *Managing for Excellence*, we have shuddered when we encountered cynical organization members who had tired of hearing lots of hype about excellence without seeing serious action from top management to make it happen. Nevertheless, many people still do take pride in working for an organization that does things well, and they will respond to the chance to contribute to that end. Consider how Scott Martin identifies vision and excellence as important currencies to Jim Bloch and trades them for Jim's cooperation:

Scott Martin wanted to persuade his colleague, Jim Bloch, to conduct a pilot test of an automated inspection machine. Jim, in his role as plant manager, was skeptical about trying the new machine before it had been proven elsewhere. Scott reminded Jim about their division's commitment to zero defects by saying, "This may be a pain now, although I believe it will work without a lot of bugs; but, most important, it really launches our effort to be the first plant in the company to be accepted as a supplier to Ford without incoming inspection. We can be ahead of everyone in the industry if we can make this work." Because Jim was excited about the potential for his plant to be the company leader in the new program, he was willing to try the untested machine.

Moral/Ethical Correctness

It is important to mention that many members of organizations will act according to what they perceive to be the ethical, moral, altruistic, or correct thing to do. Because they value a higher standard than efficiency or personal convenience, these people will respond to requests that let them feel they are doing what is "right." Their self-image is such that they would rather be personally inconvenienced than do anything they think inappropriate. This lets them feel good about themselves, so virtue becomes its own reward. For example, Brian Rooney was the purchasing manager in a high-tech division of a large manufacturing organization. Since its inception eight years earlier, the division had grown to almost $20 million a year in sales volume. The general manager, who built the organization, was beginning to recognize that growth was forcing him to consider needed organizational changes.

Over the years, more and more functions reported to the general manager, until he had 13 direct reports. None of them was happy with this arrangement, but no one wanted to give up this direct access to the general manager; nor did any of them want a narrower job.

In a series of management group meetings, the reporting structure was explored, but to no avail. There was gridlock on the subject, and everyone became increasingly frustrated. At one point, the general manager asked the group to think about the way they should be organized, independent of individual interests.

After a thoughtful silence, Brian spoke: "I don't want to stop dealing directly with you, Neil, but I have to admit that I'm hard pressed to justify why purchasing should not report to manufacturing. It kills me, but I think it would be most logical if we moved purchasing and quality control under manufacturing." The logjam was broken, and genuine exploration began to take place. Brian felt that, despite his personal desires, he had to do what made organizational sense.

Brian clearly decided to do the right thing as he saw it, rewarding himself with self-respect; but, because any transaction can be part of a complex trading economy, we need to mention some other valuable goods Brian received. He earned points from his peers and the general manager for "being a good soldier." They felt obligated to be helpful to him in the future and went out of their way to make his new position comfortable. And they admired his ability to put the organization's needs first. Brian didn't stick his neck out just to get these other valuable goods and services, but his desire to do the right thing did not go unnoticed or unresponded to.

Task-Related Currencies

These are currencies directly connected to getting the job done. They relate to one's ability to perform his or her assigned tasks or to the satisfactions that arise from accomplishment.

New Resources

For some managers, especially in organizations where resources are scarce or difficult to obtain, one of the most important currencies is the chance to obtain new resources to help them accomplish their goals. These resources may or may not be directly budgetary; they could include the loan of people, space, or equipment.

Remember Anne Austin, for example, who knew that Henry Logan was suffering from budget cuts in market research. She persuaded Roger, the product brand manager, to pay for some research on the project out of his budget. Not only would the research yield valuable data for product acceptance, it would also give something valuable to Henry, whose good will was important to the ultimate adoption of her product idea. Anne's awareness of Henry's need for funds actually stimulated her to think about how she could be helpful at unearthing resources.

Although important and useful to command, overt resources such as budgets or money are by no means the only valuable currencies; yet many organizational members focus on them exclusively when they are looking for what drives others, or thinking about what resources they personally command. Nevertheless, it is clear that, at least for some people some of the time, money is a very important currency. The chance to get a bonus, higher salary, increased budget, or other kinds of monetary rewards certainly can be an important form of currency. At the same time, it is by no means the only one, not always the most important, and even when it is highly valued, may not be sufficient by itself without some of the other currencies.

That fact alone doesn't stop some people from obsessing about the usefulness of monetary currencies, even in the face of more subtle, important currencies.

In a medium-sized, high-tech company, the president joked with colleagues about John Garner, the sales manager, being someone who understood only the currency of money. "I ought to call him Johnny Cash!" he often exclaimed. Garner's answer to every organizational problem was to pay more, and he was constantly pressing the president to put everyone on a monetary bonus system. Poor morale, low sales, slow product development, or disputes between marketing and engineering all could be solved, in Garner's view, by higher pay. He was completely baffled by the possibility that different currencies might be more valued by others, such as the engineers and scientists, who were far more driven by the opportunities for technical challenge. In the president's view, this made Garner a good salesman but a poor manager and organizational member; while sales could be directly measured and rewarded, dealing with people required greater flexibility and judgment.

Challenge

The chance to work at tasks that provide a challenge or stretch is one of the most widely valued currencies in modern organizational life. Challenge consistently tops all surveys of what is most important to employees about their jobs. At the extreme, some people will do almost anything to have a chance to work on tough tasks.

As Tracy Kidder showed in *Soul of a New Machine*, engineers at Data General talked about the game of "pinball": If you knock yourself out and work night and day on a project that is success-ful, the reward is that you get to do the same thing on an even more difficult project. They compare that with winning a free game playing pinball. The challenge itself is its own reward.

If the potential ally values challenge, it is usually not hard to figure out ways of offering it. One choice would be to allow the ally to share in tackling parts of the job that are inherently diffi-cult, or to let the ally work on something that would extend him or her. Asking the potential ally to join in the problem-solving group, or passing along a tough piece of your project for him to work on, are ways in which you can pay in the currency of challenge (and, if the person is at all competent, probably get back more than you expected).

If your boss values challenge, it would be sensible to share information about tough issues you are facing, go to him or her with tough decisions to talk over, or suggest major issues that he or she could tackle with colleagues or higher-ups. (The boss who hates challenge, on the other hand, can be protected from dealing with complex issues whenever possible.)

Assistance

Although large numbers of managers desire increased responsibili-ties and challenge, everyone has tasks on which they need help or that they would be glad to shed. This may occur because they per-sonally dislike those tasks, are swamped by the current difficulties they face, are in unreasonably demanding jobs, or for some reason have decided to disinvest in the organization. Whatever the rea-son, the chance to take some of the pressure off will be highly valued by people in this situation. Such people will respond par-ticularly favorably to anyone who can provide relief from one of the current pressures that is making their job life unpleasant.

For example, the senior vice-president of administration at a large textile company was a lawyer whose responsibilities had gradually expanded to include the personnel and information sys-tem functions. Other senior managers began to see that human resource activities were not receiving needed attention because the company's growth had expanded those areas beyond the se-nior VP's ability to handle them. They were uncertain about how to approach the executive until one of them realized that the VP had been complaining about the frustrations of getting so far away from his legal training.

She proposed that a new human resources department be created and staffed, and that a senior vice-president of human resources be hired to run it. When she made the case that the administrative VP would then be able to do the kind of high-quality legal work he valued, he was delighted at the opportunity to spend more time on the company's complicated contractual negotiations and readily agreed to adding the new position.

Another important type of assistance involves products or services provided by one department to another. These can be designed for the convenience of the provider, or customized to fit the needs of the recipients. Fitting resources to "client" needs is perceived as real assistance, rather than trying to get away with one more unbelievable promise like, "I'm from headquarters and I'm here to help!" Staff groups can create the currency of assistance by first making a sincere attempt to learn about departmental needs before demanding compliance.

Task Support

This currency is most valued by someone who is working on a project and needs public backing or behind-the-scenes help in selling the project to others. It can also be valuable to someone who is struggling with an ongoing set of activities and who will benefit from a good word with higher-ups or other colleagues. Since most work of any significance is likely to generate some kind of opposition, the person who is trying to gain approval for a project or plan can be greatly aided by having a "friend in court." A positive word dropped at the right time to the right person can be very helpful in furthering someone's career or objectives, and therefore highly valued. This kind of support is most valuable when the person receiving it is under fire for some reason and a colleague takes a public stand in support of the person or his project.

When you seek out and take advantage of such opportunities, you are mining the rich vein of influence "gold" below the surface of every organization. This precious resource won't come to you, however; you have to dig for it. For example, Larry Klein won the gratitude of a difficult colleague by asking a simple question during a meeting at which the colleague's proposal to move away from IBM as a supplier was being unceremoniously mauled. At a certain point in the meeting, when the attacks on the idea were coming fast and furious, Larry asked, "Are we jumping to a conclusion too quickly here? Do we really understand all the negatives and positives?" After a brief silence, one of the other executives suggested that they carefully list the considerations; and, in this more objective discussion, many new positive points were brought out. Although Larry's simple question was not exactly a rave review for the proposal, the sponsor of the proposal acknowledged how supportive Larry had been in the context of the meeting's dynamics. Larry's inconspicuous gesture broke down barriers and eventually led to a more harmonious relationship between the two.

Rapid Response

It can be worth a great deal for a colleague or boss to know that you will respond quickly to his or her requests. Anne Austin saw this and used it to get an appointment with John, the marketing manager she wanted to see.

Managers in charge of resources that are always needed "yesterday" soon discover that helping someone avoid the waiting line builds valuable credit that can be drawn on later. Sometimes people in this position get carried away and try to make it seem that they're always doing the other person a big favor, even when they have spare capacity! This, of course, only works as long as those with urgent requests don't know the true backlog; a valuable currency can be thoroughly depreciated by exploiting it unfairly.

Information

Recognizing that knowledge is power, some people value any information that may help them shape the performance of their unit. Answers to specific questions can be valuable currency, but broader information can be equally rewarding. Knowledge of industry trends, customer concerns, top management's strategic views, or other departments' agendas are valued for their contribution to planning and managing key tasks.

The vice-president in charge of information for an insurance company that had recently merged with another company complained bitterly about losing his office on executive row as a result of the addition of more senior executives from the new partner company. He didn't care about the status; he was concerned that moving downstairs would limit his opportunity to hear about plans or problems during casual hallway conversations. Such informal information-gathering had been useful in helping him decide what his people should be working on; and he was wise enough to realize that, despite the good use to which he could put information, he couldn't just "hang out" two floors above his new office, waiting for a chance to chat about trends.

This kind of hunger for information can create opportunities for anyone who has access to valuable knowledge and is willing to share it. Often, the higher the level of a person, the more grateful he or she will be for useful information.

Position-Related Currencies

These currencies enhance a person's position in the organization and, thereby, indirectly aid the person's ability to accomplish tasks or advance a career.

Recognition

Many people gladly will extend themselves for a project when they believe their contributions will be recognized. Yet it is remarkable how many who want influence fail to spread recognition around or withhold it only for very special occasions. It is probably not a coincidence that virtually all the managers identified in a major research study as having successfully accomplished innovation from the middle of their organizations were very careful to share the credit and spread the glory once the innovation was in place. They all recognized how important it was to pay people off in this valuable currency.

We asked a group of service managers from a large computer company how they influenced their peers to cooperate in projects that involved many departments. They immediately agreed that the first step was to figure out how to help the potential ally look good to his or her boss. They would look for ways for the ally to get credit for doing something that the boss valued—because they knew that form of recognition was crucial for gaining cooperation in their complete matrix organization.

Visibility to Higher-Ups

Ambitious employees realize that, in a large organization, opportunities to perform for or be recognized by powerful people can be a deciding factor in achieving future opportunities, information, or promotions. That is why, for example, task force members may fight over who will be allowed to present the group's recommendations to top decision makers.

Reputation

Yet another variation on recognition is the more generalized currency of reputation. At Digital Equipment, members talk about "good press" and "bad press." They understand that a good reputation can pave the way for lots of opportunities while a bad one can quickly shut the person out and make it difficult to perform.

A person who has good press gets invited to important meetings, is consulted about new projects, and is considered to be important to have on your side when trying to sell ideas. A talented person with bad press, even one in a nominally important position, may be ignored or not asked for opinions until it is too late to make a real difference. It is important to note that actual ability is only partially related to reputation, at least in larger organizations, since few will have direct knowledge of anyone's actual capacities; but, accurate or not, reputation carries potent consequences.

Often people at lower levels of a company, who think they have very little clout, don't realize how much they can do to influence the reputation of a manager who has more formal power. Speaking well or ill of the manager can make an enormous difference in his or her reputation and, therefore, effectiveness. Sales personnel display their awareness of this when they go out of their way to be nice to secretaries or other support staff members. They realize that a nasty comment about them from a secretary to the boss can create a bad impression that is difficult to overcome.

Insiderness

For some members, inside information is irresistible for its own sake. They are always eager to know what's going on in the organization. Who is getting ahead and who is in trouble? What are top management's latest concerns? What are the hottest industry trends, the newest customer developments? These "information junkies" will go out of their way to help anyone who can give them a "fix" of insider information, even if it does not help them with immediate tasks.

If your boss values this kind of information, you have an extra incentive to develop wide-ranging relationships and to keep your ear to the ground. Good things to do in any case, these activities provide you a wealth of extra-valuable currency to offer to the information-hungry boss.

Importance

A variation on the currency of inside knowledge is the chance to be in on important events, tasks, or plans. Some people gain their own sense of significance from being close to the action and will extend themselves to obtain that kind of access. For example, Martha Brewer worked as a compensation expert in a large electronics company. She could have stayed comfortably within her limited role as a technical expert; but she was ambitious and curious and did not want to be perceived by others as a backwater, soft-headed personnel type. She made an extra effort to talk to managers from all parts of the organization and regularly sought opportunities to serve on task forces and ad hoc committees that dealt with tough business problems. She wanted to be in on any issue that could make a significant difference to the future of the company. Thus, she was always ready to help any manager who would give her the chance to work on significant tasks; and her colleagues came to recognize that she would go out of her way to be helpful when they created such opportunities for her.

Contacts

Related to many of the previous currencies is the opportunity for making contacts, for creating a network of people with whom relationships are established, so that whenever the need arises the contacts can be approached to explore mutually helpful transactions. For some people, the chance to meet others is in itself sufficient reward for being helpful to the one who made the network building possible. They have confidence in their capacities to build satisfactory relationships once they have access. Facilitating such introductions is another currency opportunity for the organization member skilled at bringing people together.

Both of the authors had the privilege of being friends with an organizational consultant who was the world's greatest contact facilitator, Alice Sargent. Alice's black book was at the service of hundreds of people, including us, and she always knew someone we "should talk to" no matter what we were working on. She was selfless in her desire to be helpful; and we were always grateful for her knowledge of who was doing what, her energy in increasing her range of acquaintances, and her willingness to share them. Even on her unfairly premature deathbed she was still searching for just the right contact to help a friend's daughter decide whether to go to Pomona or Bryn Mawr, an author find an audience for his message, and a company to help package the author's training program. Many consultants and organizational members benefited from her generosity and miss her more than is possible to express. Among the many things we learned from her is the potency inherent in helping people connect to one another.

Relationship-Related Currencies

These currencies have more to do with strengthening the relationship with someone than directly accomplishing the organization's tasks. That in no way diminishes their importance.

Acceptance/Inclusion

Some people most value the feeling that they are close to others or have an easy intimacy that is in itself rewarding. Such people will be quite receptive to those who offer warmth and liking as currencies. While they may or may not place closeness over other, more task-related currencies, at the very least they won't be unable to sustain satisfactory transactions with anyone who does not preface serious task discussions with warmth and acceptance. New MBAs, eager to exercise their newly acquired analytical skills, are often tripped up when they greet a colleague who is more interested in the currency of inclusion or closeness than in more task-focused currencies.

Understanding/Listening/Sympathy

Colleagues who feel beleaguered by the demands of the organization, isolated, or unsupported by the boss place an especially high value on a sympathetic ear. Almost everyone in organizations is glad at times for a chance to talk about what bugs him or her, especially when the listener seems to have no axe to grind or is not too caught up in his or her own problems to pay attention to someone else. Indeed, sympathetic listening is a form of action that many managers do not recognize, since by the nature of their jobs and personalities they are oriented to "doing something." They don't recognize that being listened to, in and of itself, can be a valuable currency.

Personal Support

For some people, at particular times, having the support of others is the currency they value most. When a colleague is feeling stressed, upset, vulnerable, or needy, he or she will doubly appreciate—and remember—a thoughtful gesture such as a kind word or a hand on the shoulder. Some people are intuitively brilliant at figuring out just the right touch with a colleague in personal stress, sensing who would appreciate flowers, who would like to be asked home to dinner, and who would respond best to a copy of a meaningful poem or book. The gesture itself, however, is far less important than the attempt, no matter how awkwardly it might be expressed.

Unfortunately, such personal gestures could miss the mark or be misconstrued as signs of more intimate interest or personal friendship than might have been intended. An invitation to dinner at one's home, for example, could come across as an intrusion to a very private person. Although caution is in order, genuinely kind gestures usually transcend misinterpretation.

A long-time organizational member was out of the office for several days after his father died. When he returned, he was hurt by the number of colleagues who said nothing about the loss. All he wanted was the sense that others cared; when anyone inquired and said something sympathetic, he was very grateful. At that time in his life, no currency was more valuable.

Personal Currencies

These currencies could form an infinite list of idiosyncratic needs. They are valued because they enhance the individual's sense of self. They may be derived from task or interpersonal activity. We will mention only a few that are common to many individuals.

Gratitude

While this may be another form of recognition or support, it is a particular one that is valued very highly by some people who make a point of being helpful to others. For their efforts they want appreciation from the receiver, expressed in terms of thanks or deference. This is a tricky currency because, even to those who desire it, it is easily devalued when overused. That is, expression of gratitude for the first favor may be more valued than a similar expression of gratitude for the tenth.

For example, in a classic study of a tax office, sociologist Peter Blau found that the most skillful tax assessors were often asked for help by less skilled peers. Blau observed that at some point the cost to the helpers became greater (in time taken away from doing their own work) than the value of the gratitude received from the colleague they helped. "Thank you's," no matter how nicely put, were no longer enough. Nevertheless, those who fail to recognize when gratitude is expected by a colleague will soon find themselves being treated with far less liking or cooperation.

Ownership/Involvement

Another currency often valued by organizational members is the chance to feel that they are partly in control of something important, or have a chance to make a major contribution. While this is akin to some of the other currencies, for some people the chance to get their hands into something interesting is its own reward. They do not need other forms of payment.

Self-Concept

We referred earlier to moral and ethical correctness as a currency. Another way of thinking about currencies that are self-referencing is to include those that are consistent with a person's image of himself or herself. Although we have so far stressed the interactive nature of exchange, "payments" do not always have to be made by someone else. They can be self-generated to fit personal beliefs about being virtuous, benevolent, or committed to the organization's welfare. Someone might respond to another's request because it reinforces the first person's cherished values, sense of identity, or feelings of self-worth. Payment is still interpersonally *stimulated*, because the person who wants influence has set up conditions that allow this kind of "self-payment" to occur by asking for cooperation to accomplish organizational goals. But the person who responds because "it is the right thing to do," and feels good about being the "kind of person who does not act out of narrow self-interest," is printing currency (virtue) that is self-satisfying.

Rosabeth Kanter discovered a number of innovative managers who had worked long and hard to make significant changes that they knew would *not* be rewarded. In fact, several said that they had actually been punished by the organization for fighting through valuable changes that upset cherished beliefs or key executives. Furthermore, they had been aware that their efforts would get them in trouble; but they proceeded anyway because they were convinced that their efforts were needed, or because they just wanted to make their own jobs more interesting.

Comfort

Finally, there is a certain number of individuals who place high value on personal comfort. Lovers of "balance" and haters of risk, they will do almost *anything* to avoid being hassled or embarrassed. The thought of having to make a public fuss, be the target of notoriety, or the recipient of anger and confrontation is enough to drive them to the ends of the earth to remove the pressure. They are far less interested in advancement than in being allowed to do their job with the minimum of disturbance.

Derek Blansford, for example, was the administrative assistant to a department head in a large accounting firm. He was quiet and efficient, always anticipating staff members' needs and willing to go out of his way to make their lives easier. Because he hated the spotlight, Derek would always try to work behind the scenes. If a staff accountant raised his voice, Derek would cringe and turn himself inside out to end the cause of the displeasure.

Some of the more aggressive accountants noticed this character trait of Derek's and took advantage of it. Whenever they wanted an unreasonable favor, they would approach Derek in the corridor and make their requests in a slightly louder than normal voice. Usually that was enough to send him scurrying; but if it wasn't, they would become more strident and demanding. Because Derek could not hold his ground, those who employed such tactics would get disproportionate attention and service. Others in the department resented this, as did Derek, but he far preferred to make extra effort to please the demanding accountants than suffer their public anger.

CURRENCY RESTRICTIONS

Love Me, Love My Unit:
Currencies Can Be Organizational, Not Just Personal

For convenience, we have discussed currencies completely in terms of what is important to the *individual* you want to influence. But another, less direct, kind of currency is the currency of departmental or organizational benefit. When an employee identifies strongly with the welfare of his/her unit, exchanges that provide a benefit to the unit rather than to the individual can be very important.

At the same time, the person gets the psychological satisfaction of "being good," or of "doing what is right," which are by no means trivial currencies. The sense of self as a good citizen, as a benevolent, loyal person, is indeed a powerful currency for many. This kind of satisfaction is a potent payoff for cooperating with another, even when cooperation may not appear at first glance to be in that person's self interest.

In fact, in some organizations, the acquisition of a reputation for being willing to do things that do not immediately benefit the person doing them is precisely the requirement for developing the kind of positive reputation that yields great influence on others. These are the kinds of organizations in which "altruism" reigns supreme.

Ben Robbins, for example, is the least polished, least educated, senior executive at a life insurance company employing 600 people. He has risen to a top administrative position in the company, one in which he oversees 40 percent of the workforce. He is often heard to express delight that he is earning far more money than he has ever dreamed of, but he quietly worries that he has risen above his talent. Yet, whenever there is a tough problem to solve, everyone goes to Ben. They know that he will help tackle it with enthusiasm, without first asking what's in it for him. Because Ben is natural and unpretentious, no one fears that he will make fun of them for not knowing the answer in advance. Recently, Ben was formally recognized with the company's annual award to the employee who best exemplifies devoted service to others, but long before that he was informally known for his unselfish dedication. Ben didn't set out to get ahead by doing good, but his genuine concern for others has earned him considerable respect.

In such situations, a strategy of encouraging the potential ally to cooperate for personal gain is a serious breach of etiquette. That the person's reputation will be enhanced is considered a hidden benefit, one not to be overtly touted. (We might say that, for these individuals, the currency of good citizenship thus becomes an overriding one. As a result, would-be influencers sugar-coat every request with "This is what's best for the organization," which becomes a kind of invocation that allows more pointed discussion to follow.)

Different Strokes:
No Universal Currencies

Since interests vary from person to person, currencies will be valued differently. In fact, the same currency that is highly prized by one person will be loathed by another. There are individuals who will do anything for greater visibility, and others who shrink from the spotlight. Many people value challenge, but the person who prizes comfort or assistance may choke on the next one. Some people revel in gratitude for their acts, while others just want to be allowed to get on with their work.

Any attempt to use the same currency every time is likely to lead to costly miscalculation. That is what makes it so important to know just what is important to your potential ally.

Absence Can Make
the Heart Grow Fonder

Insofar as a currency is valuable to an ally, its absence or threatened removal can also be motivating. Because too many people think only of negative sanctions when seeking influence, we have stressed the positive side of currency use; but it would be needlessly self-limiting to overlook the power of withholding a valuable currency you control. Refusal to give recognition, challenge, or support can move an ally to cooperate.

When Anne Austin, for example, felt that she was not getting reasonable consideration for a marketing job, she suggested that she might take her valuable talents to a competitor. She didn't do this lightly, and she certainly didn't do it as her first attempt to create positive exchange; but she used it when she felt it necessary.

Even when employing the negative variation of currency exchange, look for a positive way to frame the currency. "I know you wouldn't want to be left out" probably will get a more positive response than "If you don't cooperate, I'll see that you're left out." In both cases, however, it is the *absence* of the currency, not its presence, that is being used as exchangeable merchandise.

What's in a Name?

As should be clear, currencies of the kind discussed here are not exact and fixed; they are also a function of perception and language. A particular "good," say, for example, *an offer to create a special analytical report,* may be translatable into several different currencies. To the receiver, it may be a *performance* currency: ("When I have the report, I'll be able to determine which products to push."); a *political* currency ("Getting the report will help me look good to my division president."); or a *personal* currency ("Although getting the report certainly won't hurt my decision making, more significant is the fact that it really shows you recognize my importance."). The same good may be valued for different reasons by different people—or by the same person.

Take another example: You recognize that the warehouse manager you want to influence values strongly the currency of *appreciation.* There can be many ways to pay in appreciation, including verbal thanks, praise, a public statement of support at a meeting, informal comments to his peers, or a note to his boss. Any of these acts can take the form of the currency of appreciation.

The value of a currency, however, is solely in the eye of the beholder. While one manager might consider the thank-you note a sign of appreciation, another manager might see it as an attempt to brown-nose; and a third might dismiss it as a cheap way to try to repay extensive favors and service.

The changeable nature of the value of currency makes it even more necessary to understand as much as you can about what is important to each potential ally—not only what he or she values, but also the *language* that reflects that valued currency. Sometimes a different way of talking about the goods—based on what you know about the ally's style and priorities—will make them more attractive.

This is a bit different from the old advice: "Sell the sizzle, not the steak." Not everyone will value sizzle, but some will value the protein, or the convenience, or the symbolic status of being able to afford steak. On the other hand, one man's meat is a vegetarian's poison, and on occasion even a silver-tongued orator will fail. If you don't have the right goods, hype will only offend. Nevertheless, it is worth careful thought about how to position goods that are available.

Bite Your Tongue: Organizational Determinants of What Language to Use

The *way* you discuss issues is determined not just by individual needs but also by the norms of the organization. How explicitly you position self-interest is different from organization to organization.

For example, in one leading computer company members are expected to be direct about what they want from others. Employees talk freely about wheeling and dealing for resources. But at another major computer company, the language is expected to be far less direct, with requests couched in terms of organizational benefits, not personal gains.

No one at the second company would say, "If you help me on this project, your career will be advanced." Instead, they will say something like, "Your area's help will increase the value of the product, and that will aid your group's getting the recognition it deserves for its outstanding efforts." The result might be the same, but the language used to get results is different.

Sometimes a good idea can be stymied because it has been described with loaded language—words whose connotations turn off the people whose support is most needed.

Mira Arthur is the director of a traditional art association, one whose members are local artists who use the association's studios and display their works for sale at the association's shop. As the organization's activities expanded, Mira sought new facilities for classes. She also wanted to establish a small museum to display classic examples of the type of art that her members created.

Unfortunately, when she mentioned her idea of adding a museum to the proposed new building, Mira encountered considerable resistance. The board found the idea of a "museum" threatening and ostentatious. When Mira saw that she wasn't getting anywhere, she backed off.

As she thought about it, Mira realized that the concept of a museum was inconsistent with board members' perceptions of the organization. She began to talk about the idea in a different way: "Wouldn't it be wonderful if, when people are taking lessons upstairs, they could pop downstairs to see how (famous artist "X" or "Y") dealt with the same kind of snow scenes?" Before long, the board approved the "extra display space" in the new building.

Inappropriate language can convert what might have been valuable to a potential ally into undesirable currency. When Leonard Hirsch talked about the assignment of new research and development groups as a form of gaining better control, he set Sheldon Marx's teeth on edge. Sheldon did not like to trade in the currency of control. When he thought that Leonard was only interested in control, Sheldon resisted. It was hard for him to see that other, more desirable currencies—learning and growth—were involved. Leonard could have achieved the organizational structure he wanted if he had framed his request in language that described the advantages to Sheldon in terms he valued.

But You Look Great in Chartreuse, and You'll Never Get Lost

Finally, the language with which a specific good is discussed can help expand an ally's view of it. For example, if you need a time commitment from a busy peer to whom you know challenge is important, show her how the task force you want her to serve on will not only be a time consumer, but will involve tackling a problem that is complex and important.

A task force wrestling with the problem of how to manage diversity in the corporation, for example, will no doubt require considerable meeting time; but it will also delve into issues of corporate mission, management styles and attitudes, recruiting policies, reward systems, and so on. While, on the surface, such an extra assignment may appear to be a big nuisance, the group will be coming to grips with fundamental management issues that can have a major impact on the way things are done in the organization. Of course, to the person whose most valued currency is *reduction of pressure,* these arguments are not particularly attractive; but, to an ambitious high performer, opportunities that may not at first be evident will be compelling when you point them out.

CONCLUSIONS—AND SOME CAUTIONS

The exchange of goods and services is the way in which organizational members influence one another. By understanding the world of the person you want to influence, you increase your chances of determining what the person needs, and, in turn, what you might give that would be valued. If you can find valuable goods or services to offer, you increase the sources of power.

Furthermore, most situations are complex enough, and flexible enough, so that there is often more room to find valuable items to exchange than is immediately apparent. A wider range of spendable currencies may be more accessible to you than you think.

In addition, the language that you use to describe your offers can increase the chances that those goods or services will meet the needs of the other party, that is, address their desired currencies. Careful, thoughtful communication adds needed precision to the imprecise process of equating your offer with another's needs.

The Dangers of False Advertising

Nevertheless, there are dangers in the process. Having a way with words is useful in any selling activity, but avoid gilding the lily or exaggerating claims. When making a sale to a stranger, there may be less fallout; but, within your own organization, an impossible promise, a claim that proves to be false, or even too much wishful thinking can damage your credibility and get in the way of future transactions. As we have tried to make abundantly clear, your reputation is a precious commodity in organizational terms. Protect that valuable asset even as you press the boundaries to complete important exchanges.

You Can't Give Me Zlotys for Gold: Some Currencies Really Are Not Convertible

Another warning is in order: Not everything can be converted into equivalent currencies. If two people have fundamental differences in what they value, it may not be possible to find common grounds.

The founder-chairman of a high-tech company and the president he had hired five years earlier were growing more and more displeased with one another. The president, a Harvard MBA, was committed to creating *maximum shareholder value*. That was the currency most precious to him. He predicted that the company's line of exotic components would soon saturate their market, and risky major research investments would be needed to make the strategic move to end-user products. Accordingly, he concluded that the company was in a perfect position to cash in by squeezing expenses to maximize profits and then going public.

The chairman was unmoved, however, because he valued a different currency, the *fun of technological challenges*. An independently wealthy man, he wasn't at all interested in the $10 million or more he would get if the company maximized profits by cutting research and selling out. He wanted a place to test his intuitive, creative hunches, not an inert cache of capital.

Their disagreements led first to bickering and then to hostility. But they were able to move beyond this, and in further exploration they realized that they would never be able to reach accord. Their currencies just weren't convertible at an acceptable exchange rate. That understanding freed them to agree that the president should leave—on good terms—after a more compatible replacement could be found.

In not every story does everyone live happily ever after.

5

Knowing What They Want: Understanding the World of Your Allies

Do Unto Others As They Want To Be Done Unto.

Maier's variation on the golden rule

Ethan Burke and Andrew Shaplen had been partners in a small advertising business for five years. Neither spent full time on the business because of other commitments, but it had always provided interesting work and reasonable income to both. There came a time, however, when Ethan fairly burst with frustration at Andrew.

Ethan was a conscientious perfectionist, who was very concerned with meeting the firm's commitments to accounts and suppliers. He was especially skilled at managing complex advertising projects that required intricate juggling of people, materials, and ideas. Andrew, who was bolder, was particularly good at inspirational selling and improvising when in a jam; but he was rather sloppy at the financial and administrative tasks he insisted on being responsible for. Although once their disparate work styles had complemented each other, this seemed less true now, and Ethan began to find fault with the relationship.

Especially galling to Ethan were the times that Andrew treated him as if he were a client whose ruffled feathers needed smoothing after some agency slip-up. Ethan would receive a call from a client or supplier asking when completed work could be delivered, only to find that Andrew was supposed to have made arrangements but hadn't; when Ethan would ask Andrew what had happened, Andrew would concoct a flimsy excuse, or say that the arrangements had indeed been made and the caller must have forgotten. He never simply admitted that he had forgotten or had not yet done it, which is all it would have taken for Ethan to be satisfied.

Several times Ethan inadvertently had stumbled on hard evidence that Andrew had not done what he claimed, but he was reluctant to confront him. Nevertheless, Ethan was beginning to "keep book" on Andrew, suspecting almost everything that Andrew said, and looking for signs of "white lies" on even unimportant matters.

Ethan was deeply disappointed at Andrew's behavior in light of their long relationship. He felt manipulated, brushed aside, and diminished by Andrew's cavalier treatment of the truth when dealing with him, his partner and friend. He began to wonder if Andrew thought that he, Ethan, was too simple-minded or naïve to catch on to these maneuvers. Or perhaps Andrew saw Ethan as too obsessive about details, which forced Andrew to say everything was under control to get Ethan to relax. "Maybe he no longer values our partnership. How can he think so little of me? Could he think I'm not doing my share?" Ethan agonized.

Because he knew that Andrew was under great strain in his other activities, Ethan did not want to add to the pressure. He worried that Andrew's other commitments might be more important than their modest business, and he didn't want to drive Andrew away. Besides, they were good friends; Ethan was afraid to offend Andrew by being confrontational or sounding suspicious, thereby causing Andrew to get angry enough to end the relationship. Their friendship was more important than business, although Ethan's good reputation with clients meant a lot to him; and he feared Andrew's sloppiness would tarnish both their reputations. Months went by as Ethan grew angrier and angrier, but he remained unable to tell Andrew.

When Ethan could no longer stand the pressure inside, he finally approached Andrew, and, to his relief, found Andrew receptive. In fact, Andrew had been engaged in a furious juggling act. He was having a hard time keeping all the "balls in the air," but because he didn't want to disappoint Ethan or fail to hold up his end of the partnership, he resorted to covering up. He didn't do it out of a lack of respect for Ethan; just the opposite!

When this came out, they discussed whether a different division of duties would make more sense; and Ethan offered to carry the whole administrative load on one of their biggest projects so that Andrew could have more time to devote to developing new accounts. In return, Andrew promised to keep Ethan accurately informed about the issues he was dealing with and to make a real effort not to resort to the kind of puffery with his partner that sometimes was needed with demanding account managers.

Andrew subsequently found it embarrassing, but much more satisfying, to be able to say, when necessary, "I'm swamped—I can't get it done in time," which allowed Ethan to take up the slack without getting irritated. Both of them wondered why they had waited so long to talk about the tension.

LOOK OUT: INFLUENCE STARTS WITH WHAT MATTERS TO YOUR POTENTIAL ALLY

In previous chapters, we pointed out the value of fully understanding the world of the potential ally. Knowing the concerns, objectives, and styles of the people you want to influence is fundamental for determining what you will need to offer to gain cooperation. The more you know, the better you can determine valued currencies, the language they speak, and the style in which they prefer to interact. Some of these things you can perceive automatically. At other times, you may need to reassess. Ethan Burke, for example, knew a lot about Andrew Shaplen's concerns because the two men had known each other for a long time. But, just as Ethan found, there are times when it is necessary to do a careful analysis of your ally's world. It is time for such a diagnosis if you're puzzled by the ally's resistance; stymied because "reasonable" approaches aren't working; or angry and beginning to assume the worst about the ally's motives and personality. This chapter will zoom in on the analytical process for determining the world of an ally whose driving forces are not immediately apparent.

Continuing to look at a situation only from your own viewpoint makes it easy to slip into the kind of tortured silence that kept Ethan from talking directly with his partner. The intense desire to do something significant or make an important change has a way of blinding hopeful influencers to what is critical to their potential allies. The resistant ally seems difficult, impossible, even irrational, because his or her behavior does not make sense to the determined influencer.

Andrew was infuriating to Ethan, whose only conceivable explanation of Andrew's behavior attributed negative motives to Andrew. Ethan concluded that Andrew must not respect him, which made him both angry and fearful of directly discussing the problem. Soon, Ethan suspected everything Andrew said, and a formerly excellent partnership was at risk. If Ethan had understood how the world—including their relationship—looked to Andrew, they might have been able to agree much sooner on how to relate to one another.

WHAT DO THEY DO FOR A LIVING?
THE POTENTIAL ALLY'S TASKS

Understanding a potential ally's actual duties and responsibilities can be a key to influencing him or her. Think about the impact of his or her job—on the ally as well as others. Does his assignment mean he has to deal with numbers all day, or with people? Do other people constantly demand things from the ally, or is the ally in the position of making many demands on others?

This kind of information can guide you to the currencies the ally values, how he or she sees the world, or the style with which to approach him or her. Andrew's tasks, for example, included dealing with demanding advertising clients—and probably reinforced any natural tendencies to stretch the truth when cornered. The same blarney that helped Andrew make difficult sales and maneuver through tight deadlines was seeping into his relationship with Ethan. Instead of reacting negatively, Ethan could have perceived Andrew's slipperiness as a strength that contributed to the success of their business—but one that was being relied on a bit too often—and used exaggerated humor to address it.

For example, if he had fully understood the way the company's tasks reinforced Andrew's wheeler-dealer style, Ethan might have said something to Andrew like, "Whoa, Pinocchio, your nose is big enough already; save the fairy tales for when we need them with the clients!" Or, "I know, I know, you arranged this already, and the check is in the mail! Come on, Andy, you don't have to make nice with me like the customers who want it yesterday." Acknowledging that demanding clients and complicated schedules made it tempting for Andrew to fabricate excuses even when they weren't needed would have eased the tension and focused the influence attempt on the right issue.

Knowing the different goals and work styles of her influence targets helped Anne Austin tailor her approach when she talked to people in sales, market research, and marketing. She could anticipate the focus of their attention and shape her approach accordingly. For example, the tasks of a brand manager, which encompass every aspect of a product's positioning, presentation, price, and so on, are different from those of a market researcher, who works with statistics, validity, scientific method, focus groups, and the like. The brand manager is called on to pull many elements together at once; the market researcher works at a slower pace to discover significant results.

But the demands of tasks alone do not account for all the pressures and concerns of individuals who are influence targets. Meredith, an assistant product manager in a snack-food company, for example, realized this when she struggled to influence a production scheduling manager whose help she needed for an experiment with a new sample size of packages. She noticed that the scheduling manager spent the day hearing product managers' various tales of woe as they cajoled for priority attention. Meredith assumed that these incessant demands were probably frustrating and depersonalizing; and perhaps the scheduling manager might like to be approached as a person who had problems, too, not just as a gatekeeper. Meredith was a warm and sympathetic person, so it was easy for her to express genuine interest in the scheduling manager. It turned out that the manager's daughter was about to be married. After only 20 minutes of listening, with genuine interest, to the scheduling manager's concerns with the match, Meredith transformed an apparent grouch into a willing helper.

Conversely, Ethan knew about the outside pressures on Andrew; but, instead of asking about them and exploring their impact, he sat back and let Andrew wrestle with them alone.

Thus, it is useful to think about many other aspects of what might be important to the one you want to influence. We will discuss several important dimensions for analysis.

Who's Counting?
Measurement and Reward Systems

In organizations, the way people behave is often dictated by the way their performance is measured and rewarded. Those who act "difficult" or negative may only be doing what they have been told will be regarded as good performance in that function. The salesperson who is furious because the plant manager resists changing priorities for a rush order may not realize that part of the plant manager's bonus depends on holding unit cost down, which is easier to do with long production runs. The plant manager's response doesn't necessarily arise from a disregard for pleasing customers or overall company sales goals.

Similarly, the MIS manager who resists the plant manager's pet scheme for automating production costing may be responding to the project backlog measure by which she is judged. Less complex projects that don't require design from scratch may make it far easier to plan and control backlog, so she may be avoiding a desirable but necessarily lengthy project. And, in turn, the chief financial officer who balks at the MIS manager's requests for the latest equipment may be judged by certain financial ratios that will be harmed by adding capital equipment that takes many months before it begins to provide proportionate returns.

In all of these cases, the starting point is an understanding of the potential allies' performance criteria as a means to determine how you might be able to add value or alter your request to fit their requirements. In some instances, it might be possible to raise questions about the reasonableness of the measure, since departmental measures designed from the top or left over from the past may have unanticipated negative consequences. In such cases, the organization might eventually want to alter the measures if their negative impact to the company was made clear. But often, in the short run, the other's way of being judged is a given that has to be worked with, or around.

Surrounded: Their Environment

Other factors that shape task demands include the degree of contact with the organizational environment, top management, headquarters, the sales force, the factory floor, exotic or temperamental equipment, the media, and so forth. Each of such contacts, or lack of them, is likely to create pressures that affect the way the person looks at problems and requests. The manager who has to deal with customer complaints on a regular basis may be far more receptive to appeals that involve quality improvement than the manager who never sees customers but is in close contact with the controller's office.

Surrounded: Their Worries

In addition to looking at the environmental forces that affect your potential ally, you could think about what the person's anxieties might be. Ask yourself what it is that makes the person you want to influence toss in bed at 2 A.M. At the least, every one in an organization ought to be able to answer that for his or her boss. If you don't know, think about it. You never will get what you want from your boss if you can't quite pinpoint what it is that worries him or her most.

The young engineers at a consulting firm wanted more say on the layout of space in their new office building, and greater control over projects. But because they had no idea what mattered to Dan Stein, the founding partner and president, they were quite ineffective at influencing him on the matters they cared about. They organized an employees' committee, which sent him recommendations; but he never responded. Because they hadn't thought through what the president's worries were, the engineers completely missed his preoccupation with keeping billing rates up while maintaining quality. With both his investment at risk and his name on the company's letterhead, the president had a lot to lose if things did not go well. What he perceived as the engineers' "bellyaching" about their comfort and convenience was not a high priority worry for him. Yet the issues they wanted addressed were certainly related to company performance. If they had framed their concerns in terms of quality improvement, or improved billing time, they would have received far more attention—and action.

Is your boss worrying about long-term competition from Asia, or about meeting next week's payroll? Is it the merger rumor mill keeping him awake, or fear of his boss's wrath for missing a budgeted expense number? Does she worry about the impact of exotic new technologies, or whether she has the nerve to confront old Charlie on his nasty political games? The answers to these and similar questions determine your approach.

Shit Happens: Task Uncertainties

Another indicator of what might be important could be those aspects of the potential ally's job that have the most uncertainties associated with them. In organizational life, control is valued. The bigger the uncertainty, the harder it is to keep control, so it is the areas of greatest uncertainty that receive the most attention. You often can gain an ally by finding a way to help the person get control of a part of his or her job that is currently uncertain.

In one traditional textile company, for example, plant managers spent a great deal of time worrying about the high amount of machine downtime. The manager who tested a successful new system of preventive maintenance (which, not so incidentally, gave responsibility to machine operators rather than to a separate repair crew) increased his influence in the organization. He had eliminated a major source of uncertainty, and his fellow managers were very grateful.

WHERE ARE THEY HEADED?
CAREER ASPIRATIONS AND PERSONAL BACKGROUND

Besides the organizational factors that are part of the potential ally's world, there will of course be many personal concerns that arise from the person's previous experiences and current goals. If you already know the person well, it isn't hard to figure out what might be important to him or her; but problems arise when you have had little previous contact or, worse, your prior relations have been unfriendly.

Friendly or antagonistic, familiar or unknown, the potential ally's world will be more transparent if you get the answers to some critical questions. For example, is the ally on the fast track or stuck indefinitely in his or her current position? Is he anxious to make his mark or more concerned with preserving a calm atmosphere in the department? Will she be around to live with the consequences of cooperating (or refusing to), or will her successors be the major beneficiaries—or victims?

While being careful to avoid stereotyping, you might also examine what you know about the ally's personal history. Educational background can be helpful, including what the person studied and where. A manager without a college degree or, in some organizations without an MBA or other advanced degree, could be sensitive about his or her perceived "deficiency" or about possible slights to his or her intelligence.

The ivy-league liberal arts graduate might care more about culture and polished manners than an engineer who graduated from a big state university would. The accounting major may prefer careful discussions of data and detail more than the marketing major would. Of course, it would be foolish to base your approach entirely on such preconceptions, but they may give you helpful clues to start a more careful diagnosis.

You might also gain valuable insight if you know where the person worked previously and what his or her former jobs involved. The manager who has never been outside of manufacturing is likely to have a world view different from that of the manager who has moved into manufacturing after stints in personnel and marketing. The manager who has worked for IBM or GE will look at problems differently from the manager who has spent his or her whole career in the same medium-sized company. And the manager who has spent some time working at European and Japanese subsidiaries probably will have a different perspective from the one who has never left Detroit.

How successful was the potential ally in his or her previous jobs? Does he see himself as highly competent or still learning? Is she a fast-track performer brought in to fix things, or did she move slowly into each position and remain there a long time? All of these will likely affect how the potential ally will react to new ideas, major changes, or large projects versus more modest ones.

It can also be helpful to know what negative career experiences left unpleasant memories that shape how he or she performs today. When was the person "burned," and how? Was he a victim of a bad manager who fired him arbitrarily, making him gun-shy? Did a subordinate let her down in a crucial situation, or did a peer stab her in the back after promising support? If you discover that such a critical event took place, be sure to take it into account.

Prescription Lenses: How the Ally Defines the World

Although not always easy to detect from a distance, the potential ally's assumptions about such key issues as leadership, motivation, competition, or change, once known, help you determine what he or she values. The potential ally, for example, who believes that people are inherently lazy and need to be closely watched is likely to value control and predictability, while one who believes that most people want to do a good job is more likely to value currencies of challenge and growth. The ally who believes that anything is negotiable operates quite differently from the one who holds fast to a few eternal truths, no matter what the situation.

STAY TUNED: GATHERING DATA ABOUT THE WORLD OF OTHERS

What Did You Say? Language as a Clue to Valued Currencies

Because any argument or request is more likely to succeed if it is framed in the currency valued by the person you want to influence, any clues that help identify the other's important currencies will be useful. One of the best ways to tune in rapidly to another's currencies is to listen closely to the language the person uses. The choice of metaphors often can be revealing of the person's preoccupations.

For example, Anne Austin (see Chapter 2) wanted Roger, the brand manager of the shampoo line she was working on, to finance additional market research by her division. Because she had noticed that Roger seemed preoccupied by how his boss would view things, she used language that pushed the appropriate buttons in Roger: ". . . you *know* John will ask. It's probably a good idea to spend some money on research so that we're ready for John." Anne had picked up on Roger's sensitivity to his boss's view of him, and she used that knowledge to show how her request would give Roger more of a currency he valued. She didn't waste her time telling Roger his peers would like him more or that his job would be easier. She transmitted her request in the communication channel Roger tuned in to.

When a request for help is met immediately with an inquiry about who else will be involved, you know that political concerns are that person's currency. Another might ask directly, "What's in it for me?" which reveals concern for self and suggests that a blunt, direct response will probably work best. Yet another manager will respond with questions about how the request fits in with the company's mission, which indicates that person values corporate over personal goals—and perhaps will welcome the opportunity to be a good citizen.

It is remarkable how often the hopeful influencer will completely miss obvious clues to the potential ally's hot buttons. Many resistant allies telegraph their concerns by the way they respond initially to a request. For example, an ally might say, "What I'd be worried about if we did that . . ."; or "I don't think the finance people would buy it"; or "My concern here is . . ." Each of these statements is an invitation to further dialogue but is too often misread by the influencer as stubbornness. Instead of asking exploratory questions that might reveal the currencies that have to be traded for cooperation, they argue; and that puts an end to their hoped-for influence.

The style of language used—metaphors, images, jargon—can be revealing; but that which is *not* said—whether they are avoided topics or just nonverbal cues to feelings and attitudes—can tell you a great deal, as well. Tuning in to others' feelings is a communication skill you should practice, and it is especially important when trying to figure out what is important to a potential ally. Whether you just learn to shut up when your boss's neck gets red (a sign that he is feeling harried), or you watch for the widened eyes that indicate growing interest in the tack you are taking, careful attention to the nonverbal cues can help you determine which currencies to use and how to make your requests in language that will elicit the desired response.

Being sensitive to nonverbal cues is easier said than done. Time and again in our training workshops, we find participants eager to demonstrate how skilled they are in reading the concerns of others, but then they promptly get sucked right into selling their own views rather than determining the ally's views. Here's a sample:

Dorothy, the sales manager, wants Hank, the operations manager, to support her request for a new phone system. He resists: "The last thing we need around here is new phones. The old ones work fine. I've got real equipment problems in the plant, and I don't need expensive phones that will be obsolete again in two years."

Dorothy gets hooked by his resistance—a familiar occurrence—and starts to press harder: "You're always against change; come out of the dark ages. If you got out of the plant once in a while, maybe you'd see that our salespeople need a way to get through with customer orders!"

Dorothy's extensive experience with Hank should make it evident that arguing harder and attacking faster only increases his resistance, but she is so intent on showing why she needs new phones that she zips right by Hank's concerns. In just a few sentences, he has sent important messages that she doesn't hear. He is focused on the equipment needs of the plant and his ability to meet schedules. Obsolescence of equipment is on his mind, which suggests that he has worries about his own ability to keep up with changes. Would he respond, perhaps, to some recognition for what he's accomplished in the plant with chewing gum and baling wire?

If Dorothy could step back and listen instead of launching a counterattack, she might realize that Hank is sending an SOS; but it's in code, and needs amplification. Even a simple, "Oh, are you having trouble getting your capital budget approved?" could improve the strained communication. How much better it would be if she asked about the state of the plant, or indicated her appreciation of the way he'd held things together!

Afterwards, when we point out to Dorothy what she has missed in her determination to beat Hank into submission, she looks sheepish because it is so "obvious"; but it takes discipline to avoid doing the same thing as soon as the next exciting project comes along and some colleague fails to see it her way.

In Front of Your Eyes:
Other Sources of Data

For some of the categories of information about the potential ally, the data are self-evident. The ally's tasks may be common knowledge or readily gleaned from the organization chart. The measurement and reward system may be well known, especially if the person works in your area or in a related one with which you often do business. If the potential ally has a similar background to yours, say the same field of education at a comparable university, or comes from the same social segment, it may take less time to find common ground because you make similar assumptions and have similar values. And, if the potential ally is someone with whom you presently have a good working relationship, chances are you already have a good idea of what is important to him and how he views the world; or you know how to ask when it is not clear.

Even when the person whose help you seek is a stranger, he or she may "advertise" so clearly that it is hard to miss what is important. Who hasn't encountered a fellow employee who manages to mention his (high-status) undergraduate college within the first five minutes of conversation, no matter what the topic? It doesn't take great psychoanalytic insight to figure out that status is probably an important currency to that person.

A management professor had to meet an executive for the first time in order to ask a big favor. One entire wall of the executive's office was covered with enormous stuffed and lacquered sport fish. The spaces between the mounted fish were crammed with photographs of fishing trips. With a giant blue marlin glinting in his direct line of vision, the supplicant professor could not miss the message about this man's consuming interest. Even the world's worst salesman would have known that common ground could be established by inquiring about fishing.

The professor, torn between his need for the favor and a reluctance to grab the all-too-easy catch being served on a platter, had to exercise exquisite self-control not to ask with a straight face, "Don't you think deep-sea fishing has become too easy with all the modern sonar equipment?"

Unwilling to fake interest in fishing, but unable to ignore the invitation to mention it, the professor searched desperately for a comfortable way to acknowledge the executive's interests without phony enthusiasm. Finally, he combined his own interests with the manager's, and asked whether the manager had learned any organizational lessons from the sport. An interesting conversation on planning and patience ensued. The professor was able to remain authentic while responding to the manager's preoccupation; and the favor was granted.

For those you do not know, and who do not make it so easy to learn what currencies they value, other colleagues may be able to supply information. As a communications manager at a large computer company put it, "When I have to approach someone I don't know, I ask someone who knows him what he's like, what he cares about, what his hot buttons are, what I should definitely not say. At the very least, I don't want to step on any land mines." With a bit of ingenuity, it is often possible to find someone you trust to be a helpful source.

Just Because It Waddles and Quacks Like a Duck Doesn't Mean It's a Duck: The Dangers of Stereotyping

All of the factors already discussed can provide clues to what might be important to your potential allies, what language they are likely to use and respond to, and what style of interaction they might prefer. Although any such information can be invaluable, it is important to sift through everything you hear and treat it only as clues, not as certain information. Be careful not to assume any one factor determines all currencies; people respond to many complex pressures. The actuary who cut his teeth on numbers may indeed prefer crisp, statistical reports; but we know high-level actuaries who are eloquent about the limits of numerical analysis and the need for intuition when making important decisions.

Similarly, though many plant managers are rewarded for holding down unit costs and therefore resist special orders that interrupt long runs, that isn't automatically the case. Human resource managers often are attracted to prepackaged training or compensation packages that address management development problems, but some we have consulted with are quite different, and want unique, situation-based approaches. For every category, there will be plenty of exceptions; proceed with caution. Nevertheless, the more information you can glean about the target of your influence attempt, the greater your chances of making the right approach. And there is no doubt that, although individual personality shapes behavior, the person's organizational situation is an equally important factor.

We are not suggesting that it is necessary to compile a complete dossier on each potential ally you try to influence. Often, all you need are a few pieces of information to have a good idea of where you should focus. If, for example, you know that the person you want to influence just joined your organization after three years at Digital Equipment Corporation, and left because the chaos of working in their loose, free-form matrix was maddening, you can probably guess that a businesslike, disciplined approach will be appreciated. Conversely, if the person just left IBM because the structured, disciplined style made her feel straitjacketed, then injecting some fun into your pitch might be just the right touch.

Especially when you think you're up against someone who doesn't appear susceptible to influence, the more you know about the person, the greater the chance you will find currencies to trade. If the ally is working under heavy time pressures, you will know enough to avoid rambling, problem-solving conversations. If, however, the ally likes to philosophize about the meaning of the Federal banking system, you will realize the need to be patient and allow enough time for the meeting in which your request is likely to evoke such a profound dissertation.

Even if you can't always find a currency to offer an ally, there are still good reasons to know his or her world. If you can understand the pressures the person is under, or why he acts as he does—even when you can't do anything about it—you're ahead of the game. Without that kind of insight, it's natural to attribute unwelcome behavior to negative personality characteristics. Ethan Burke, for example, began to see Andrew as manipulative and insulting because otherwise his behavior was too puzzling.

Similarly, the plant manager who won't agree to meet the rush order can appear momentarily hostile or essentially contrary. The person who doesn't return your phone calls is assumed to be trying to show how important she is; or the one who listens to your requests but doesn't respond is labeled weak or devious. Organizations are filled with people who judge their noncooperative colleagues harshly, label them as inherently bad persons, and write them off. When you write off a potential ally as suffering from a congenital—and incurable—personality disorder, anger and impotence are generated. These are hardly the foundation on which to build close relationships or to influence potential allies.

It Had to Be You: The Negative Attribution Cycle

As tempting as it is to perceive another's actions as negative and unreasonable, such a response has major problems for influence because it interferes with the ability to understand the potential ally's world. In turn, that diminishes the possibility of finding what currencies the ally values, making influence less likely.

Figure 5–1

THE NEGATIVE ATTRIBUTION CYCLE

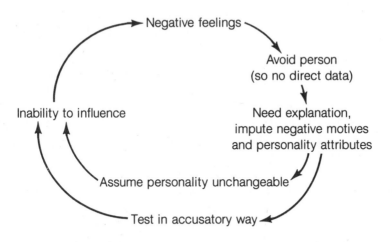

Figure 5–1, "The Negative Attribution Cycle," depicts the process by which this occurs.

Distancing the Other:
Get Away from Me

If you have no relationship, or a poor one, with another, then it is natural to avoid him. One of the basic laws of relationships is that people tend to interact more with those they like, (and to like most and interact most with those who are like them). In turn, people tend to avoid interaction with those who are dissimilar. While this makes life pleasanter and more predictable, because it avoids the discomfort of trying to overcome unfamiliarity or belligerence, unfortunately it tends to cut you off from information about someone whose help you may need.

Thus, the very people about whom it is most important to gather data that reveal their interests are those who are the furthest away and, therefore, the least likely to be understood. Difficult potential allies might well value currencies that make exchange possible, but it is hard to know that if there is little contact or discussion.

Just because someone is at a distance doesn't mean your need to make sense of his behavior diminishes. Especially if an alliance is needed in order for you to accomplish your objectives, you have to have some way to explain the puzzling or displeasing behavior. How do you make that happen?

Imputing Motives and Intentions:
The Presumption of Evil

One of the natural ways that people explain puzzling behavior of others is to attribute motives that make sense of the behavior. They explain the behavior by assuming that it is driven by internal forces, rather than organizational factors. For example, it is more common to account for a colleague's cautious behavior by saying, "She's afraid to take risks," rather than by looking at her boss' constant criticism of new ideas, the organization's cultural imperatives not to make waves, and the precise daily targets by which she is measured.

It is common to equate what a person *does* (his behavior) with who he *is*. So, when he acts in a way you don't like, you immediately label him a "jerk." Although everyone does it, premature negative labeling makes it difficult to gain insight into the potential ally's currencies. When you conclude that another person is impenetrable or intractable, you close the door to influence. If, "That's just the way Chris is," becomes the definitive "explanation," the negative attribution cycle is in high gear.

Further Decreases in Interaction:
Quicker Get-Aways

As the assumptions-about-personality concrete begins to harden in this way, any inclinations to interact diminish. Why waste your time on a person whom you believe has negative traits and can't change? Because you have concluded that a person who can't change would only be hurt or angry at being confronted with the offending behavior, you write off that potential ally for all time.

In the unlikely event, however, that you do raise the issue, it is extremely difficult not to do so in a negative, accusatory way. If resentment has built, you tend to deliver your direct comments in an attacking style that relieves your frustrations rather than helps the other learn something useful. By this time, even if your original belief about the potential ally's inability to change was wrong, your attack just precluded any chance for a positive response, and you walk away from the exchange feeling vindicated. While such an outburst provides a momentary release of frustration, it is not exactly a formula for building a trusting relationship where influence can flow both ways.

For a sad example of this downward spiral, take the case of Mark Buckley and Oliver Hanson.

Mark Buckley had recently been promoted from within the company to the position of president of Magnacomp's financial services subsidiary, Vitacorp. Soon after taking office, he became increasingly unhappy with the behavior of Oliver Hanson, the Magnacomp group vice-president in charge of Vitacorp. Oliver, a meteoric star at Magnacomp, repeatedly went to Mark's subordinates for information. Mark found this maddening; because, on the basis of these apparently casual conversations, Oliver would leap to conclusions and begin asking Mark annoying questions about "the problems" in Vitacorp.

Since Oliver was unfamiliar with Vitacorp's operations, Mark found his questions always slightly askew. They seemed to reflect more about the politics of Magnacomp than the real problems facing Vitacorp. After several experiences like this, Mark decided to take action; but his indirect attempts to hint at the issue with Oliver were met with irritation. Oliver would mutter something about needing to have a feel for what was going on.

Mark concluded that Oliver's meteoric rise must be due to the fact that Oliver was an inveterate meddler who wanted to get the dirt on everyone so that he could make himself look good. This made Mark extremely cautious around Oliver, and he made every possible excuse to reduce the contact between them. "The less information I give that power-hungry SOB, the less harm he can do!" he thought. Their relationship became quite strained, and Mark began to wonder why he had ever wanted to be president.

This portrait of organizational life has been painted many times. Not only do many employees resent interfering bosses, but virtually everyone encounters someone (or several people) whose annoying ways do not seem capable of change. Before we offer advice on how to avoid this negative cycle, we think it would be instructive to tell you how differently Oliver Hanson saw the events we just described from Mark Buckley's point of view.

Oliver was put in charge of Vitacorp as a developmental assignment. He had ideas, based on his general knowledge of financial services, about ways to improve Vitacorp's performance; but they were a result of expertise in diagnosing financial statements rather than in-depth knowledge of Vitacorp's actual business. Early on he sensed Mark's resistance to his conversations with people down in Mark's organization; but since he wasn't an expert on the business, he felt he needed a first-hand feel for the way managers thought. He had no intention of interfering, but he wanted more of a basis for judging how to assess the progress of Vitacorp. Furthermore, because Magnacomp's culture was very political, Oliver assumed that Vitacorp would have the same kind of jockeying for position in the ranks that he had seen at Magnacomp. He believed that only a very naïve manager would neglect to develop his own sources for deciphering the political maneuverings in a company he was responsible for.

With this set of assumptions, Oliver was surprised and disquieted by what he perceived as Mark's secrecy and withdrawal. "What's he got to hide?" wondered Oliver. "I'd better spend even more time talking with the troops, or I'll really be flying blind." Thus, Mark's response to Oliver's behavior made the situation worse.

Oliver *was* amenable to changing his style, but Mark never gave him the chance. Once he decided that Oliver was a died-in-the-wool politician and meddler, Mark believed he couldn't broach the subject for fear of having it used against him. Why be open with someone who can't be trusted?

Stop, in the Name of Love! Alternatives to Creating Distance and Limiting Influence

One of the ways to avoid getting into the kind of negative cycle that limits influence is to recognize the pattern as it develops. Whenever you find yourself assigning negative personality traits to an uncooperative colleague or boss, take it as a warning that needs further investigation. That difficult person may indeed turn out to be a totally immovable object; but until you have thoroughly tested that notion, you can't know if it is true.

One obvious way to develop intelligence about another is to ask colleagues whether they see him or her the same way as you do. Their views might be more detailed, more detached, and maybe more insightful; and they will protect you from reaching inaccurate conclusions.

Unfortunately, colleagues are not always the most useful source, although their views, when different from yours, can prevent you from premature hardening of the arbitrary conclusions. There are two potential problems with colleague opinions:

Birds of a Feather

The people whose opinions you most trust are quite often those who see the world most similarly. It is the sharing of biases and assumptions that usually makes for trusted colleague relationships, which increases comfort but reinforces distortions. When Mark Buckley asked his most trusted senior vice-president about Oliver Hanson, he was treated to a portrait of Oliver remarkably similar to his own, confirming the "wisdom" of his vice president.

Indirect Data Sources:
I Heard It Through the Grapevine

Even when a person asked for an opinion is not so similar that prejudices are merely shared and reinforced, often they can provide no better evidence than you already have. Their responses to your queries may be based on a few observations and some rumors rather than on firsthand knowledge. Unless the colleague is one of those rare people who is not uncomfortable asking others directly about puzzling behavior and has done so with the difficult ally, the reliability of the observations may be suspect. Thus, it is not always as easy to get useful evidence from colleagues as it appears.

I THOUGHT YOU'D NEVER ASK:
THE ALTERNATIVE OF DIRECT INQUIRY

To solve this problem, take the direct route—to the horse's mouth. Despite the natural fears of being bitten, when in doubt, just ask. To do so, however, requires that the inquiry be a genuine attempt to solve a problem and not a thinly veiled accusation.

To do that (and not just fake it, which seldom fools anyone), you must drop any negative judgments you've made and adopt a working assumption that the potential ally does not view his or her behavior as deliberately bad. Most people view their own behavior as reasonable and justified, no matter how it may appear to others.

People seldom perceive their actions in the negative way that they are seen from outside. Although the same people might label others in a parallel way, their self-perceptions do not reflect any of the negativity that others might see. Just as Oliver Hanson did not see himself as power-hungry and interfering but rather as wanting to explore unfamiliar territory and protect himself from getting caught in political traps, others have comparably favorable explanations of their own behavior.

For example, Tim sees himself not as resistant to all change but as careful to insure no big mistakes. Myra does not see her quick putdowns of anyone who disagrees with her as defensiveness but as holding high standards and wanting to save time.

When real estate developer Donald Chiofaro accused Massachusetts State Transportation Secretary Fred Salvucci of slighting Chiofaro by refusing to return phone calls, Salvucci told the *Boston Globe* that it was just a way of preserving important relationships: ". . . when there's nothing new to say, I generally don't return calls. I'm not going to undercut my engineers while they're working on a problem." In Salvucci's eyes, he was not being petty or displaying his power. The trick to unhooking yourself from your negative views is to assume that the potential ally thinks his or her behavior is quite reasonable, and your job is to understand that reasonable person's rationale.

If you find yourself starting to draw conclusions about the motives of someone you are trying to influence, try stepping back and taking a different approach. Say to yourself, "This is an intelligent, reasonable person who, for some reason that I don't understand, is not cooperating. I am beginning to act as if his motives were _____. Let me treat that only as a hypothesis, not as fact." Then, think how you might test for the truth of that hypothesis. What questions can you ask that might open up the discussion?

Often, a direct question may be all that is needed. You get into trouble when you have such a negative view that the only question you can think of would make things worse. Mark Buckley couldn't ask Oliver Hanson, "Are you really a power-hungry, back-stabbing meddler?" Ethan Burke couldn't ask Andrew Shaplen, "Are you deliberately lying, concocting flimsy excuses, and manipulating me because you don't respect me?" Such loaded questions can only provoke the recipient rather than begin an exploratory discussion.

Once you have reached a negative conclusion about someone, it is hard to go back to neutral inquiry. The bad taste left by having to deal with such a rotten apple makes it difficult to clear your palate, and lingering doubts remain. Work on understanding an ally's world when you are still puzzled, rather than after you have tried and convicted the person in your mind.

Ethan should have approached Andrew as soon as his pattern of "improvising" answers became clear and said, "Hey, I'm your partner; you can tell me if you've missed something. I can't understand what's keeping you from just letting me know what's happened." Or, perhaps he could try a more straightforward, "You seem uncomfortable about admitting even a small screw-up. I don't see why. What gives?"

Mark Buckley might have approached Oliver as soon as he heard the first couple of reports from subordinates that Oliver had asked them for information and said, "Oliver, I wonder if you know the position you've put me and my people in by assuming that they know, and told you, the complete story of what's happening in the division. I'm baffled as to why you feel you need to do that. What's the deal?" The conversation that might have ensued would have been far more pleasant at that time than after Mark decided Oliver was an inveterate meddler.

In our experience, despite the natural fear of openly admitting there is something you don't understand (especially to a person whom you think might be out to get you), this kind of openness works well for several reasons. First, the potential ally is likely to be surprised by your genuine interest. Because people in organizations rarely bother to ask others exactly how they see the world, those asked are often grateful. They appreciate your willingness to show confusion, and, in return, give you the information you need.

Second, most people are grateful for the chance to "tell their story," to explain themselves and their situation. As consultants, we repeatedly find that managers aren't accustomed to having an unlimited chance to tell it as they see it. When we show interest, they pour out far more than other insiders have predicted. This only works, however, if you are genuinely interested in what the other has to say and aren't just going through the motions of using a technique you picked up in some book.

It has long struck us as odd that so many organizational members believe they can fool anyone when they want to, but nobody can successfully fool them! (That leaves too many who are nobody's fools.) In general, we agree only with the premise that few are taken in by insincerity, so don't fake interest or confusion if you don't feel it (or can't drop the negative assumptions you've made).

Finally, perhaps the most important advantage of sincere, direct inquiry is that it builds openness and trust into the relationship, which aids all future transactions. It is easy to get so caught up in influencing potential allies that you fail to learn from them; asking what is important to them helps keep you in a more open-to-be-influenced posture, which increases their confidence in you. Again, however, faking interest is probably worse than not asking at all.

Bigger Than a Breadbox: If You Think You Know the Motive

Sometimes you are not at a complete loss as to what might be driving the reluctant ally, but you don't want to leap to the kinds of conclusions that will harden opposition. It is possible to test your intuition in an exploratory way.

For example, suppose you have a hunch that a potential ally is being pressured by his boss. Something about the way he seems to be constantly looking over his shoulder suggests that the boss' heavy hand is getting in the way. Could you talk directly to the person and say something like, "Casper, I have been puzzling about your hesitancy to back this project, especially since I think it has potential benefits for both our areas. I was wondering whether part of the problem is that you think Otto is going to climb all over you if you do anything that could affect your quarterly financials. Is that why we're having trouble connecting?"

Even if your hunch is wrong, this kind of direct query is likely to serve as the opening for an interesting conversation. If your question comes across as genuine, and does not imply that a negative answer will confirm your conviction that he is a wimp, then, whatever his answer, you have created the likelihood of learning more. If he responds that his boss has nothing to do with it, that is as much an invitation to ask what the problem really is as it is a defeat for your hypothesis. And if he confirms your suspicion, then you can help him strategize about how to overcome his boss's concerns.

Another way to engage allies in direct discussion of their interests, concerns, or currencies is to look for what appear to be mixed messages. Does the person say one thing and do another, or say nice things but in a tone fraught with hostility? For example: Your boss has been proclaiming that the future of the unit depends on people taking more initiative and being more entrepreneurial, but then she micro-manages and requires that you get her approval for every small act. Instead of concluding that she is hypocritical (or that she means it but can't let go), and then giving up, try a direct approach, one like this, "Linda, I'm really confused; and, because my confusion is interfering with my ability to do what I think you want me to, I want to try to understand better what you really want. At our staff meetings you have been stressing that you'd like us to take more initiative and do what needs to be done. But there are a number of things on which you still insist that I come to you for approval before I can go ahead. These seem to me to be places where I could take action in a responsible, enterprising way; yet, when I do, there isn't much latitude. Can we talk about this, because it's puzzling, and I could be more effective if we sorted this out."

THE WAR BETWEEN ELLEN BATTLES AND BILL BARKER _____

The more you value the relationship with the person you want to change, the harder it can be to say just what you want. Yet it often makes things worse to hold back, and it is an enormous relief to get issues out in the open. Quite often, the ally's position seems far more reasonable when it is explained. The experience of Ethan and Andrew, who discovered that they felt much better after direct discussion of their colleagues' bothersome behaviors, is by no means unique. Listen as Ellen Battles describes the severe problems she had with her colleague, Bill Barker, the many negative conclusions she leaped to, and the way she finally made peace on acceptable terms:

"I had difficulties with Bill from the moment we met. I was hired as assistant quality control manager by Ron, the associate quality control manager. I was to be responsible for the third shift; Ron had the second; and Bill, who was plant quality control manager, the day shift.

"I remember my first meeting with Bill. Ron took me into Bill's office and said, 'I want you to meet Ellen.' Bill was writing as I walked in and hadn't looked up until Ron's introduction. He then gave me this cold stare, didn't smile, just said 'hello,' and then resumed his writing. That was that!

"I don't know how much of that was merely Bill's style—harsh—with everybody, or whether it indicated his resentment at my being a woman or his not having been involved in the hiring process.

"I had been interviewed by Ron, which made sense because he would be my boss, and by Jerry, the divisional quality control manager, who was Bill's boss. I remember at the time being surprised that they jumped a level and did not have Bill talk to me; but I thought it was just the way they did things.

"Midwest Technologies was not the most progressive company. It was an old-line manufacturer of production machinery. The management group was exclusively white male; I was low in the organization but the highest-ranking woman. Other women were on the production floor, but none had risen to management.

"Since I had the night shift, I mainly saw Bill in the morning when I was finishing up. Our interactions were brief, and consisted of my reporting any problems. I felt that he was highly judgmental and always looking to find faults. I sensed that I could be fired at any time. I don't think Bill was very comfortable with women and saw them as appropriate in only two places; management was not one of them."

I Try to Talk with Bill

"After three months of this, I was fed up, so I went into Bill's office and said, 'I suspect that you aren't happy with my work. I want to be a good contributor and would like to hear what you would like me to do.' He seemed taken aback and quickly responded, 'I have no idea what you're talking about; I am perfectly happy with your work.' I wasn't totally reassured, but didn't know where to go from there.

"Then, two weeks later, I met with Jerry, Bill's boss, to review some troubles we were having meeting quality standards with one of our key customers. In the course of the conversation, Jerry said, 'Bill has come to me and wants you fired.' I was flabbergasted; but I told Jerry that I'd tried to talk to Bill, and he denied there were any problems. Jerry just shrugged and we went back to working on the quality problem. After that, my fear of Bill was so high that I stayed out of his way as much as I could."

Bill Makes a Pass

"A couple of months later, I attended a convention in Chicago with Ron and Bill. We made the rounds of the hospitality suites one evening; I stuck to ginger ale, but Ron and Bill did a bit of drinking. Nothing that heavy, but Bill was much friendlier than usual; he almost seemed to treat me as a person. When we got back to the hotel, he followed me to my room and tried to make a pass at me. I was furious! He was treating me like an object and I felt betrayed and disillusioned. He claimed he was drunk, but I think he was sober and using that as an excuse. He didn't say anything about it the next day, but after that it was difficult for him to do anything right as far as I was concerned."

My Relationship to Jerry

"The following year I was promoted to a position that put me in charge of all the analytical quality control work for the plant. Normally, I would report to Bill; but, in essence, Jerry ran that plant. Although he was divisional quality control, his office was in the building next to our plant; and he made it clear that he was the final decision maker. Jerry needed Bill to handle all the details, so in practice Bill was more like Jerry's assistant. I never saw Bill as my boss, and nobody else did either. When I had a question, I went straight to Jerry.

"I developed a very strong relationship with Jerry. He was sort of a mentor to me. I think that I reminded him of his daughter. He would often talk about the difficulties she was having on her job; I think he saw helping me get ahead as a way to vicariously help her."

A Taste of His Own Medicine

"It was an accepted practice around the plant that we could take off around 3:00 on Friday afternoon. Since I had a small child at that time, leaving early was important to me. Inevitably, around 2:00 every Friday afternoon, however, I would get a call from Bill telling me he would be by around 4:30 to go over some things he wanted to check with me.

"This really pissed me off because these were small nitpicking details; and, in almost all of the cases, I was right. I thought he was just being punitive. 'He's trying to bother me,' I concluded; 'I'm not going to let him get my goat.' So I started to keep a list of questions during the week. When our meeting ended at 5:00 and Bill was ready to leave, I would say, 'I'm glad you stopped by because there are quite a few things that I need to check with you,' and pull out my list. I would keep him there until 6:30 P.M. After three weeks of that, he stopped calling me on Friday."

My Move to Line Management

"After four years in QC, holding various jobs, I decided that I needed line experience if I were to move up the ladder at Midwest Technologies. I went to the plant manager and asked to be production supervisor on the third shift. He agreed. I knew that Bill wanted to move into production as well; but, because of his cold interpersonal style, no plant manager would take him. In my new job, Bill and I still had some interaction; and periodically in meetings he would come up with something that would blindside me. I think he was jealous of my success."

A Promotion

"I did well; and, after a couple of years, I was promoted to second shift supervisor. I caught the eye of Greg Hollins, who was then production vice-president. After a management retreat one day, Greg pulled me aside and asked me to meet with him. Over a drink he said, 'I want you to be technical services manager.' It was a new position, and I didn't know what it entailed. Greg explained his objectives, 'Ellen, we are having relationship difficulties with our key customers. They are concerned with quality and with customizing their products. You know both those areas. But I also want you to look into any other area that causes us problems. You have carte blanche to look at anything you want.'

"Technically, I reported to Jerry, the head of QC, which put me on the same level as Bill. But, in essence, I was working for Greg. He would call me in every two days and ask me questions and give me new assignments. I was really his eyes and ears in the plants.

"Although exciting and challenging, this job put me in conflict with Jerry and Bill. As my former mentor, Jerry didn't like the close relationship I had with his boss. As for Bill, not only was he jealous of my advancement, but he resented the scope of my job.

"My work involved a lot of QC issues that involved Bill, but my wide jurisdiction meant that I was unfettered by rules and regulations. Bill was a person who 'went by the book,' and my freewheeling style drove him crazy.

"Bill started to withhold information from me. Eventually, even Jerry would hold meetings and exclude me. When I approached Jerry about this, he blew up and said, 'Why should I invite you? You don't really work for me. You take your orders from Greg.' Both of them communicated with me only in response to my questions. They never volunteered anything; there was no cooperation.

"I continued doing my job, but it was very difficult. At the same time, the company was under a great deal of pressure to improve its performance. In fact, there was going to be a top-level management meeting in which managers were to present what we would do to make the company first rate."

The Reconciliation with Bill

"I realized that I needed Bill. In fact, given our differences in style, we could be a perfect team, so I decided to go to him and lay it all on the table. I went to his office and said, 'Bill, I need to talk with you. I want the door closed and the Kleenex box out.' He was startled and taken aback; I went on:

"Bill, I want to know what I can do to make our relationship better. I have a lot of respect for what you do. I'd sell my soul to be able to understand all the processes as well as you do. Your ability to see that things are taken care of—that all the ducks are in a row—is incredible.

"What I'm trying to say is, you have great talents; and I have some, too. If we worked as a team, we'd have everything covered because we are just such exact opposites."

"I was crying by this time but continued, 'I don't know where our problems started; there's a lot of hostility here. I think you are being secretive, hiding things. We're working against each other rather than as a team. I think that a lot of this started with misunderstandings you didn't intend. But I took it wrong, and it escalated.'

"Bill just sat there, shocked. Finally he said, 'When you got promoted to your present job, nobody knew what it meant. Neither Jerry nor Greg sat me down and told me what the implications were for my career.' He revealed his fears that I wasn't telling him everything. 'You tend to work on your own and not with the group, and I feel left out.'

"At that point, he began to cry, too; but he continued to discuss his concerns about where he stood with top management and what his future with the company was.

"After about an hour, during which we reviewed the history of our relationship and looked at all the places where it went wrong, we agreed to go into the meeting with top management and tell them we intended to be the best damn team in the company. To begin our new relationship on firmer ground, I said, 'And the crap stops here. Whatever went before is dead. We start fresh. And to keep this from happening again, if I piss you off, you come to me before you carry a grudge. You say, 'Damn it, Ellen, why did you do so and so,' and I'll so the same. Agreed?' Bill agreed readily."

The Beginning of a Beautiful Friendship

"Because Bill and I were not used to communicating with each other, I set a day and time every week to meet with him and go through what work we did, what problems we had, and what we planned to be working on the following week, so each of us would be completely informed about the other's activities. At the close of the meeting, we shook hands; and we could tell both of us felt relieved and happy about the exchange.

"At the top-level planning meeting, I spoke for both Bill and me. I outlined our plans in positive terms (rather than complaining about the past). In the middle of my report, Jerry said, 'But we never excluded you, Ellen.'

"Bill, sitting next to Jerry, said in a quiet but firm voice, 'Yes we have, Jerry, and we did it on purpose.' To me, this act cemented our contract and started to build a solid friendship."

Who Put That Fence in the Way?
Barriers to Directness

What keeps people from reaching such mutually satisfying agreements in comparable situations? Why is it so hard to ask directly what it is ultimately crucial to know? If you can explore others' concerns and situations directly, then it is far easier to find exchange possibilities; even when the relationship is not well-developed, it can be useful to inquire. Why doesn't it happen more often?

One of Ellen Battles' barriers to directness was that she had once tried to talk with Bill and gotten burned, so she wasn't eager to try again. Furthermore, she had concluded he couldn't deal with women as peers and was out to get her, so there seemed to be no point in trying to establish a good relationship. It never occurred to Ellen that her own success and behavior in the job might be contributing to Bill's reactions. Her relationship with Jerry, then Greg, cut Bill out. She learned in retrospect that Bill was very bothered about not knowing where he stood, and it isn't surprising that her drive and determination were threatening to him.

The pass Bill made could be interpreted as an insult and was by Ellen; but it might also have been seen as an attempt—awkward and inappropriate, to be sure—to find some way to connect with her. While Ellen was more than entitled to reject unwanted advances, her anger blinded her from the fact that Bill was not only cold and antagonistic toward her. Might she have deflected his pass but turned the attempt into something more suitable to a collegial work relationship? When she approached him with openness and recognition of their mutual dependence, he responded in kind.

There are several reasons why people in positions similar to Ellen's fail to use direct inquiry and discussion until despair forces them to a last-ditch attempt. Many just let the relationship die.

Who's Been Eating My Porridge?
Accusation, Not Inquiry

Barriers get erected when the other is not behaving as desired, and the first few approaches have not produced desired results.

Then the negative conclusions begin to form, and they have amazing staying power. Future inquiries turn into statements with strong negative overtones. Just as when a parent "asks" a child, "Why can't you keep your room clean?" inquiry laced with accusation seldom produces useful information.

For example, at a fledgling high-tech company, Steve Armstrong, the marketing vice-president, and Gunter Keppel, European director, were constantly at war with one another. Keppel believed that the products made in the United States were not sufficiently elegant for the European markets ("too klugy," in the jargon of the trade); and he refused to sell them until they were redesigned in Europe. This meant that there were delays in selling products that mattered to Armstrong, but European sales of the redesigned products were strong.

Armstrong was frustrated at his inability to influence Keppel; and, as a result, he pronounced him a power hungry, Teutonic war lord who would not listen to reason. Whenever Armstrong asked why components that were good enough for the United States and Japan weren't acceptable to Europe, he did it in a way that implied that Keppel was impossibly stubborn and arbitrarily defying Armstrong's expertise. "How can you argue against a successful product line?" was not an inquiry but an accusation, and it never failed to produce the same response from Keppel. Keppel would smile politely, say he would look into it, then do just as he pleased.

As a result, Armstrong never heard Keppel's explanations of the complex, long-term relationship issues involved in selling components to companies in Europe. Keppel was absolutely certain that a long-term strategy was the only one that made sense for Europe, and he was concerned about placing any component that wasn't exactly right. Further, he had found a few extraordinary engineers, who were making important technical extensions of the products' capacities, and he believed that the entire company would benefit from the results. Because Armstrong convinced himself that Keppel was motivated only by power, he shut himself off from the kind of critical information that would have allowed both of them to explore mutual benefit possibilities."

Say It Isn't So: Confusion Between Understanding and Agreement

Although exploration is required when the other's behavior is not quite comprehensible, it is tempting to argue when the other person says something that isn't "correct" from your point of view. When the other person is so plainly "wrong," it is natural to want to shift from listening and probing to persuasion or argument, like Dorothy did when trying to sell Hank on a new phone system he didn't want. If you don't step in, the other person might come to incorrect conclusions—or, heaven forbid—become convincing. The danger of really listening to anyone is that you might have to change your opinion, which is unsettling when you are trying to change his or hers.

Nevertheless, it is possible to work at understanding without conveying agreement. The English language does not afford us the convenient "ah so" of the Japanese, which means that the listener understands but takes no position on the matter, so we have to be more careful to make our position explicit. It can be helpful to say something like, "I don't think I see things the way you do; but if we are going to work well together, it's crucial for me to understand where you're coming from. If I'm silent, it doesn't mean I'm agreeing or disagreeing, just concentrating hard on understanding how you see this issue—or biting my tongue so I don't jump in to challenge you before I understand properly! Let me know if you think I'm not getting your views." Or words to that effect.

The patience to work towards this kind of understanding can make it possible to find opportunities for exchange where at first there appeared to be none. Knowing the world of the potential ally, however, is only part of what is needed. You also need to be clear about your own needs and interests, in order to increase the likelihood that you will find currencies to offer for those valued by the ally. Understanding your world and the power you control is the subject of Chapter 6.

6

You Are More Powerful Than You Think: Understanding Your Own World

"If you haven't got a penny, a ha'penny will do."

Pre-inflation concept for making
the best of available resources

Leslie Charm, now a successful entrepreneur, franchisor, and turnaround expert, has always been full of energy, nerve, and a willingness to take risks. He expected to use those qualities upon completing an MBA at Harvard Business School. But his first position after college was that of analyst in the five-person private loan placement department for Prudential, which at the time was an old-line, bureaucratic insurance company. The extreme mismatch between his and the company's personality was evident from the beginning.

Les had worked since he was a teenager for his father's leather manufacturing company, and it was always his practice to begin his workday early. On his first day at Prudential, Les arrived at 7:30 A.M., raring to go, but no one was there. He hadn't asked, and no one had thought to tell him, about the gentlemanly nine-to-five workday. Nor was he pleased with the conservative, stiff atmosphere when everyone did show up.

Dick Gill, the senior vice-president of the division and an experienced, lifelong Prudential employee, called Les to his office that day and greeted him with, "Welcome to the Pru. When are you leaving?" Taken aback, Les asked what Dick meant.

He replied, "An ambitious Jewish boy like you isn't planning to make a career at a place like this. So how long do you plan to stay?"

Les decided to meet honesty with honesty. "How long do you want?" he asked.

"Two years," was Gill's frank reply, "By which time you'll have learned the business and will have done enough deals to pay me back for letting you learn."

Les thought that a fair-enough arrangement; but within two weeks he was champing at the bit. He hated the required paperwork and the routine-filled, bureaucratic way of life the others seemed to accept. He wanted to meet entrepreneurs all over eastern Massachusetts, create a network of contacts for himself, and be out making complicated loan deals. How could he make the two years bearable or, better yet, enjoyable and educational?

As Les thought about his options, he realized that he was the new kid on the block, an alien in a conservative land. His formal position was two levels below Gill, and he was not in charge of anyone else. The situation did not hold much promise for getting the freedom to do what he wanted in a style that he preferred.

Then Les remembered his only other work experience outside his family's leather business. A week after Les got his bachelor's degree in business administration from Babson College, his father died. Les took a year off to sell the company before entering Harvard's graduate school of business. Six months later, the business was sold; and Les found himself without a job. After only one month, the embarrassment of collecting unemployment propelled him into taking a job in the asset-factoring division at the First National Bank of Boston. The interviewer who hired Les sent him to a low-level, credit-approval job.

During his first week at the bank, Les' boss, Dick Ajamian, invited him out for a drink. After some polite conversation, Dick suddenly said to Les, "You must be going back to graduate school in September." When Les didn't protest, Dick continued, "That's fine with me. Don't worry about it. Look, you can do your present job in two days a week. I'm 31, and I want to go places in the bank. I want you to help me, to be my tool for getting ahead. I'm going to get you into our management training program, which will allow you to see every department in the bank. You'll meet lots of people, so it won't waste your time. I'll use the training program as a cover and send you into all the asset-factoring departments. You'll look for every weakness in the system you can find and report back to me every week. That way I can strengthen the division, and you'll find it more interesting."

Les readily agreed; and, as an outsider without preconceptions and with a fresh viewpoint, he was able to spot big holes in the system then in use. Even better, he met many important people in the bank, who served as useful connections in his later ventures.

Best of all, Les learned that it was possible to initiate a nego-tiation for something he wanted by offering a win-win proposi-tion that appealed to the interests of the other party. The opportunities Dick Ajamian had provided at the bank could serve Les as a model to get where he wanted at Prudential.

Although Les nominally reported to Dick Gill's subordinate at the Pru, Les' boss preferred to make his own deals rather than supervise others. Les realized that Gill was the person to influ-ence, since he was the company's expert in bringing in new busi-ness. Gill might be interested in getting some help finding new accounts, especially the unusual deals that wouldn't ordinarily find their way to the company. If he could work out an arrange-ment with Dick, Les might free himself from the job constraints he found so irritating, meet all kinds of entrepreneurs and fi-nanciers, and, in return, provide valuable business to Dick's area.

Since the department was small and it was easy to approach anyone in it directly, Les spoke to Dick. "Dick, I see you know everybody, but I'm betting you could use help in bringing in new deals. I'll do that for you, but only if you'll meet two conditions: Nobody tells me what hours to work, and you'll have someone take care of all the related paperwork except for the actual deals. I don't want to face office bullshit and spend time filling out forms. If you do that, I'll bring in deals like none you've ever seen. If they look good to you, let me fight the battles upstairs to have them approved."

Dick said he would support Les once Les' efforts proved suc-cessful. Until that time, Les was on his own. When Les said he understood the conditions, Dick agreed to the exchange.

Les spent the next five years with Prudential, working the way he liked and producing the highest volume of loans in the division. Although he worked hard, he rarely appeared at the of-fice and conformed not at all to the customary requirements. When he did show up, he was wearing a turtleneck; then he'd casually saunter into the executive dining room for lunch. His ex-pense account, which he used for wining and dining potential and not-so-potential clients, was always the highest in the office. And he delighted in tweaking Dick. One day he strolled in at 9:00 A.M. and answered Dick's, "What are you going to do today?" with, "Oh, I'm done for the day; I've already finished two deals."

Even Les' eventual departure involved important exchanges. After five years, he went to Dick to tell him he was leaving. He didn't know exactly what he was going to do, but he was looking to start his own business. "Have I got a deal for you," Dick replied. "Stay five more months, which will let you finish the big deal you're working on and give you time to train your replacement. In return, I'll give you an extra day off each month to do your own business—one day the first month, two the second, and so forth—at no loss of pay. I'll cover for you." Les agreed. Although this arrangement was not prescribed by the Prudential policy manual, both Les and Dick got what they wanted, and the company benefited.

POWER SOURCES: YOU ARE PLUGGED IN

Our basic premise is that your power comes from having access to resources that others want (because you gain influence by engaging in mutually beneficial exchanges). This turns on its head the commonly held concept of what it takes to have influence. Too many people, whose only focus is formal authority, believe that power rests in the ability to say *no*. Although it is sometimes necessary, constantly taking a negative approach can actually diminish influence. Real power comes from knowing when and how to say *yes* and from focusing on more ways to be able to say it.

Acquiring the power to say yes requires that you know your own world, as well as your potential ally's. Until this point, we have assumed that your world is perfectly clear to you; but, unfortunately, we often see employees who lack Les Charm's clarity about what they want and what they bring to the table—the resources they command. Although they want influence, they aren't aware that they may be doing certain things inadvertently that diminish their potency.

You probably are more powerful than you think. You have untapped resources that careful diagnosis can reveal; then, like Les Charm, you can use them to gain influence even in difficult situations. We will show you in this chapter how to increase your resource pool and influence repertoire by looking carefully at the elements available when you know your own world *and* the world of your potential ally.

WHAT DO YOU WANT ANYWAY?
GAINING CLARITY ON YOUR OBJECTIVES

The first step to increase your power is to figure out exactly what you want. That is easier said than done. Most significant influence attempts usually have more than one goal; the problem comes in deciding which goal is most important and which can wait for another day.

In general, it is important to think carefully about what you want from each person that you are trying to influence. Decide in advance the *minimum* you need from each. Because, in most cases, your "wish list" will contain more than the potential ally may be willing (or able) to give, it's important to know the difference between what would be "nice to have" and what is absolutely necessary.

First Things First:
What Is the Primary Goal?

Think of Les Charm's goals when he realized he was not enjoying his job at Prudential. He wanted to meet many people who could help him later when he went into business. He wanted experience in complicated, financial deal making. He wanted to be free from the usual company constraints and paperwork. He also wanted to be able to act unconventionally and feel he had not sold his soul to a large company.

Although Les eventually was able to do all of these things, he needed to figure out what his main priorities were. If being unconventional were his main goal, Les might have focused on that and created an adversarial relationship with Dick. Then, he would have lost the chance to get out and explore new deals. By focusing on freeing himself from routine paperwork, he could get the time to meet people who would be potential loan candidates. The chance to behave in an unconventional manner would come when he proved himself, which he did.

Remember how Anne Austin refrained from showing everything she knew in a calculated strategy to gain a marketing job? Allowing her marketing colleagues to offer their expertise, she realized, would in the long run serve her objectives best because it would help her get the new product out. She acknowledged the limitations in her background ("I'm not a marketing expert . . .") and even soft-pedaled some of her knowledge to leave room for the marketing audience to "own" the product by making their own contribution.

Being willing to set aside your personal needs, even temporarily, isn't easy. Too often, we have observed managers who became so personally invested in a project that they forced it to be done only their way, rather than collaboratively, and then tried to grab all the credit. Likewise, people often become obsessed with winning the argument and thereby lose sight of the larger goal: getting support for their project.

Peeling the Onion:
Being Aware of Your Real Objectives

At issue here is not just failure to separate out personal issues from the larger goal. Lack of clarity of one's own priorities can also cause problems. For example, consider the way that Carl Lutz defeated himself.

Carl was an information systems vice-president in a large financial services company. He had steadily moved up through the organization and, being ambitious, coveted the post of senior vice-president.

He was shocked and upset when he was twice bypassed for that promotion. Although Carl was very bright, those who worked with him found him unpolished and single-minded, which made them suspicious of his ability to handle a job that called for considerable political finesse and personal sensitivity.

Carl had little patience with the kind of delicate, indirect style used at the top echelons. He attacked those who practiced such behavior as "always currying favor, being concerned with style—not substance—and failing to have the courage of their convictions."

When Carl was passed by the first time, his boss tried to explain why he had not been selected. But Carl was so caught up in wanting status that he couldn't hear. He stubbornly insisted that he had been treated unfairly, and his loud, angry outburst only served to further convince others that he was "impossible" to work with. As a result of his inability to learn, Carl was eventually asked to leave.

Even worse, his failure to think through his priorities prevented him from realizing that he really enjoyed complex, technical tasks, rather than management duties. Ironically, the division would have been happy to give him more responsibility on major system design projects, which he would have enjoyed and excelled at.

The lesson learned is not that you should set aside personal needs; doing so is both impossible and counter-productive. Personal involvement is necessary for the processes and changes this book advocates. Without a personal "investment," you won't have the drive to set goals and see them through. It is important to recognize your needs and accept them as legitimate, not drive them underground and beyond your conscious control.

In most situations where people seek major influence, the

initiators have needs above and beyond the task objectives. They may also need visibility for themselves or their department, association with the project as a way to "make a name for myself," approval, or respect. These extra, personal needs not only can provide the energy to stick through the rough spots, but can also serve the organization. Les Charm, for example, actually needed more autonomy to reach the loan objectives that justified his freedom from conventional constraints. His was a case of personal needs dovetailing with professional objectives. By contrast, Carl Lutz's personal needs ranked higher than the job-related tasks, which produced the unnecessary conflict.

In a very different situation, Ethan Burke (whom you met in Chapter 5) had to sort out his objectives with his partner, Andrew Shaplen. Although he intensely disliked Andrew's exaggerations and untruths, Ethan was stuck in the belief that preserving his friendship with Andrew was even more important than changing Andrew's behavior. Ethan raised the issue only when the problem became so disturbing that the friendship was threatened.

By making friendship his first priority, Ethan was more reluctant to criticize Andrew than to watch the business suffer. He could have redirected this priority in a positive way, by saying something like, "Andrew, nothing matters more to me than our friendship. That's why I have to talk to you about a problem I've noticed. I want to get this cleared up so we can stay as close as we've always been. When I learn that necessary arrangements haven't been made, you often tell me that you did the work even when there's good evidence you didn't. That's driving me crazy. I don't mind if something's not done, but it worries me when you won't tell me straight. I start to worry about what you must think of me. What's going on?"

There is a paradox here: The friendship ultimately would have exploded if the differences had not been addressed, which means that *quality* of relationship was probably even more important than friendship at any price. But only because friendship was so important did Ethan finally raise the issue and save himself from ending the partnership in reaction. Careful sorting of priorities is all the more difficult when personal feelings and work are intertwined.

More Than One Way to Skin a Cat: Flexibility in Goal Attainment

Even when they know their primary goals, people can lose influence by being too inflexible in the way they go about achieving them. Sometimes people with an exciting idea and high commitment become more single-minded than is necessary. They lock in on a detailed vision they've created and ignore the variations that also could work. Thus, they miss the chance to get half a loaf—or sometimes an improved, though different loaf—through the adaptation of their allies' ideas.

Rosabeth Kanter found that people who had carried out important changes in their organizations were both highly persistent and flexible. They stuck to the *essence* of the desired end state they envisioned but were open to change as they dealt with the many stakeholders whose cooperation they needed. Occasionally, even the fundamental vision changed as encounters with reality brought to light new limits and possibilities; but, more often, it was the details and pathways that changed while the vision remained intact.

Les Charm, for example, knew that he wanted to start his own business. He thought he would work for another company only two years before setting out on his own, but he ended up staying more than five. Because he was given considerable freedom to work as he wished, he not only continued to learn, but enjoyed the time more than he had expected. He eventually reached his goal of getting out and starting a company; but he did more along the way as an employee of another organization than he had anticipated, and he left behind good feelings and considerable accomplishment at the insurance company.

Whose Job Is It? Expectations of Your Role and That of Your Ally

People can limit their potential power when they arbitrarily define the boundaries between themselves and their potential allies. By defining it too rigidly, they may cut off options that could be crucial in reaching their goals. That was initially the case with Arthur Ryder.

Arthur's boss, Theo Snelling, although competent in many ways, could never seem to get memos out. This meant that decisions weren't adequately communicated to the organization. It wasn't that Theo couldn't make decisions; he just had trouble sitting down and writing the directive. Theo was European-born, unsure of his English, and insistent on composing the perfect message, for which there was never enough time.

Arthur felt more and more frustrated about this. Complaining to Theo resulted in apologies but no actions. Although memos weren't the most important issue in the department, they—or the lack thereof—were critical enough to be an increasing annoyance.

Arthur finally realized that he was locked into a too-rigid notion: "That's Theo's job and he should be doing it." Although he was technically correct about the formal responsibilities, he was limiting progress by observing imaginary boundaries. When he realized this, Arthur went to Theo and offered to write the memos himself. Since he had majored in English in college, this was no great chore. This positive exchange resulted in multiple wins: Not only were the memos out quickly, helping reinforce departmental decisions, but Arthur was building credit with Theo that could be drawn upon later.

There are several reasons why conventional job descriptions constrain people. One is the changing world of work. The historical contract (or exchange) between organizations and individuals was, "Do your job and the company will take care of you." The emphasis was on staying within the lines and boxes of the organizational chart and not interfering with anyone else's carefully circumscribed job. But, as we pointed out in Chapter 1, these rigid boundaries are dissolving. People have to do more than what is listed in their job descriptions because no single set of rules can anticipate all the changes flowing by. As a result, it is now initiative, rather than conformity, that is required.

There is another reason for the tendency to hold onto the misguided expectation that others, especially superiors, should be without flaws. Who doesn't dream of the perfect boss: the manager who is considerate but doesn't forget the task, who can criticize without being harsh, and who is capable of giving autonomy without casting subordinates adrift? But such a wise and omnipotent superior exists only in imagination, which leaves the hope-filled subordinate trapped in an organizational box. If bosses don't "do what they're supposed to do," what can someone lower in the hierarchy possibly do?

Unfortunately, standing back and criticizing, rather than seeing opportunities for exchange, means giving up potential influence. As an example, take a look at the way Martin Evans did himself in.

Martin Evans found himself reporting to a division head who was not appropriately diplomatic when dealing with key outsiders. Evans happened to be extremely good at diplomacy, always able to find just the right words to smooth out potentially difficult relationships. It irritated him that his boss was so clumsy at what Evans could do instinctively.

Instead of jumping in to help his boss, Evans criticized him to others and let the division head dig himself into numerous holes. When pushed by a colleague to help out, Evans insisted that "any division head worth his salt should be able to deal with these kinds of things." He refused to cover up for his boss or even anticipate what might be coming up and prep him for meetings.

The division head eventually offended so many people that his failings rubbed off on the division, which was perceived as self-absorbed and short-sighted. Even though the head was eased out after two years, the division's reputation remained poor, and it received fewer resources than it needed from the rest of the company. Evans was glad to see his boss go, but he suffered along with the rest of the division from the resulting poor reputation and reduced resources. His unwillingness to help at what he short-sightedly defined as his boss' responsibilities hurt his own career.

You've Got the Goods: Being Aware of All That You Can Deliver

If the basis of influence lies in what you can give that a potential ally needs, then you are only as powerful as the resources you command. Most people—even those far down the organization—control far more goods than they usually recognize.

Again, it is in their relationships with superiors that people fail to recognize the resources they can provide that the crucial senior partner needs. They tend to focus on "doing quality work on time" and ignore the other vital currencies the boss needs. They too seldom do what Les Charm did: determine the boss's critical needs and then figure out how to meet them.

It is worth emphasizing that, when you are genuinely aligned with your boss's goals and interests, you can push hard for what you want. You can disagree with your boss and be praised for it! As long as you are delivering what your boss wants or needs, you can make demands, talk straight, and effect change.

But just what do you have that your boss needs? What currencies do you command? Although every boss will have particular interests that are unique, there are some universal currencies, beyond those we mentioned in Chapter 4, that most bosses would be delighted to receive. Think of those you control:

□ *Not having to worry about the subordinate's area; knowing the person will deliver,* as Les Charm did when he found new customers.

□ *Knowing the subordinate will deliver in a way that takes into account political factors in the organization,* as Les Charm refused to do when he thumbed his nose at conventions of dress.

□ *Being able to rely on the subordinate as a sounding board; someone who makes sure the boss doesn't "shoot him/herself in the foot."*

□ *Being able to rely on the subordinate as a source of information, from other parts of the organization as well as from below. Keeping the boss informed of problems; making sure "there are no surprises."*

Because so many people distort what they tell their bosses in the belief that the boss wants to hear only what will please him or her, managers are always in the position of wanting, and needing, reliable information about what is going on in the company. The subordinate who proves to be a reliable source of information, who is good at anticipating others' reactions and can warn the manager about land mines, and who brings potential problems to the boss' attention is likely to be valued and trusted.

When Mort Buzzell, head of the tax division at a large law firm, first called the new managing partner with news about a battle between two secretaries, the managing partner asked why Mort was telling him about this seemingly insignificant problem. "You don't have to do anything about this now, but if the partners who these secretaries work for get involved, it's useful for you to have the background," Mort answered. Within six weeks, the managing partner began seeking Mort out to "chat about the organization." He had discovered the value of having a reliable advance source, and Mort was able to build a strong relationship with a partner he had not known well before he took the initiative.

There came a time when the managing partner decided to fire a senior employee, but he knew it had to be handled in a way that didn't arouse negative reactions from other partners. He asked Mort to have a drink after work and run through several scenarios with him. Mort pointed out some possible pitfalls. The managing partner was extremely grateful, as usual, and Mort's stock rose once again.

□ *Representing the boss (accurately) to other parts of the organization,* which frees the boss to do other things.
□ *Being a source of creativity and new ideas.*

Any manager who is not trying desperately to hang on to the status quo will value a subordinate who brings new ideas and approaches to problem-solving sessions.

Vlad Czernak was a physicist who had moved into a management position in a manufacturing company. His training in physics and his natural intelligence gave him the ability to "turn problems upside down," to take what others assumed and relax the constraints. When a problem needed to be tackled, the plant manager always got Vlad involved and kept him fully informed.

When Vlad would say, "This is probably a dumb idea, but what do you suppose would happen if we . . .," everyone would pay close attention. His thought processes worked like those of a naïve, fresh kid, as if he didn't know what was considered impossible, which led him to question the routines that everyone took for granted. It was Vlad, for example, who had realized that the usual clean-up process at the end of the day was causing more contamination of the product, rather than less, which led to an entirely new process that increased yields considerably.

□ *Defending and supporting the boss' (and the organization's) decisions to your own subordinates.*

It is tempting for many employees to blame any tough decisions on "the boss" or on the invisible "they" at the top. Thus, managers are grateful when a subordinate "sells downward," rather than subtly undermining the boss' credibility by implying that all unpopular decisions are forced from above.

□ *Taking initiative with new ideas; preventing problems instead of waiting for them to happen.*

In an era of rapid change, there is even more need than in the past for subordinates who can take initiative, rather than wait for instructions that inevitably arrive too late. The willingness to jump in to prevent problems is valuable and often dramatically noticeable.

Betsy Barnes was only 19 when she started work as a receptionist at a management consulting firm. One afternoon during her first week on the job, she discovered that a set of slides for an important client presentation had not been delivered. She called the photo lab and was told that the slides had never been received. When she insisted that they had indeed been hand-delivered two days earlier, the lab supervisor replied that was impossible and Betsy would just have to look around her office for the film.

Betsy dug through a pile of unfiled materials and found the receipt from the lab; she called them back to insist that they should look harder. They gave her the runaround again, but she hung in, insisted on talking to the manager and, over the phone, guided him through a search for the missing film. When he had finally located the film, Betsy persisted in pressing the lab to do a special rush job so a courier could pick up the finished slides that afternoon in time for the company president to take them to the presentation.

By chance, the president walked by Betsy's desk as she patiently but very insistently demanded that the lab look harder for the film. He was amazed that on her own, this new, young employee was so conscientiously anticipating the disaster of not having the slides and making sure they would be ready. Not only did he award her an instant bonus, but he also mentioned to the office manager that Betsy obviously had more potential. Within two months, she was promoted to a more responsible position, managing materials sales.

□ *Performing above and beyond what is required.*

This is a traditional way of building credit with any boss, but it is still fundamental. When Les Charm asked to work directly at finding profitable loan opportunities, and then delivered, he was given extraordinary latitude by a manager who appreciated the results and was willing to bend the rules to accommodate a star performer who provided more than expected.

□ *Providing support and encouragement, "being on the boss' team."*

Managers do not always find it lonely at the top, but the person in charge will often find it impossible to explain exactly why he or she had to make certain decisions and how the power to affect others' lives can be a tough burden. Managers often especially appreciate a subordinate's loyalty, encouragement, or general willingness to give the benefit of the doubt. Even bold, strong leaders value having someone around who will stick by them through thick and thin. President John F. Kennedy, for example, counted on Dave Powers, a Massachusetts "local" with a great sense of humor, for companionship and general support.

Although this list has been far from exhaustive, awareness of such needed currencies allows a subordinate to move from just "making a request" (which makes one dependent on the grace of another) to creating credits that can be exchanged for outcomes in both parties' interests.

In the first section of this chapter, we stressed the importance of knowing your own goals and gaining a clearer picture of what you need. While that is crucial, it serves only as the first step. It is only the beginning of your strategy for dealing with the person you want to influence. Focusing only on what you want means that the change will be defined in terms of meeting *your* needs, rather than the potential ally's, which is unlikely to be a successful influence strategy.

If you see clearly what you want (and if these demands are reasonably within the scope of what others can deliver), you are free to focus on what others need from the transaction. Then, by examining what resources you command, you can decide how the exchange can meet the others' needs. Not being able to deliver a valuable currency is a formula for powerlessness. Let's look at how Jim Clayborn defined what currency to trade in and created a resource to pay with.

Jim encountered a problem with Wes, his boss, who had a tendency to withhold information. Once a professional poker player, Wes tended to keep his cards close to his vest. This meant that Jim often heard first from subordinates about new plans coming down from corporate headquarters, which wreaked havoc on Jim's credibility and influence with his subordinates.

For example, Jim found out from one of his people that corporate was planning major divestiture of another division. The subordinate was clearly surprised, then embarrassed, that Jim hadn't yet heard.

Jim's previous attempts to ask Wes to keep him better informed had produced no results. This led Jim to fear that Wes saw him as demanding and insecure. To get better information, Jim needed to provide something Wes valued. Rather than put his request into terms of what he needed for himself, Jim went to Wes and said, "We've talked before about the importance to our department of being seen as knowledgeable and on top of issues. As you've said many times, we get credibility by being 'in the know.'

I agree with that and want to deliver, but sometimes I can't. When things are breaking and I don't hear from you, the department and I look foolish. Could we set up a 15-minute meeting each Tuesday morning where you can quickly brief me on what's coming down the pike?"

Phrasing his request in terms of Wes' best interests—rather than just Jim's—finally did the trick. Jim offered Wes currency—departmental reputation—that Wes valued enough to prompt him to hold regular meetings.

POWER OUTAGES IN MAKING EXCHANGES

Fear of Flying: Reluctance to Assert Legitimate Claims

Jim set out to create currencies that would be valuable to his boss. Others, however, experience power failures because they don't know how to collect on obligations others have incurred toward them. Bill Heatton, the frustrated R&D manager from Chapter 2, for example, believed the change he made in his own organization automatically obligated Ted, his counterpart in marketing, to comply with his requests. But Ted failed to acknowledge any debt, and Bill didn't know how to collect.

Ethan Burke (Chapter 5) was similarly reluctant to draw on past obligations his partner incurred toward him. Ethan's emotional and *personal* reaction to his partner's behavior clouded his judgment; he never considered that Andrew might feel grateful for Ethan's hard work. Ethan's attention to project details freed Andrew to pursue sales, which gave Ethan potential clout that he had overlooked. Andrew needed Ethan's skills and recognized how much he depended on him. But, for a long time, Ethan was afraid to point that out.

Another person reluctant to collect debts was Sheila Sheldon, a curator of an important collection at a major art museum. She became very unhappy with the way other department heads treated her when she realized that she accommodated so many of their needs but they didn't respond well to her requests. "I'm always going out of my way for people, lending staff members for projects, researching questions, or giving up storage space. But I can't bring myself to remind them when I want something. They should know! That's the least I can expect if they're good colleagues. Why can't they live up to their obligations?"

Sheila's model of influence and relationships depended solely on her colleagues' awareness of what she had done, its value to them, and their goodwill, any of which could be lacking. Did they realize how much she had inconvenienced herself for them? Did they think she was only doing her job? Did they find the usefulness of her gestures far more modest than she had thought? Had the fact that she always "suffered in silence" made them completely oblivious to her efforts and her need for reciprocity, or led them to believe she was happy to be self-sacrificing? Because she wouldn't raise the issue, she had no way of finding out.

It isn't necessary to become a miser, hoarding currency and constantly reminding people what they owe you in order to stake legitimate claims when others fail to notice your efforts. At the very least, initiate a direct conversation in which you ask bluntly but politely if your view that reciprocity is being ignored matches theirs. Until your unreciprocating colleague understands your side of things, you are tossing away the ball before the match has started. Raising the question doesn't guarantee the response you desire, but at least it unlocks the court.

Avoid Dancing in the Dark: Know Your Work Style and Match It to Your Ally's

All people have a certain work style, a way of solving problems, dealing with others, and getting their jobs done. Some people prefer careful analysis before action; others like to blast through and patch up any holes later. Some managers want subordinates to come to them only with solutions, while other bosses want employees to seek help when the problem is still developing. In building a working relationship, some people like to get to know a colleague first before dealing with the task, while others feel they cannot consider closeness until there has been some successful work interaction.

Preferred styles come from training and past experiences, from the demands of jobs, and from individual personality. Cultures create work styles, too. In many Asian and Latin countries, no work can be undertaken until colleagues have consumed many cups of tea or coffee and exchanged gossip. In parts of the United States, however, people get impatient if the tasks aren't tackled early and socializing saved for later.

In most cases, there isn't one "right way" to interact, declared in heaven and engraved in stone. Or, to put it more subjectively, people often *do* feel there is *one* right way—theirs! Like the fish who is unaware of the water because it is always there, people often are not aware of their styles; it feels so natural, it must be inherently correct. But, in dealing with others, it is important to be aware of your style and that of the person you want to influence.

Mike Impacienza, production vice-president of Weavers, Inc., never realized that he and Simon, the company president, had different—and contradictory—work styles. Mike, accustomed to handling minute-by-minute crises in his department, had a tendency to mention whatever was on his mind when he would see Simon in the hall. "I think we'll need a new cutting machine and I can get a good used one for under $50K—Okay?"

Simon, whose background was in finance, would get bent out of shape with these on-the-fly requests. "For God's sake," he thought, "I usually say 'yes' to everything; but at the very least, why can't he write up a three-page request that lists the options?" Even when Simon made this request of Mike, Mike saw it as "unnecessary bureaucracy" and did it only when he "had time" (which was seldom or never). Mike, by stubbornly working in the casual style he preferred, got turned down more times than necessary. Being sensitive to Simon's style would have made him much more effective.

Not being fully aware of your style can keep you from considering other possible approaches. Sometimes, for example, a person finds that a bullying, threatening style makes others reluctant to disagree and therefore assumes that it is always appropriate. When they try it with someone who is not so easily intimidated, they are shocked at the strong reaction.

At the other extreme are people who try to do everything with honey because they have over-learned this way to catch flies. There are others whose style dictates they make all of their influence attempts face-to-face, which may not fit the more remote style of the potential ally and may also prevent the use of other forms of influence that utilize intermediaries. Being unaware of your style can lock you into doing only what worked in the past rather than enable you to make a careful diagnosis of whether it fits the present situation.

Being sensitive to your own style can also give you clues to what may be causing difficulties in a work relationship. Most of the time, when we see what are called "personality conflicts" between people, different work styles are the actual cause. Like a Greek tragedy, Jack Walters and Tony Carlino played out that kind of mismatch to its unfortunate end.

Jack Walters had recently been named vice-president of marketing. This was a lateral transfer from production, with the twin goals of broadening his experience and using his considerable skills in the crucial (but underdeveloped) marketing area. With his engineering training and production background, Jack was used to solving problems himself and only taking them to his boss when he was stuck. He liked things tidy and wanted to be on top of all issues.

Tony Carlino, the company president, had come up through marketing. His experience (and personal style) made him comfortable with messy problems. He wanted to hear about difficulties when they first arose. He didn't necessarily have to solve every problem himself; he was amenable to a subordinate's saying after they had discussed the various options: "I hear your input and certainly will consider it carefully, but I want to handle this on my own." What Tony needed most was to be kept informed and to feel that he had been listened to.

Jack's and Tony's opposite styles led to polarization, then suspicion, distrust, and even paranoia. When Tony was concerned about something, he would ask Jack if there were any problems. Jack would "hear" this as "any problems that you can't solve?" and would say no. Tony would think that Jack was keeping information from him and would probe even further. Jack would feel his competence was being questioned and would become even more circumspect.

From Jack's point of view, the problem was Tony: "Damn it," he thought, "He is paying me good money to be head of marketing; why doesn't he let me manage? I guess he really wants to run marketing himself." Jack's failure to recognize the part that his own style played in this problem meant that the problem grew and grew, until the point that Tony saw Jack as not only disloyal but sneaky and untrustworthy. The problem "ended" one day when Tony strode into Jack's office and fired him.

Although differing work styles are often enough to cause serious problems, sometimes it is style or personality that is blamed for genuine differences of substance. For example, Claude Bebear, head of Axa-Midi Assurances, and Bernard Pegazy, chairman of Midi, were in a huge battle over company direction. In *The Wall Street Journal*, an article about this, entitled "A Clash of Egos Strains a French Marriage: Country's Biggest Firm Shows Signs of Breaking Up," claimed the charisma of Bebear and the technocratic, autocratic style of Pegazy were the source of their difficulties, but then revealed that the real problem was different ideas about the correct *strategy* for the recently merged company. "Bebear wants to eat up the group's financial assets to grow in insurance . . . Pegazy took 30 years to build up his group, and he doesn't just want to be at the head of a financial rump within the group," reported a company official.

Thus, what is attributed only to ego and style can be a manifestation of real differences in strategic plans. We do not want to minimize business disagreements as a source of influence disputes, since they do cause their own kinds of problems. Nevertheless, there is enough to genuinely disagree about without allowing work *style* to become an extra problem in achieving influence. Stay aware of your style and how you are influencing, or failing to influence, others because of it.

For Every Season:
Increasing Your Influence Repertoire

Although most people limit their power because of a too-narrow definition of the range of currencies that they can deliver, they also can lose power by overspecializing in only one style of interaction. We have stressed the importance of an open and collaborative style in dealing with potential allies. Although usually the preferred style (especially with people who will be needed in future interactions), at times it becomes necessary to use threat and confrontation (carefully) in order to set the stage for a mutual exchange. More than merely a willingness to be tough, since threats with no resources behind them are empty, doing this successfully also requires a sense of how your own worth expands possibilities. In Chapter 2, Anne Austin threatened to quit if John didn't consider her for the marketing position. Because Anne had built her credibility *and* credit to the organization, the threat carried some weight. You don't want to get into the position of barking a threat only to hear the calm retort, "Got a dime? Call someone who gives-a-shit!"

In the following case, Chris Hammond was forced to take tough actions because of the intransigence of her boss. Note the way she marshalls resources and uses a confrontational style to achieve mutual gains.

"When I was a sales trainee, I knew that if I didn't make the Computex Sales Award, my career at Computex would be ended. Although they wouldn't fire me, I would just be a sales rep, twiddling my thumbs for however long I stayed. You have to make your numbers or nothing happens to you. So there I was, with a

manager who had 20 items that he needed to make to achieve his
budget by the end of the quarter and who was trying to make sure
that I didn't make the Computex Sales Award. Sales trainees
aren't supposed to make the sales award; and if I did, then he
should have promoted me to a sales representative. So I asked his
secretary what budget numbers he needed. I wasn't being devious; I was really trying to support him. I wanted him to succeed
because that was the only way I could succeed. But I had to do it
with a power play because he wouldn't treat me seriously.

"So I read the numbers and said to myself, 'Okay, he can't
make it in these six areas.' As it so happened, I had an account
which was going to make the numbers in four of those areas. Then
I called up every single lead that we had received in the office
over the last four months and on which no one had returned calls,
identified the ones that were going to close in a month, and found
15 accounts.

"As a sales trainee, that wasn't what I was paid to do; I was
paid to learn. But I was tired of being a sales trainee; I was determined to be a sales rep and sell and make the Computex Sales
Award—and be the only sales trainee to do it that year.

"Another dimension entered into the situation. My manager
had a fair-haired boy, a sales rep and the only individual whom
he had personally hired; he wanted him to make the sales award.
Since I was leaving on July 1, if I made the sales award, to take a
job at corporate headquarters, my manager reasoned that I should
give 50 percent of anything I booked to the sales rep. The motives
behind this request were pretty transparent to me. So I told my
manager that I didn't think that was fair unless he was willing to
give me 50 percent of all the sales rep's bookings, since I had
done a considerable amount of work and could document it on
two banking orders he had. In effect, however, I was being asked
to give the rep a split so that he would make the sales award, and
I was getting nothing for it. That was a key link in my strategy,
since exposing my manager would not be advantageous for either
the manager or the sales rep.

"I went to the district manager and asked whether I would
make the sales award if I closed such and such accounts. He said
yes. So I said that was not what my manager told me, that he had
told me I would have to give 50 percent to the sales representative. The district manager asked why, and when I answered, he
looked at me in total disbelief. I explained that I didn't think it
was fair that the sales rep should make the award on behalf of my
efforts, and if that was the case, the company would not get any of

the business I had found. I would leave the company today, take my vacation pay and go. The district manager said to go back and talk to my manager. What none of them knew was that I had already pulled this off, that the bookings were in my drawer and this was not idle conversation. I could make good on any deal I worked with them, and I knew what they needed to make their numbers to look good to their bosses.

"So I went in to my manager. There were two weeks left in the quarter and he was scared now because he wasn't going to make his numbers. I said to him, 'I have a problem. I really want to go back to headquarters, and I need your help. I need to make the sales award. You know that and I know that. I can't go back to corporate as a turkey who hasn't succeeded in making the sales award. I believe I've put forth the sales effort required to do that. I also believe I should go back as a sales rep. I believe I've earned that. Now I think I can make the following budget numbers for you, and I can bring in these two accounts. All that I need from you is the assurance that I will receive the Computex Sales Award if I do it. Otherwise I'm not going to work another day.'

"He looked at me and finally said, 'If you get those orders in, you can make the sales award; and yes, if you bring in that business, then you're more than qualified to be a sales rep.' What he was banking on was that I didn't have the orders. I walked into his office with them two days later.

"What motivated me for the most part was realizing that they were not taking me seriously and not paying attention to what I was doing, to how many accounts in which I was involved were closed as a result of my efforts. I also wanted them to know that I was fully aware of their attempt to use me. That kind of approach is a very strong power play and a high-risk strategy, but if you succeed, you are given much more respect and higher levels of managerial credibility."

Chris followed a high-risk strategy that could have backfired at any of several junctures. In some companies, going over her boss' head to the district manager would have been seen as inappropriate and possibly even grounds for dismissal. The sales manager she cornered might have retaliated by refusing to recommend her for promotion to sales rep or by spreading negative rumors to others in the organization with whom she would be dealing in the future. Further, she might have made a permanent enemy of the sales rep who had been promised credit for her work. These are all the potential costs that one has to take into account before selecting such a strategy.

Nevertheless, when faced with a situation in which there was little left to lose and everything to gain, Chris correctly diagnosed her boss' most valued currency (his sales quota); stressed the currencies she commanded or could command (sales to customers not yet approached by anyone at Computex, her boss' reputation with the district manager); and made an exchange that got her what she wanted, helped her boss, and was good for the company. (It is worth noting that she was not insensitive to the organizational culture; managers at Computex are valued for playing exactly that kind of "guts ball," and Chris has continued to do well there).

The choice between collaboration and confrontation is only one set of alternatives for increasing your influence repertoire. Another set involves the time pressure for results. Chris was under external pressures that forced her to move quickly. Tom Owens, on the other hand, was successful because of his willingness to be patient.

Tom Owens was a customer service district manager at GE Med Systems (and one of Rosabeth Kanter's original group of managers in her research for *The Change Masters*).

Tom had been trying for several years to get a new recruiting program adopted for this service organization. He wanted to recruit college graduates and provide a full year of classroom and field training before placing them in field offices to install and repair sophisticated medical products. He was convinced that the increased complexity of products meant that technical degrees or on-the-job experience was no longer sufficient background.

Tom took the idea to his general manager, who supported it. But before anything got started, the manager was transferred in a reorganization. Tom then decided to set up a pilot for this program, which he funded by taking money from his subordinates' expense budgets. He tried to reassure them by promising that he would only need the funds for a short time, and that they would benefit from helping to train the new staff. When a new general manager was appointed, Tom won his approval to include the program in the long-range plan, but without any provision for funding. Nonetheless, Tom continued his pilot program and tried to convince others of its merits. This dragged on for two years.

Finally, a peer of his was selected as the next general manager; and this manager agreed to fund the program—but only if Tom could convince his four other peers in the service organization to give their support and adopt it in their regions. This presented Tom with a big challenge.

He invited all of them to a meeting. First, however, he determined what changes they wanted in their functions; and he used these as agenda items for the meeting. It took three days of discussion and negotiation, but Tom was able to get their agreement in return for his support on matters important to them. Although the new general manager was surprised, he kept his part of the bargain and obtained the several hundred thousand dollars needed to expand the recruitment and training pilot into a full-fledged, company-wide program. The subsequent program has been very successful, and it has continued to be fully funded even in a period of budget cuts.

Unlike Chris Hammond, Tom was patient and nonthreatening. Yet he did not let go of what he was certain would be a beneficial activity for the company. He stuck with it through three general managers and a tough-sell to his peers in order to prove the program's viability to the boss who could fund it. In the meantime, he had mobilized the currencies he did control (the budget of his department, including lines assigned to his subordinates), used them to demonstrate the value of the training program he advocated, and thus created a new currency (good performance) that helped him trade with his peers.

SUMMARY

To achieve all the power of which you are capable, you need to understand yourself as well as your potential ally. What exactly are your task or project goals? Which are of primary importance and which can be set aside if necessary? What are your personal and career goals, and do they help or hinder task success? Are you using all available resources? And, finally, what is your style? Is it compatible with the style of your ally, and is your way of getting work done partially causing the problem that you hope to solve? All are questions that need careful attention if you are to be as powerful as possible. Then you will have the capacity to gain influence by making successful exchanges.

7

Building Effective Relationships: The Art of Finding and Developing Your Allies

The stranger within my gate,
He may be true and kind,
But he does not talk my talk—
I cannot feel his mind.
I see the face and the eyes and the mouth,
But not the soul behind.
The men of my own stock,
They may do ill or well,
But they tell the lies I am wonted to,
They are used to the lies I tell;
And we do not need interpreters
When we go to buy and sell.
The men of my own stock,
Bitter bad they may be,
But, at least, they hear the things I hear,
And see the things I see;
And whatever I think of them and their likes
They think of the likes of me.

"The Stranger"
Rudyard Kipling

Rudyard Kipling was fonder of the devil he knew than the devil he didn't. At least the devils you know are strangely comfortable. Their assumptions and ways of viewing the world are familiar. Their behavior, though reprehensible, is predictable; and they can be influenced by known methods. They provide a kind of reassurance because they can be counted on for similar perceptions and values. The world certainly is easier if you only have to deal with those who think like you.

Alas, we live in "interesting," and, therefore, not easy times. Organizations are filled with people who are "strangers," who view the world differently, because they work for differing functions and managers, are a different sex, age, race, ethnicity, have different training and experiences—all the things that require diverse expertise be brought to bear on complex organizational problems. The forces we described in Chapter 1 require a wider range of people, backgrounds, and views than was the case in Kipling's time. Then, members of the British Administrative Services were trained to "think like the Queen" so that they would know what to do when messages and instructions took too long to arrive. And, since they were recruited from the same narrow class, they already had a running start toward cohesiveness and ease of dealing with one another. Current conditions require more effort to build effective relationships with the range of people whose cooperation is needed.

Although, occasionally, transactions can be so clearly beneficial to both parties that the relationship between the parties is irrelevant, most of the time there are many ways in which a poor relationship affects the likelihood of influence. For example, a poor relationship:

□ Decreases desire to be influenced
□ Distorts accuracy of diagnosis of each other's currencies, intentions
□ Increases burden of proof on:
  □ Other's performance
  □ Delivery of promises
  □ Value of what is offered for exchange
  □ Timing of repayment
□ Decreases tolerance for the ambiguity inherent in making exchanges of different goods and services
□ Reduces willingness to engage at all; raises spitefulness: "I'd rather go down in flames than help *that* bastard!"

These are big handicaps when trying to achieve influence. If all relationships worked from such disadvantages, organizational life would come to a standstill. Luckily, only the most unfortunate have *no* relationships that are solid and trusting. Most organizational members know one or more people with whom they can be open and direct, and realize the benefits of that kind of relationship. Problems arise with all those colleagues who are not so trusted, or trusting. It's bad enough when you deal with strangers who are unknown; complications multiply when you seek to influence someone who has a negative reputation or with whom you have personally had a bad experience.

SOURCES OF RELATIONSHIP PROBLEMS

Bad Blood: The Relationship's History

One problem arises when there have been negative interactions between the two parties in the past. Events may have occurred that are interpreted by one side or the other as "proof" that the other party is not trustworthy, likable, or a good colleague.

For example: Jill Richards ran the headquarters systems support group for a large insurance company. When given the opportunity to work with Tony Marini, the head of methods and procedures, she refused, citing her past dealings with him in his previous role.

Jill had "caught" Tony misrepresenting her views to top management as a way of bolstering his arguments for a changed procedure he was trying to institute. Someone who attended the meeting later told Jill what Tony had said there; when she confronted him, he denied it. Jill offered to go to the executive with Tony to clarify her views, but Tony backed away, promising to "straighten out the misunderstanding" on his own. As a result of this experience and others like it, Jill declared that she would never cooperate with Tony, saying: "He's a backstabber and can't be trusted at all. He'll say anything to get his way." Even when Tony came around with good ideas, Jill refused to cooperate.

Sometimes it is not even necessary for a person to have actually done harm to another to be mistrusted. Tony, for example, had acquired a reputation around the insurance company; and there were colleagues of Jill who knew the "book" on Tony, so they avoided him. Reputation may or may not be deserved, but it can strongly affect ability to get work done.

We have already examined some ongoing relationships where the parties were familiar with each other but decided they "knew" each other's reputation only too well. Ethan Burke and his partner Andrew Shaplen, Mark Buckley and Oliver Hanson, Ellen Battles and Bill Barker all had beliefs about their counterparts that served as filters for interpreting behavior. History gets in the way.

Sometimes, reputation is not personal but departmental; anyone from methods and procedures, for example, is seen as a spy and know-it-all, in spite of the fact that each member of the department is a unique individual with personal characteristics. The way in which your department or division is seen can rub off on you and color the way you are seen. This is particularly true if you are developing a relationship with someone from another department who perceives yours in a negative way.

It's Not the Situation; It's Your Personal Style

Personal style conflicts are another source of difficulty that interferes with cooperative relationships. As we have explained earlier, what is often attributed to personality is really situational; but there can be corrosive chemistry when dissimilar operating styles come in contact with each other.

When Jack Starr and James Bloch are in the same room, they each cause the hair on the back of the other's neck to stand straight up. Jack is a political infighter who long ago cultivated a tough, confrontational style with everyone because "you can't let the bastards get any edge." James is a quiet, principled man who would never put his own personal interest first and doesn't like anyone else in the organization to do so; he prefers resolving differences by quietly reasoning together. He sees Jack as gratuitously nasty; Jack sees him as sanctimonious and repressed. They long since have stopped listening to each other; everything the other says is suspect.

CONVERTING PROBLEM PEOPLE TO ALLIES

Whatever the source of relationship problems, the challenge you face is how to turn difficult people into working allies. Whether the problem is that you don't trust the potential ally or that the ally doesn't trust you—or both—you *must* lay the important groundwork that will help improve the working relationship. The goal is not to build friendships, where magically your bitterest enemy is converted into your best friend. Remember, the nature of alliance is for the parties to accept that they may have very different objectives and styles, but can find some common ground on which to conduct limited, mutually beneficial, transactions. Although friendships sometimes grow as a byproduct of getting past old wounds and doing business with each other, the goal is only to create working relationships satisfactory enough to get tasks done to help the organization.

Overcoming Mistrust and Negative Attributions

How can you build good working relationships? Problems usually arise because *mistrust* has entered the relationship, or because one party *attributes negative motives* to the other's behavior. As we explained in Chapter 5, when that happens, the natural tendency to avoid the mistrusted other person reduces the very contact that might inject new, more favorable data into the relationship. The absence of favorable data then becomes a fertile breeding ground for more mistrust and negative attributions, and so on in a vicious negative cycle. Somehow, the cycle must be broken. We will describe two approaches to improving relationships: working on *tasks* together, or discussing the *relationship* directly.

Hey, I've Got an Idea: Let's Forget This Ridiculous Personal Stuff and Go to Work!

Perhaps the most common attempt to fix poor relationships is to overlook feelings and concentrate on working together at some tasks. Successful joint accomplishment can improve trust and foster a better relationship.

Of course, when there is a poor relationship and neither party can order the other to engage in a joint effort, often they never actually do find a cooperative task. Like Jill Richards did, the most dissatisfied person usually just avoids the other, or stalls. But even when two combatants agree to tackle some task together, there is little guarantee that they will improve their relationship.

Unfortunately, the very problems that created the original difficulties are likely to get in the way of cooperation on a task. This is similar to a divorcing couple trying to negotiate their own settlement. If they could talk reasonably to one another, the property would not be hard to divide; but if they could talk reasonably, they probably wouldn't be getting divorced in the first place. It is very hard to work well with a person who does not trust you or you do not trust.

Nevertheless, circumstances sometimes force people to work together, and they find that the task demands are so compelling that they can put aside their differences, and, as a by-product, an improved relationship emerges. When that happens, both parties are pleasantly surprised and can build from there. But the odds are not great that such a fortuitous outcome will result.

Speak Up: Direct Approaches to Resolving Relationship Problems

If, by their nature, poor relationships depend for continuation on reduced contact, the obvious solution is to increase the amount of contact and make a direct attempt to patch the difficulties. When this is done well, it can make a very big difference in the way two parties deal with one another.

Because Ellen Battles, from Midwest Technologies, was desperate to solve her difficulties with Bill Barker, she tried directness as a last resort. With hindsight, we could ask why the same approach would not have worked sooner, and why she had to wait so long to tackle directly the tensions with her colleague. But, during the course of our consulting in organizations, the reluctance to discuss openly a poor relationship appears remarkably often. A number of factors determine the appropriateness of dealing directly with relationship problems rather than trying to carry on with the tasks.

When to Proceed with a Task or Initiate a Direct Discussion to Improve a Relationship

The following list graphically depicts the conditions for "getting down to business" versus those for doing a little relationship work first.

Task	*Relationship*
Animosity is mild	Animosity is strong
Task can be accomplished even with animosities	Feelings block task success
Culture represses explicitness	Culture supports explicitness
Task success likely to improve feelings	Even with task success, feelings won't improve
Ally can't handle directness	Ally welcomes directness
Your style not suited to directness	Your style suited to directness

Let's look at each of these factors.

Heat Waiver: Degree of Animosity

When prior animosity is too great between two people, it gets in the way of their working together on any task. The feelings bubble to the surface at the slightest provocation and drive out real work. Any disagreement deadlocks decision making, and both parties look for ways to prove how bad the other is—and how virtuous they are.

On the other hand, when animosity is moderate, the pull of a difficult task may carry both parties past their feelings. They "get interested," and the work proceeds despite the reservations of each about the other.

We Did It! (You Couldn't Have Done It Without Me)

When a good job is done, both parties may come to feel better about each other. Despite the conventional wisdom that liking produces successful teamwork, the opposite can be true: Successful joint performance leads to greater liking. Winning teams like their teammates; losers look bad to each other. Or, as many social scientists have pointed out, attitude often follows behavior.

There will always be those who, unhappy with their colleagues or bosses, can rationalize even great joint success and discount the contribution of the disliked ally. It is tempting to see any new, more desirable behavior as an exception, caused by circumstances rather than any "real difference" in the disliked person. Claiming that "he was just on good behavior" is less disconcerting than revising strongly held beliefs.

Don't Mention It: Degree of
Explicitness Sanctioned by the Culture

Some company cultures foster an open style and encourage the confronting of differences of all kinds, task and interpersonal. Members are expected to let each other know what is on their minds, and anyone who doesn't speak up is considered to be weak and unduly constrained. When someone is unhappy with what a colleague or boss has done or said, he or she takes a direct approach, face-to-face, using as much heat as is felt. Such organizations are generally expressive and animated; problems are settled quickly and everyone moves on to the next issues. There is often a special name for sessions where people take each other on, such as confrontation meetings, heart-to-hearts, off-line meetings, green-light sessions, shoot-outs, or shirtsleeve seminars.

Unfortunately, this kind of culture is less common than cultures that discourage straight talk. Many organizations reinforce members for being circumspect, holding disagreements down, and avoiding sharp interpersonal confrontation. In these kinds of cultures, disagreements are "managed" so as not to be embarrassing, and it is considered bad form to speak directly to a colleague about your relationship. Thus, even those who would be personally inclined to talk straight learn not to do so. They may learn to send subtly encoded messages that protect the receiver and allow denial by the sender. Since interpersonal communication is difficult under the best of circumstances, great distortions arise, with no direct way to correct them.

Me and My Big Mouth;
You and Your Rabbit Ears

Your style, and the way it interacts with the style of your potential ally, is another important factor in determining whether or not to work directly on the relationship. Some people are skilled at raising relationship issues, while others are ham-handed and in no time manage to insult the person with whom they are trying to patch up. Some allies welcome a direct discussion about relationships, while others are too shy or uncomfortable to participate in open discussion of differences. And, as a further difficulty, not everyone is good at figuring out what the other party really prefers; often, they assume reluctance when there is eagerness, or eagerness when there is great reticence.

Les Charm, the entrepreneurial MBA you met in Chapter 6, used a very direct approach to create the kind of working relationship he wanted. He was fortunate because the division head he negotiated with was a deal maker by profession, so Les' directness was appreciated. Imagine Les Charm trying to talk that way with Bill Barker, the circumspect and rule-bound quality control manager with whom Ellen Battles struggled for years. Ellen's early attempts at rapprochement resulted in Bill's denying everything and then trying to get her fired.

Your objective should be to find a style that fits with your inclinations and is compatible with the style of your potential ally. If you don't assess the style of your potential ally and adapt to it, you'll limit your influence, as did Maria Cuore, division personnel manager at a large computer company:

Until recently, Maria reported to the group president, with whom she had a very satisfactory relationship. They shared a common vision, real concern for making the company a human, caring place, and a joint willingness to have Maria provide him with feedback on his effectiveness and personal style. In a reorganization, the group president's layer was removed. As a result, Maria would now report to the marketing division general manager, Rob Farr, who would report to the company president. She reluctantly agreed.

Farr was more concerned with the bottom line. His style was very different from her old boss; Maria (and several other managers) had found it rather difficult to relate to the new general manager. He was not particularly warm, didn't easily make small talk to ease interactions, and preferred distance to closeness. Uncomfortable with conflict and confrontation, Farr believed in dealing with organizational problems by creating and using formal systems rather than informal, face-to-face negotiations. Further, he managed by keeping things very close to his vest; he did not readily share information.

This style was not only uncomfortable to Maria personally, but she believed that it was inconsistent with the humanistic changes that the company was trying to introduce into the division culture. The reorganization had prompted such wild rumors to blaze through the division that productivity was off. Yet, it never occurred to Farr to call a meeting of everyone, explain the changes, and answer questions. While to Maria it seemed an obvious solution, it was not Farr's style.

Maria decided that she needed to have a good working relationship with Farr in order to be effective in the division. It was important that he feel comfortable with her and trust her enough to let her persuade him to handle the upcoming changes in a way that would take care of the people in the division.

Although Maria's concerns were on target, she found herself stymied when she tried to act upon them. Her natural instincts were to get close to Farr by going to see him and offering to work on their relationship. She first sounded out the group president to see what he knew about Farr's concerns with and impressions of her; the group president reported that Farr said everything was fine. Nevertheless, she went to Farr's office and announced:

"Rob, with this reorganization and all the changes that we will be going through, you and I really need to work together. I want to be able to give you what you need. Why don't we have lunch together soon and discuss how I can better meet your needs?"

Farr reacted by putting his hands out in front of him, palms forward, as if to push her away, and replied, brusquely:

"Everything's fine. You're doing a great job. I have no complaints. No need for us to discuss this . . ."

Maria felt very frustrated because she could sense that Farr wasn't really comfortable with her, but she realized that her direct attempt to address the relationship was only making things worse. If Farr had been willing to talk about the relationship over lunch, they probably wouldn't have had a problem in the first place.

In fact, her desire to feel good about coworkers before tackling tasks, and to do so by socializing and chatting first, was exactly what was putting pressure on Farr. Because he wasn't especially comfortable with or skilled at this kind of interaction, it was a mistake for Maria to lead with Farr's uncomfortable territory. While she was a professional at discussing relationship issues, he was a pro at crunching numbers and building systems. She liked dealing with ambiguity, feelings, and hunches; he preferred structured problem solving. Even the setting she proposed, over lunch, was far more comfortable to her than to him; he would probably feel trapped in that situation.

Maria's ideas of how Farr should deal with problems like the rumors and anxiety were certainly not a very good fit with his style and strengths. Trying to do things Maria's way would probably make things worse. Maria began to realize that, if she wanted influence with Farr, she would at least have to approach him in a way that was more comfortable for him. He was probably more locked in to his style than she was to hers, although the idea of shaping her interactive style to his was not exactly a thrilling prospect.

Eventually, Maria was able to back away from the negative feelings she was developing about Farr and see that, just because he was different, it did not mean that he had no skills for, or interests in, doing what the organization needed to develop its people. It was just that Farr's style would need support to help make him effective; and, as the human resources manager, that created an important role for her.

Maria could not be effective with Farr, however, unless she found a way to be on his side and to be a good ally to him rather than a buffer between him and the organization. If she saw her mission as one of throwing herself into the breach between him and the organization, he would feel undermined; rather, she had to see herself as his loyal strategist and helper on tough people problems that would have to be solved to make the reorganization work. How could she help him think of ways that he could meet these human needs in his own style?

Maria also recognized that she could increase her credibility with Farr not by being friendly and personal first, but by making significant work contributions and letting the relationship follow. If she helped Farr in ways that he valued, his feelings for her would probably warm up; though he certainly was not going to become a cuddly dispenser of "warm fuzzies." While this strategy didn't guarantee results, she couldn't force him to become what he wasn't, and trying only made it less likely.

She realized that the way to get work relationship issues on Farr's agenda was to put them within a crisp task framework. She needed to show him how such matters had important consequences for the division's financial plans and needs. Arguing that a humanistic culture was an end in itself would be a waste of time; she had to demonstrate the connection between the culture— attitudes, skills, and morale—and the division's performance.

As a result, she gave careful thought to a memo she would send to Farr in advance so that he could prepare himself for a meeting and not feel ambushed or surprised. It would go something like this:

To: R. A. Farr

From: M. Cuore

Re: How HR can assist in an effective reorganization to maximize productivity and financial performance

Following are the changes that the division will implement in the next six months. [Include a list]

As a consequence, the following list encompasses what I believe will be required of HR to provide the needed support. [Another list]

Can we meet for 30 minutes to discuss any modifications you have to the list, and how we can best help you?

Maria planned to propose a regular weekly meeting "to monitor progress and plan HR strategy in support of ongoing developments." She would be careful not to sound as if she wanted a meeting for the sake of meeting, or to improve relationships, but to get work done.

This major accomplishment would not be without its costs to Maria. She would find this more structured, businesslike approach far less fun than her former, preferred style. She hopes that Farr will gradually loosen up, but she doesn't know whether that is realistic. For now, she is choosing to be effective rather than personally comfortable. But she has managed to begin to contribute to Farr in his new role and, therefore, to the company. It isn't clear whether the exchange can be sustained when it is not her natural preference; but the possibility exists that, just as Farr may slowly warm up, Maria will find pleasure in enlarging her professional repertoire to include a flair for details and a bottom-line orientation. That might make her current discomfort a worth-while investment in an even more successful career.

Letting Sleeping Dogs Lie: Fears of Direct Discussion of Relationship Problems

There are many reasons other than the listener's resistance that people are reluctant to raise relationship problems directly with a difficult ally. Concern about hurting the other, fear of retaliation, worries about possible embarrassment in future dealings, fear that the initiator is really the one at fault and will be told that in no uncertain terms—or just plain dislike of unpleasant encounters—all are reasons we frequently hear. The question you must answer is whether the potential pain caused by an attempt to tell the ally your concerns is worse than the very real and present pain of continuing on in an unsatisfactory way. In general, we believe that the actual "confrontation" is seldom as bad as anticipated; therefore, we encourage directness.

There is risk in putting everything on the table, but there are also risks in letting tension, mistrust, and animosity build. Unaddressed relationship issues have a way of exploding at the most awkward moments possible; just because the risk of doing nothing is not immediately visible does not mean that it isn't just as real as the risk you take when you confront the problem. Furthermore, dealing directly with such problems tends to create faster and more complete resolution. Thus, for the remainder of this chapter we will demonstrate how to manage and minimize risk when you tackle problems in your relationships with your boss and colleagues.

USING EXCHANGE PRINCIPLES TO ADDRESS RELATIONSHIP PROBLEMS

In explicating direct discussion of relationship problems, we do not want to imply that talk is a complete substitute for action. Talk has to be backed with action, both as a way of creating good (or better) will, and to follow up on whatever is agreed upon. You don't want to be seen by others as someone to whom "talk is cheap." We will proceed on the basis that the reader understands the importance of delivering on promises.

The process of working directly on the relationship to facilitate task exchange is very similar to the influence process for tasks described in previous chapters. It involves:

□ Knowing your own world (your goals and intentions) and making it clear to the ally;

□ Understanding the ally's world, by unhooking from attributions about his or her personality and then exploring what is important to the ally;

□ Making exchanges that remove the difficulties that have prevented task exchanges in the past.

Let's look at each of these steps in more detail.

Know Thyself

The process of knowing your own goals and intentions starts with a careful examination of what you want the working relationship to be. Are you looking for a way to discuss work needs? Would a more open relationship help you do a better job? Do you expect personal closeness or just the ability to discuss work needs in a businesslike way? Knowing just what you want can save considerable aggravation and prevent an approach to the ally that is awkward, confusing, or unnecessarily irritating.

Say What You Want

Once you know your goals and intentions, state them explicitly to your potential ally. By being up front about your objectives, you try to break the negative mindset the other has about you. It helps avoid misunderstandings about what you are up to and increases the possibility that other communications will be more accurately received.

You need open with nothing more than, "We don't seem to be working very well together; I'd like to spend some time with you to see what I could do to take the tension out of our dealings."

When Tom Jeeter became upset by something his boss told him a colleague, Mark Stobb, had said about him, Tom called Mark and said, "Are you free now? I just learned you have a problem with me, and I'd like to get it straightened out. I wish I'd heard it directly from you, Mark, but it sounds as if we should talk. Okay?" Mark quickly agreed to meet with Tom and clear the air.

Expense Account

It is helpful to be explicit early on about exactly how much the strained relationship *costs* both you and the ally. What are you prevented from doing, and what does your colleague lose as a result of the difficulty in working together? What are the costs to the organization? Such an accounting helps lay the groundwork for further discussion and motivates the ally to do something about the problem. After all, if you can total up the costs to the ally of not being able to work together, it is harder for him or her to just dismiss the problem as a "personality difference" that isn't worth talking about.

For example, Tom might have also told Mark that he was trying to address quality problems, that Mark's putting him down made it harder to move a resistant organization and made Tom unwilling to get Mark's views ahead of time. For example, Tom might say, "Since that reaction makes it less likely that your views will be included in our work, Mark, I'd guess you might want to iron this out so that you'll have a chance to give proper input."

Leave Your Attributions at Home

Specifying costs to your ally leads you into assumptions about what is important to him or her. It is crucial, then, to work at unhooking yourself from any negative attributions you are making about the ally's motives. You have to adopt the idea that there is probably a perfectly reasonable explanation for the ally's difficult response, and your objective is to discover it so that you can take appropriate action.

We have earlier discussed how easy it is to attribute the worst possible motives to someone you are having trouble with; whatever it takes to keep from doing it is worth trying. Say to yourself again and again if you have to, "If Shirley were here now and could speak for herself, she'd think she was perfectly justified to act as she has." It is astounding how often that turns out to be true.

Have you concluded that, because she abruptly walks out of meetings with you, Shirley doesn't like to work with you? It may be hard for you not to see that as a form of calculated rudeness; but Shirley may only be acting as she does because she fears becoming argumentative or bursting into tears when she gets upset.

Her unceremonious departure may have nothing to do with you; but if you believe that people should have their say and always make graceful exits, it can feel like a slap in the face. Fight your own temptation to assume the worst; there's always time to revise your assumptions downward.

As we have suggested earlier, the behavior you find unappealing may be caused by situational circumstances that are not visible to you. Bruce's mistrust of you may reflect suspicions planted by his boss, or the accounting department's general view of engineers. Until he sees that you are not just another wild-eyed engineer, he may treat you with the kind of skepticism that gets your goat—and makes you just nasty enough to discourage him from wanting to know you better.

It is also possible that you are inadvertently causing the very reaction you do not like. Occasionally, problems are one-sided, but seldom is there purity on one side and fault wholly on the other. Perhaps Shirley avoids spending extra time with you because you tend to flirt a bit when business is done. While you may do it innocently, as a way to show how friendly you feel, she is made uncomfortable by flirtation in a business setting, so she gets out before you have a chance. Or maybe you are a woman who likes to needle colleagues after getting to know them, but she finds your humor too biting; so she beats a hasty retreat to avoid getting nasty in return.

If you always assume that the problem resides in the other person, you compound the problem. No matter what words you use, your tone will be accusatory, and the no-longer-potential ally will be defensive in response. Once that happens, the original problem is even messier because it is now intertwined with self-protection. Furthermore, the assumption of negative motives will make you less open to real exploration with the ally if you ever *do* raise the issues between you. It is hard to listen to *and hear* someone you believe to be deliberately difficult—and wholly at fault—which reduces any probability that the differences will ever be addressed.

I'd Really Like to Know What's Bugging You

If you can let go of your negative assumptions, you free yourself to genuinely explore the world of your ally. You can either diagnose the factors in the situation that might be causing the difficulties, or begin to make direct (but nonjudgmental) inquiries about that world. Notice the difference between "asking" Shirley,

"Don't you know how rude you are to me when you stomp out of meetings?" and saying, "I'm puzzled about our relationship. What happens at the end of our meetings? You often turn on your heels and get out fast without saying anything. What's that about?"

Better still, add an admission of the possibility that you may be part of the problem: "Am I doing something that makes you want to leave?" In general, if you are willing to own up to the possibility that you are a part of the relationship problem, you reduce defensive denials and make real exploration possible.

This doesn't always work; sometimes the other person will be unwilling even to admit that there is a problem. The relationship may feel so strained, the colleague may be so convinced you are incorrigible, or may be so resistant to discussion of negative feelings, that even open discussion by you of possible "fault" gets nowhere. However, directness remains the best bet for increasing willingness to explore a relationship problem.

Consider how Stan Sandler, an irascible financial adviser, handled a difficult relationship.

Stan and an associate were forced by a client into working with an outside tax lawyer. At their first meeting, Stan instinctively disliked the lawyer; he found him shallow and glib. Stan knew he wasn't hiding his feelings very well, but he thought he was asking sharp questions that would lead to a meeting of the minds. Stan noticed that his associate was very uncomfortable. He uncharacteristically scowled at Stan several times during the first one-and-a-half hours of the meeting.

At a break, when the outsider went to the men's room, Stan asked his associate why he seemed so angry at him. The associate appeared to be uncomfortable with the question. Stan said, "Was I being too hard on that guy?"

The associate replied, "Are you kidding? You were impossible. Every single thing he said, you disagreed with and put him down. You're screwing up an important relationship, and I don't know how to stop you."

Stan looked at his associate and said, sheepishly, "Why don't you tell me to go shit in my hat next time? I was afraid I was being impossible; I guess I was."

The associate breathed a huge sigh of relief, smiled, and became far more supportive. Stan was not only able to be more tolerant of the lawyer, who, Stan conceded, actually knew a few things; but he also earned a much freer relationship with his associate. The associate subsequently went to bat for Stan on occasions when others in the office condemned him for being closed-minded or negative—a byproduct of his brilliant and irascible style—by referring to the "shit-in-my-hat" incident as proof of Stan's openness to influence.

The exploration of your ally's world, then, is designed to let you understand enough about how he or she perceives things so that you can genuinely say that, if you were in that position, you would see things similarly. You don't necessarily agree with the conclusions drawn by the ally, but you can see how he or she arrived at them. Getting to that point is remarkably helpful in taking the sting out of a tense relationship. It isn't always possible to get there, since on some occasions greater understanding only makes the other person seem more obnoxious or offensive but is a worthwhile target to keep in mind.

I Did It My Way

If you are able to understand the ally's position, then it is easier to take the next step, which is to make your own world visible to the ally. What are the forces and assumptions that led you to the behavior or style that the ally is not happy about? Can you help the ally see your framework in the same way that you have seen his or hers, that is, with understanding, if not acceptance? This is far easier to do if you have first demonstrated *your* understanding.

There is a danger that you will be perceived as making excuses, which is not your objective. It is to be clear about what has been going on with you so that the ally will have accurate information about the world that is shaping you, in order to find ways to overcome differences or reach an agreement about how to work together. Acceptable reasons, not rejectable excuses, are your goal. That will help the ally see that the negative attributions he or she has made about your motives may not be correct.

For example, suppose you have been needling Shirley, and she has said that it is to avoid becoming nasty with you that she abruptly leaves meetings with you. You might say:

"I can see how that would bug you, Shirley, and I see now that it is out of consideration that you leave, not as an insult. Maybe it would help if you knew that, in my family, we express fondness for each other by teasing. We don't do it to harm anyone, and we never do it to someone we don't like; so it certainly isn't intended to get your goat. I guess that there's no way you could realize that I meant no harm; if *I* felt someone were really trying to put me down all the time, I'd have trouble controlling my reaction, too!"

What Can Be Exchanged?

Now the question becomes, "What can I do to alter my behavior so that my ally will allow more of a task relationship to grow?" What you want from the ally is a willingness to engage in transactions around your task goals; what you can give in return will depend on what your ally wants, but it probably involves some kind of new behavior from you.

For example, let us look at the problems between Brian Woods and his long-time partner, Dennis Longworth.

Friends since high school, Brian and Dennis were equal partners in an international, financial services holding company with a dozen subsidiaries. Each looked after one of the two biggest subsidiaries and shared, to varying degrees, management of the others. Although they were highly successful, recent events had crystallized Brian's dissatisfaction with his relationship to Dennis.

Brian had been feeling for some time that Dennis was unconcerned about the partnership and possibly even avoiding him. Dennis, a lawyer by training, was not available when Brian needed expertise or support. Both Brian and Dennis were traveling to different countries a good bit of the time, serving their international clientele, and were extremely busy. But, in the early years of their partnership, they had found ways to be available to each other when needed. Increasingly, however, Brain felt that Dennis was so involved in his activities that, when Brian wanted help, Dennis was unreachable.

A crisis in Brian's main subsidiary brought matters to a head. Brian needed Dennis's support to deal with a very knotty problem; he had left word for Dennis at his hotel in Denmark to rush home for a key meeting, but Dennis had not showed up and had never even bothered to call. Brian was so upset that he was considering a proposal to end their long partnership via a buyout; but, in a last-ditch attempt to straighten out the relationship, Brian scheduled a weekend meeting with Dennis. They invited an old friend with considerable mediation skills to help them.

It was very difficult for Brian to express just what was bothering him. They went back a long way together, as friends as well as partners. With some prodding, Brian revealed that he felt abandoned by Dennis and finally managed to say how disappointed and angry he had been when Dennis hadn't shown up or called. Dennis responded, astonished, "When I realized that I couldn't possibly get back in time, I tried to call; and when I couldn't reach you, I sent a telex to my assistant, Marsha. I assumed she had told you."

This set Brian off even more. Marsha was Dennis' cousin, and Brian didn't trust her at all. He had been upset when Dennis hired her, had complained for some time that she was a schemer who wanted to make trouble, and this was just the "proof" he needed. There must be some sinister reason why Dennis would try to use someone Brian so distrusted to send a message about missing a crucial meeting. Dennis, calm and detached as always, tried to explain again about the mechanics of different time zones, international phone calls, and sending the telex. Several rounds followed, with Brian getting no satisfaction. Dennis' detachment exacerbated Brian's upset feelings over what he perceived as Dennis' lack of commitment, which just made Dennis pull back further.

Finally, with some help from their friend, they were able to look at the underlying problem of the relationship. Brian wanted to be certain that he could count on Dennis' support in dealing with particularly knotty problems, and he considered a willingness to be physically present at times of crisis the way that a partner should show support. It wasn't even Dennis' legal expertise that was crucial to Brian; it was Dennis' presence and emotional support that Brian sought.

Dennis was unaware of how important it was to Brian that he demonstrate his commitment at critical times. To Dennis, the 50–50 partnership arrangement, with no controlling vote, showed how much he valued and trusted Brian. As far as he was concerned, the unusual arrangement of an equal partnership with loosely defined and varying responsibilities was positive proof of his support. Furthermore, Dennis believed Brian's reaction to Dennis' absences and Brian's dislike of Dennis' assistant were irrational. Why get up in arms over an assistant in light of the enormous financial stake they shared? Dennis had assumed that Brian understood how busy Dennis was with his main subsidiary and would learn to deal with certain problems himself if Dennis could not make it. As a result of these differing assumptions, the costs of the strains in the relationship were so high that Brian was contemplating a split that Dennis didn't want at all.

As they explored their assumptions and feelings, they began to see that it might be possible to accommodate each other. Brian said he was willing to keep an open mind about Marsha and he accepted the fact that it was convenient for Dennis to use her as a communication channel when he was on the road. He also agreed to be clear about when he had to have a direct, personal response and when it would be nice but wasn't an emergency. Dennis agreed to make phone calls on important issues, even if it meant calling Brian at home in the middle of the night, and to make extra efforts to be present whenever it was important to Brian. The partnership, and friendship, survived.

Because the issue was so emotionally loaded for Brian, he did not find it easy to start by understanding Dennis' world and working to achieve acceptance of its meaning to Dennis before leaping to conclusions about Dennis' motives. It took a lot of heat and some help from their friend to get to the point where each side understood enough about the other to figure out what kind of exchange could be made. But they avoided a potentially disastrous outcome when they were able to talk directly with one another, see what needed fixing in the relationship, and then trade concessions.

HEY, KNOCK IT OFF! INFLUENCING THE ALLY TO CHANGE BEHAVIOR

The case of Brian and Dennis suggests that it is possible to use exchange principles to do more than just repair a relationship enough to address task exchanges. The same approach can be used when you want to use influence to change the behavior of someone you are dealing with. That kind of influence is problematic for many organizational members; when the boss does something you don't like, how do you get him or her to stop? How do you get a colleague that you deal with daily to alter behavior that annoys you or makes it hard for you to do your job?

Sally's boss supervises too closely; can she back him off? Robin's coworker interrupts constantly; can he be persuaded to let Robin complete a thought before jumping in? Terry's associate says negative things behind Terry's back; can that be stopped?

Just One More Chance: Exchange in Behavior Change

At the risk of sounding like the child who has found a hammer and wants to treat everything as a nail, we believe that the same general approach to exchange can be used successfully in this particular kind of difficult influence situation. As usual, you need to be clear about what you want, about the ally's world and the reasons for his or her behavior, and then find something valuable to offer in exchange for the new behavior.

Using exchange to alter behavior, however, has some wrinkles of its own. A lot takes place when an involved, interdependent party tries to tell the other party that current behavior isn't effective. We will try to sort it out using the experiences of Brian and Dennis where possible, then proceed with other examples that will show how the complexities can be utilized to positive effect.

I Did It on Purpose: The Intentionality of All Behavior

In this discussion, we make the assumption that all people behave with intentions, expecting that what they do will get them what they desire. At this level, exchange is always going on, whether or not the results are as intended. People do whatever they do hoping that, in return, others will behave in certain ways, yielding a profit on the exchange. Dennis remained detached, expecting that Brian would learn to deal with many problems himself, and in return, Dennis would be allowed time for complicated dealings elsewhere.

No Reason to Change

When people are achieving their intended results, they are likely to continue the behavior. Getting them to change requires that you either offer something that produces a more desirable result, or increase their costs to the point where the good results aren't worth it. As long as the ally is getting his or her intended results, your not liking a particular behavior is not a good enough reason for the ally to change. (If you have a close relationship, your disapproval of the behavior might matter, but only if its cost to your ally is greater than the positive results otherwise obtained.)

In the case of Dennis and Brian, Dennis assumed that all was well with his behavior, and he would have continued it indefinitely. At first, even when Brian complained, Dennis did not see that there was a real cost and resisted Brian's interpretations. Because he did care about Brian's reactions, however, he began to pay attention.

Minor Repairs Welcome

If, however, your ally is not satisfied with the returns from some particular behavior, he or she is likely to be looking for a way to change the behavior. If only all behavior that offends you were of this type, behavior change through exchange would be relatively easy; all you would have to do is point out to the receptive ally some alternative behavior that would be more likely to achieve the intended results, and then stand by to lend a helping hand as needed.

Only the Shadow Knows:
Uninformed About Unintended Consequences

Unfortunately, as was the case with Dennis, allies do not always know that the behavior in question isn't working, especially if the person who is unhappy about the behavior is keeping that fact quiet. The ally may sense that something is not right in the relationship but won't necessarily decode that it is due to some offending behavior. Allies who have no clue that you are bothered will charge ahead even when they aren't getting especially satisfactory results.

I've Got a Secret:
The Power of Information

When trying to influence a colleague's behavior, you automatically have a currency that he or she values: *information* about the cost of the behavior to that person. Since the behavior affects you, you are the expert on the consequences of the behavior, which means that you have something the other person needs in order to be effective with you.

This creates an opportunity. You can trade this important information, along with information on how the ally could achieve the intended effect on you, for new behavior on the ally's part. Of course, you will have to discover just what effect the ally intended, which may be obvious or hidden, in order to be most constructive in helping him or her reach the goal (and you, in turn, reach yours). That means you will need to diagnose the colleague's world, to see if you can discern what he or she intends. Everything we said earlier in this chapter about not attributing motives applies equally here.

If you assume the worst about the motives of the colleague, you make it very difficult to gain influence. You either need to go through a diagnostic process that lets you conclude what "reasonable" goal the ally had in mind, or you have to ask.

Sally's boss supervises too closely. Is he a controlling SOB who wants to crush Sally's spirit? Or does he worry about quality performance and think that close supervision is a way to insure it?

If it is the latter, you can see where Sally has leverage: She knows that his style makes her nervous and resentful, which gets in the way of her doing quality work. She can show him that looser supervision would achieve his goal better than his current practices. But if she assumes that he is really a controlling jerk, she will probably act in a way that makes him feel he has to supervise even more closely. For an example of how to provide information about costs of behavior in just this nonblaming way, examine the case of architect Steve Hart and his colleague, Karl Appel:

Karl acted in ways others saw as sneaky and manipulative whenever he wanted something. As a result, everyone in the firm avoided dealing with Karl whenever possible, and made fun of him behind his back for always having something up his sleeve.

Steve decided that his work life was being made too unpleasant by Karl's behavior, so he took him aside. He asked Karl whether he knew how he was seen by others in the firm, and if he knew what his nickname was.

Karl was curious; when he learned that he had been dubbed "the cunning fox," he responded, "That's double-edged. Foxes are smart, but that probably means you can't trust them."

Nodding his agreement, Steve admitted that he had reluctantly come to the same view; and he asked Karl whether he wanted to be treated as someone who had to be watched carefully.

When Karl answered "No," the stage was set for a reasonable conversation about what might be done. Karl intended no harm; he had thought he was just avoiding conflict or hurt feelings by his maneuverings.

In this particular instance, the cunning fox shortly thereafter decided on his own to move on to another organization—maybe to try his manipulations on a new audience, or perhaps to start fresh without a negative reputation. The reason he gave was, "Times have changed, and new blood is needed around here." In any event, Steve was happy with the outcome, which he had achieved by making clear to Karl the costs, in reputation, of his way of dealing with others. Steve had never accused Karl of being a manipulative person, only of behaving in ways that were *interpreted as* manipulative, possibly unfairly. That allowed Karl to come to grips with the issue without having to defend himself to Steve.

Charity Pays

In fact, it is probably always a good idea to make charitable assumptions about the motives of the person you want to influence, since negative assumptions usually gum up the relationship further; but, when in doubt, ask. For example: "Mr. Ditka, you check my work once an hour. Could you please explain what you're trying to accomplish by that?" Or, if you can imagine a benign hypothesis, "Mr. Ditka, I've noticed that you seem to check my work hourly. Are you concerned about the quality of what I do and worried that I will make the department look bad?"

Similarly, Robin might say to the colleague who always interrupts, "You jump in a lot. Are you really eager for me to listen to your ideas?" Or, Terry can ask the negative associate, "Are you saying negative stuff about me behind my back because you want me to get the message without giving me an opportunity to retaliate? Are you concerned that I can't take it if you tell me directly how I screwed up?" Of course, there is no guarantee that any of these colleagues will answer honestly; but, if the question is not loaded with negative innuendo, at least the dialogue is opened. From there, you can explore further.

What I Do When You Do That Voodoo You Do

Sometimes it is enough just to tell the person whose behavior you want to change precisely how his or her behavior is affecting you. You don't have to understand the intentions; you just come right out and say how some specific behavior affects you and ask if that is the effect he or she intended.

Robin could say to the interrupting colleague, "You often don't let me finish my sentence, which just makes me want to slow down and be sure I get every thought in. I don't think that is what you want to happen."

Terry can say, "When you talk about me behind my back it gets me to plot revenge and look for ways to embarrass you publicly. Can that be what you're hoping I'll do?"

An open, direct, and honest explanation (without acrimony) is better than retaliation, which just perpetuates the cycle, because it gives the ally a chance to say gracefully that a very different outcome was intended; and mutual exploration can begin. In general, you should begin your feedback to a colleague with less interpretive statements, and only get to inferences about intentions when the straightforward report of consequences doesn't take.

Pretentious? Moi???
Casting Stones from a Glass House

Just to make life complicated, another possibility must be mentioned. Sometimes, the ally's offending behavior is being prompted by a pet (or unconscious) behavior of yours! All the considerations of intentions/results/awareness we have been discussing may apply in reverse; you may be acting in a way that gets from your ally a response you don't intend. In the worst of all possible worlds, that response is the very one you have been finding disagreeable in your ally; and you don't know that you are the cause of it! What a revolting predicament . . .

It Takes Two to Tango

It is not uncommon that the one who wants influence may, in part, be causing the behavior that he or she doesn't like. Sally's boss may indeed have a general tendency to overcontrol; but, in the case of Sally, he does it because her work is sometimes sloppy and she doesn't check it herself. She may well be right that it would improve if he backed off, but he was motivated in part by her past performance.

Robin's colleague may indeed be impatient and spontaneous, but he interrupts Robin because Robin is laboriously slow at expressing opinions and insists on spelling out every detail when a more freewheeling brainstorming method is appropriate.

Terry's associate may indeed talk about people behind their backs, but is prompted to it with Terry because Terry flies into a fury whenever anyone tries to give direct feedback. Neither party is totally innocent or at fault; it is the interaction between the two that perpetuates the "undesirable" behavior.

This kind of reciprocal pattern is quite common. A's behavior is disliked by B, which causes B to do things that A doesn't like; so A does more of it, which makes B do more, and so on in a closed loop. If, at any point, someone asks A about the problem, A will be thoroughly convinced that it is all a result of B's impossible behavior. B, however, would give an equally convincing reply about how any reasonable person can see that it is all A's miserable behavior that is at fault. Talking to only one of this pair gives you only half the story.

The troubles between Oliver Hanson and Mark Buckley we described in Chapter 5 are an example of this phenomenon. Because Buckley believed Hanson was bypassing him for information, he withheld as much as possible. This caused Hanson to worry that he was flying blind and thus probe people at lower levels, which confirmed to Buckley that he should withhold more, and so on. Each man's natural tendencies were reinforced in precisely the opposite direction by the other, who then exhibited even more of the very behavior that prompted the other's irritating behavior.

This kind of negative cycle is so common that we feel safe in suggesting that you adopt it as your working hypothesis when you want to change a colleague's behavior. As a general practice, to your statements about the impact of a colleague's behavior, add the question, "Am I doing anything to cause this?" If you can't genuinely entertain the possibility that you are part of the problem, asking the question will only come across as manipulative; therefore, don't bother if you don't mean it. But consider the possibility that no matter how outrageously irritating the colleague's behavior, and no matter how many of your other colleagues agree with your opinion of it, you may in part be prompting it!

Besides reducing your colleague's defensiveness, that assumption carries other advantages. If you already know what you do that the colleague doesn't like, you have the basis for an exchange. If you are surprised by what you are told, you may have learned something useful, since the colleague has information about the consequences of your behavior that you didn't have before. You can choose to ignore it if you like, but knowing gives you more choices. And, best of all, if you can identify what you are doing that the colleague doesn't like, you now have the perfect currency to exchange. *You can offer to alter your behavior to better suit your colleague if the colleague will alter the behavior that bugs you.*

This could be an exchange of behavior of the same kind: "If you'll avoid shouting when we disagree, I'll keep my voice down, too." Or it could be an exchange of something different but valuable: "If you'll stop putting me down to other people, I'll stay late and help you finish your reports when you ask." In either case, you exchange something valuable you have in return for the new behavior you want.

Brian, for example, exchanged his acceptance of Marsha as a communication link and his agreement to be clear about the urgency of his requests, for Dennis' commitment to stay in touch and be there in person when urgently needed. Each gave the other something he wanted.

Sally could promise her over-controlling boss more care in doing her work and better self-monitoring of quality in return for greater autonomy. She could agree to periodic inspection to give him assurance of quality control in exchange for less frequent observation. Or she could offer to accept some coaching to improve her skills in return for less looking over her shoulder.

Similarly, Robin can offer to lighten up and step up the pace in brainstorming sessions if the impatient colleague will agree to interrupt less—and not get mad if Robin can't stand an interruption and insists on finishing. (The "real" Robin and colleague made just such an agreement after a discussion of their respective childrearing—Quaker and Jew—in regard to interruptions and spontaneity made both realize that no rudeness was intended. Eventually, they were able to stop and laugh whenever Robin started dotting all i's or the colleague jumped in in mid-sentence; and both hooted when it was Robin who would get excited and begin to interrupt.)

Terry can offer his back-stabbing pirate the assurance that he will hold his temper when being criticized if the associate will confront him directly and not conduct whisper campaigns. These kinds of exchange agreements are not always possible and are frequently broken in the heat of events, but they allow the possibility of reopening discussions if one side violates the agreement. Even if no agreement is possible, owning up to your part while making clear the impact of the other's behavior on you is a serious gesture toward an improved relationship and increased trust. In several instances where no explicit agreement was reached, we have seen the relationship slowly improve afterwards, as if each side decided that it was worth the effort to be more accommodating and gradually reduced the behavior that had provoked the other.

Can I Help?

If you can make an exchange, you may be able to reinforce it by discussing what you can do to be helpful to your colleague who finally decided to change behavior. When it turned out that Sally's boss also worried about his own tendencies to overcontrol, and said that he wanted to give her more latitude but slipped automatically into his habit of close supervision, she was sympathetic. She asked if it would help if she signaled him by looking at her watch. He laughed and replied, "No, that's too subtle. Why don't you just say, 'I'm not ready for you yet, Charley,' and I'll back off."

It takes a considerable amount of skill to get to the point where the colleague, or boss, will be willing to admit that he or she needs to work on improving the new behavior; but the non-blaming, information-sharing, self-revealing approach we have described has helped many people to create that kind of collaborative influence. At the very least, it is useful to go back to your ally after initiating an exchange in which you gave such feedback and ask how he or she is feeling about it. That gives you an opportunity to smooth any feathers that might still be ruffled.

First Among Equals? Getting an Edge from Giving Helpful Feedback?

There is even a complication in giving useful feedback, however. Although it appears simple, an exchange of information for new behavior often carries a rider that can make the exchange seem uneven. The person who is given the feedback about the heretofore hidden negative impact of his or her behavior can easily feel one-down for not having known. To accept such feedback is to admit that he or she has made a mistake and is not perfect.

In most organizational settings, no matter who gives the feedback, awkwardness can enter the relationship as a result of the recipient's concern about appearing weak in front of a subordinate, flawed to a boss, or one-down to a supposed peer. Any hint from the person giving feedback that his or her awareness of the ally's "flaw" has led to feelings of superiority can set off uneasy tremors in the relationship—and a desire to right the imbalance. Even genuinely helpful and supportive "sharing" of "information" can be perceived as a put-down by an insecure colleague; this makes it all the more imperative that feedback on behavior be delivered as a genuine act of caring and not as a subtle put-down.

Can't Buy Me Love: The Need for Genuine Concern

It may not be enough, however, to just have good intentions. Informing a colleague of the ways that particular behavior keeps him or her from achieving desired goals is unlikely to be effective if the message is not delivered with genuine concern for helping the colleague perform better. The words of the message matter far less than your intention in sending it. Even highly resistant or difficult people can sense when someone who delivers bad news is looking out for their welfare rather than using the occasion to inflict some punishment or revenge.

What we have found, and personally tested in many organizations, is that it is possible to say almost anything to anyone, no matter how high their organization level, if you frame it in terms of how their behavior is getting in the way of accomplishing *their* goals, *and* you convincingly convey your genuine desire to give them the information they need to move toward their objectives. Although there are people who will shoot the messenger (especially when the messenger is more vulnerable than a third party who may be the source of the bad news), most people will quickly recognize and appreciate the person who has cared enough to say the very worst. And, a quick reminder that shooting the messenger will not help solve the problem usually suffices to get all but the most rigidly defensive recipient to back off.

Talking straight in this way is useful in positively affecting others' behavior because it provides them with data they need, data that they often cannot get in any other way. That is literally true when the data are about your reaction to some aspect of their behavior, since only you know what that reaction is. If the information you provide is indeed useful to the receiver, you will be creating some obligation because reciprocity will induce the person to feel obligated for the learning you have created.

Furthermore, your willingness to deliver the tough stuff in a direct but supportive way is a sign of courage and risk-taking that almost always wins eventual respect. Since many organizational members will never deliver their negative feelings directly (choosing instead to talk *about*, rather than *to*, the person whose behavior they wish were different), or, in some cases, will deliver plenty of negative messages but without any attempt to show concern or be helpful, using exchange for influencing behavior is less risky than it appears.

Of course, this kind of directness only works if the other person actually cares about the behavior and its impact on you and others, which is not always the case. There are organizational members who will get sadistic pleasure from the knowledge that they are somehow making your life miserable, or who just don't care about some aspects of the organization the way you do. Because they value different or incompatible currencies, the information you are providing them about the effect of their behavior is not valuable to them (except to tell them more about what matters to you). In that situation, if you cannot find a currency they value, and show how their behavior prevents them from getting what they want, direct methods of feedback will not work.

Sometimes, however, people who appear to be impervious to feedback are not as indifferent as they first appear. If no one has been willing to test their reaction, it is hard to know whether a direct approach to feedback will work. We cannot guarantee results, but we urge you to expand your willingness to test the waters. The rewards from converting a formerly irritating colleague into one with whom you can more comfortably work are considerable.

8

Exchange Strategies

"'Tis better to give than to receive."
"Never give a sucker an even break."

"What goes around comes around."
"Let the buyer beware."

"You scratch my back and I'll scratch yours."
"All's fair in love and war."

"A stitch in time saves nine."
"Opportunity knocks but once."

> Common sense advice about exchange strategies,
> so easy to follow even a child can do it

Up to this point, we have examined the steps that lead up to the exchange process, which include knowing your ally's world, being clear on your own objectives and resources, building trusting relationships, and matching your resources with your ally's desired currencies. The next logical step is the actual discussion with your ally of the exchange and the strategies to follow; we now address this step of the influence process—perhaps with more clearcut guidelines than are offered in the contradictory aphorisms above.

It is important, however, to acknowledge that the exchange begins to take place before this step; in fact, it has been going on throughout the previous steps; and it is only because we can't discuss everything at once that we separate the process into different chapters. Every influence-related contact you have with anyone who eventually becomes an ally is part of the eventual exchange. Whether it is simply a smile the first time you are introduced, or an all-out effort to ask about the other person's interests so that you can find something to offer in return for the cooperation you want, each interaction feeds the likelihood of successful exchange.

Not only does your general reputation and relationship with the potential ally affect the exchange, but the process of inquiry is already shaping the reception you will get when you finally make your request and offer. How and what you ask, whether and how you listen, the kind of interest you show, and the sincerity of your concern for addressing the ally's real interests all become part of the exchange process. You smooth the way or make the terrain rough by the way you go about your early diagnosis and relationship development.

The *quality* of your diagnosis also greatly influences how well the actual exchange will go. The more you know about the ally's interests, style, and preferred language, and the better you select what to offer for what you want, the easier the transaction is likely to be. As with any kind of negotiation, the most important part is the planning. If you have badly misdiagnosed the situation, clever "techniques" probably won't save the day; Eskimos aren't likely to buy many ice boxes no matter how slick the pitch.

Thus, you need to plan your exchange strategy carefully, as well as to carry out the actual exchange discussions in a way that takes into account your previous relationship with the other, eases the transaction, and leaves the relationship improved for the future. This can be a complex process, even though the actual transaction may be completed in a few sentences.

TRADE POLICY: PLANNING YOUR STRATEGIES FOR EXCHANGE

Although many of the strategies for approaching exchange discussions have been mentioned in earlier chapters, they are worth reviewing now to help you focus carefully on what conditions determine which approach to take. To be an effective influencer requires versatility in selecting among exchange strategies.

How difficult it will be to make an exchange depends in part on the degree to which interest between you and your potential ally converge. As we have suggested, it is always easier to start with an exchange strategy that demonstrates to the ally the benefits that will result from cooperation, without your having to do anything more; but that usually requires a fortuitous set of circumstances. We will explore this strategy first, but then we will move on to ways of addressing the ally's interests when the benefits of cooperation are not as evident.

Showing How Cooperation Helps the Potential Ally Achieve Existing Goals

If it can be done, show the potential ally how cooperating with your request will help him or her achieve other goals (i.e., pay off in a valued currency). For example, an area manager who wanted more current information from his regional manager, but didn't want to appear to be prying or criticizing the regional manager's close-to-the-vest style, decided to frame the request in terms of the genuine need for information to help defend the region's decisions to skeptical branch managers. Because this very currency was one of the regional manager's objectives for the year, the suggestion that there be a regularly scheduled staff meeting was seen as helpful rather than as a time-consuming nuisance. The area manager had known enough about his boss' currencies to frame his request in a way that would be seen positively by the regional manager.

Free-Market Exchange: Clear Mutual Gain

When it isn't possible to identify in advance the ally's direct benefit from going along, the most straightforward alternative is to plan a direct offer of something valuable to the ally in return for something you need or value. If both sides readily see the advantages of the outcome and believe each "payment" of time, trouble, or resources is approximately the same, the exchange is equivalent to going to the store and exchanging money for a desired item that is "fairly" priced. Neither side is doing the other any exceptional favor; value is exchanged for value.

If there is already a good relationship between the parties, neither has any reason not to trust the motives or integrity of the other, the right goods and services are available to both sides, and mutual interest is readily apparent, this direct approach is the best strategy.

Free-market exchanges can work even when a good or longstanding relationship does not exist; and they can also involve quite different currencies as long as they are seen as equivalent.

For example, Anthony Amici, the plant manager of a small company, very much wanted to have a more personal friendship with the company's president because Amici knew he worked best when he had considerable social contact with his boss. Otherwise, his feelings about authority figures got in his way, and he couldn't take the appropriate kind of initiative.

The president, however, was not in the right frame of mind to get chummy with Amici. Whenever he walked through the plant, he noticed bottlenecks, inventory stock-outs, and piled-up parts-in-process. He wanted to see more initiative from his plant manager in attacking these problems. Lacking that, the president felt annoyed and wanted to avoid Amici for fear of exploding at him.

When Amici finally diagnosed the problem, he proposed a series of lunch and dinner meetings with the boss "to discuss how to shape up the plant." These meetings provided the president with assurance that Amici was on top of things, gave the president a chance to make suggestions, and, in turn, gave Amici plenty of time to socialize and build the kind of close relationship that allowed him to be effective. Thus, a reasonable exchange was made, though in different currencies.

Uncovering—and Exchanging for—Hidden Value

When the benefits are not readily apparent to a reasonably willing partner, the clear mutual gain is hard to sell. Some effort to discover and reveal less obvious benefits can lead to satisfying exchanges.

An enterprising production manager wanted to obtain his general manager's approval to introduce automated technology into the plant. Knowing that the standard payback analysis based on labor savings would not be fully convincing, he analyzed the impact of faster turnaround time on preventing lost orders. Using this innovative capital expenditure method, he was able to persuade the general manager that the automation would be in the interest of the division.

Such an approach is becoming increasingly common. Organizational members who want to persuade colleagues to support an innovation are seeking new measures that reveal hidden benefits or demonstrate hidden costs that can be saved. For example, J. Douglas Phillips, senior director of corporate planning at Merck, was cited in *The Wall Street Journal* for using cost studies of turnover to justify investments in work and family benefits. He "says such bottom-line demonstrations add to his 'internal credibility' in promoting such programs as day-care centers and lunch-time employee forums on teen-age drug abuse."

Compensated Costs

An alternative strategy calls for acknowledgment that costs will be involved and development of a plan to compensate the potential ally for those costs. Although not highly motivating, this approach may be the only way to engineer an exchange when you don't have resources available that the potential ally wants. It is only possible, of course, if you can find something to use as compensation.

A project manager, for example, might propose budget transfers to buy time from a market research group that would prefer not to undertake a research project that the product manager desperately wants. Or, the person requesting a special report from an analytical group could offer to compose a rough draft using unanalyzed data that already exist, which would reduce the load on the analysts by providing the approach and format for them.

In any circumstance, it is necessary to be able to inquire or diagnose what the potential ally's costs of compliance will be in order to determine whether you can help defray the costs in some way. For example, a secretary wants early morning flexibility of arrival time from her boss, who would just as soon she be there when he arrives. But she knows that even more important to him is her willingness to stay late when there is an urgent job to complete, so she agrees to that in return for being allowed leeway in the mornings when her day-care arrangements require an extra 10 to 15 minutes. Both get what they want by exchanging in the same currency: time available for work. The cost to the boss is compensated by the gain of time in tight situations.

How to Make Hidden Costs Visible

It is not always readily apparent what an ally's noncooperation will cost you and the organization. The potential ally sees only the inconvenience to him or her, not the costs on your side. This can be especially difficult when you want something from your boss, because you do not want to sound whiney or threatening in specifying consequences; or it may arise between peers because you don't realize that the potential ally cannot see what appears obvious from your vantage point.

In these circumstances, it is necessary to plan a way to make clear what the costs to you are, and to convey that as you discuss your request. Not all allies will respond to your inconvenience when they become aware of it; but when you have a reasonable relationship, this kind of information can help create more responsiveness.

FLY NOW, PAY WHEN? STRATEGIES THAT USE THE TIME VALUE OF CURRENCY

Another set of strategic considerations involves the way to utilize past or future obligations to achieve desired goals. Strategic use of time extends what is possible in alliances.

Building Credit:
Saving for a Rainy Day

An old joke about banking says that banks only want to lend money when you can prove that you don't need it. The grain of truth in the joke relates to the need to be able to repay the loan, at least at some date in the future. For this reason, it is often wise to invest current resources so that when there is future need, it will be possible to borrow, or draw on savings. The same reasoning applies to exchanges in organizations: Whenever circumstances permit, it is prudent to accumulate obligations from others long before you have any idea of asking for anything in return. Before you get to the actual exchange, it helps to have made investments in future considerations.

This is easiest when your job puts you in the position of commanding valuable resources that others want so that you can naturally do task favors for many people. The people who decide information system priorities, control the scheduling of production, or provide valuable services to line managers are constantly building credits, especially when they alter priorities or give extra service to help others out. The best way of building credit is by doing useful tasks in return for future obligations to help you do your job better. That keeps the focus on real work, not influence for its own sake.

Although not all jobs have such an advantageous positioning, it is usually still possible to discover alternative ways you can help others. As we have made clear, because different players value different kinds of currencies, many opportunities exist to make an extra effort to be helpful, considerate, or thoughtful *in advance of* needing the help of others.

Think of the many ways Anne Austin (Chapter 2) built obligations by providing information, ideas or, assistance to people whom she didn't know she would ever call on for help. The person with energy, some ability to determine what might be valuable to others in their work, and an inclination toward creating multiple alliances can find daily opportunities to earn credit by being useful.

We can look, for example, at the middle-level manager who inadvertently built credit by assiduously clipping job-related articles of potential interest to the wide range of organizational members he knew and sending the clippings "FYI." He was naturally interested in people and ideas, and he took the time to chat with others and remember what they were working on or excited about. When he subsequently noticed related articles that could help, he sent them along. As a reader of many magazines and newspapers anyway, he was able to convert his natural interests into an activity that he genuinely enjoyed and that was always appreciated. Although he never cynically sent the clippings just to build support, he did earn credit from others for his thoughtfulness; and his subsequent requests for his own department and projects always received serious consideration and, often, approval.

Sleaze Alert

There are situations in which the ally you want to influence doesn't value any work-related currencies, or you have no access to any that he or she does want. That means you will be forced to find more personal currencies to deposit to your "account" if you want to build credit.

There is a danger, however, from seeking nontask-related ways of creating obligation, even though it is sometimes necessary. It is unfortunately tempting for employees who realize the power of having credit in the reciprocity bank to use the process of doing favors in a self-promoting way, currying obligation for its own sake. Even when this works, there are often considerable costs to reputation that cannot be overlooked.

For example, the head of physical plant in a service organization, not usually a position of great power, volunteered to organize the December holiday party each year. As part of the festivities, he always arranged to have a photographer in attendance who wandered around the party taking pictures of managers and their families. A few weeks later, the people who controlled resources or were otherwise central would get an enlarged photo "with compliments" of the physical plant manager.

Because there was some doubt whether this gesture was an act of kindness or a ploy to build obligations, many coworkers acted cautiously toward this manager. His good will was valuable for getting office equipment moved or repair work done, so no one confronted him about this "little game"; but many were uncomfortable in dealing with him.

Although he didn't use his credit in an overt way, by mentioning the photos when he made subsequent requests for his department, still his purpose was to build goodwill that could serve him later. When he needed something during the year, he was seldom refused, although people grumbled because they felt trapped. As a result, he got what he wanted; but he was never fully trusted in the organization and was never promoted.

On a far grander scale, Robert Moses was reported to have used the resources of his position as New York Commissioner of Parks to create subtle obligations among reporters, commissioners, and politicians. When he wanted to push through a project, people to whom he had catered found it difficult to oppose him. Limousine rides, fancy meals, meetings in spectacular places were all used by Moses to court supporters or neutralize detractors before he put the bite on them. As a result, he built roads and parks on an unprecedented scale. At the same time, he rode roughshod over the poor, disrupted neighborhoods and spent vast public sums to further his personal vision of New York.

Moses used many other influence techniques, including covert, indirect ones, such as burying clauses into complex legislation that later gave him almost unlimited power; but he also knew how important it was to have relationship savings in the bank to withdraw in tight situations. Apparently, he was also charming enough—and dealing with sufficiently seducible allies—to allay concerns about the sincerity of his intentions. It is possible that, in complex public situations, with so many differing constituents and interests, only a skilled manipulator can make anything happen; but the process produces enormous cynicism and public costs that make the enterprise questionable. As we have maintained from the start, any tool can be abused.

It is easy, of course, to overdo unrequested favors, especially if the recipients suspect that the favors are being done only to create obligations, or if the favors are not valuable to the person receiving them. Many years ago, for example, Dale Carnegie advised people to win friends and influence people by, among other things, learning their names promptly and using the name frequently in early conversations, since "everyone likes the sound of their own name." Anyone who has ever had a newly converted disciple flood a conversation with "Yes, Seymour, it certainly is a swell day, Seymour. Would you, Seymour, be interested in hearing about what a fine fellow you are, Seymour?" knows how readily the currency can be debased. Once again, we emphasize that insincerity can cancel out the benefits of what might otherwise be an effective way of building exchange credits.

Calling in Past Debts

If the person you want to influence happens to be one for whom you have done things previously, and the debt level is sufficient to cover whatever it is that you are asking for, exchange should be relatively easy. This assumes that the potential ally recognizes the debt previously incurred, and believes it to be at least equivalent in value to the cost of what is being requested. If the relationship is good, you can even collect in excess of the existing debt; since, among trusting colleagues, the accounts can swing from black to red and back again depending upon circumstances.

Although the concepts in this book are relevant for any influence attempt, a great deal of organizational exchange happens more or less automatically. Elaborate exchange discussions only take place when you need something out of the ordinary. Thus, it is useful to signal to your potential ally early on that the transaction at hand is unusual and calls for special attention. It is not just a routine part of your job, and it is important enough to spend time on.

Interesting problems arise, however, when your signal is ignored. What happens when a request is made of a debtor, but the debtor does not acknowledge that there is any obligation? Confusion can arise in organizations where there are strong norms against making exchanges explicit. The past "lender" may believe that an obligation is created, while the borrower may see past help as just part of the lender's job and therefore perceives no debt. It can be very deflating to suggest that a past favor deserves a current response and be told, "Big deal. You were just doing what you're supposed to do." That is especially discouraging when it comes from your boss, who isn't aware of what it has cost you to deliver on a request.

If it is not an accepted practice to discuss such issues, it can be difficult to resolve these differences without elaborate circumlocution. At the marketing department of a consumer goods company we have consulted with, members report many such put-downs when they try to influence higher-ups in other divisions.

Instead of being able to say, "Hey, I've got your marker"; or, "I've knocked myself out for you in ways you don't even know about because I didn't want to burden you; how about some consideration in return?", influence attempts are approached indirectly, with statements such as "Oh, I thought we had established a good working relationship, with lots of give and take."

Subtle allusions to past transactions, "teamwork," and the like substitute for direct discussion of the apparent differences in perception; or influencers give up in frustration before they have exhausted all possible avenues of influence.

Each organization tends to have its own language for conveying strong expectation of a response. At one consumer goods company, members convey the importance of an issue by saying, "This is a strike issue," even though there is no union involved. At another organization people say, "I'll go to the mat for this one." "This is a biggie," is another way that members of a certain company signal that they are not making a routine request. Somehow or other, you need to use the organization's shorthand or jargon to indicate the seriousness of what you want. Of course, it is always possible to cry wolf once too often; be sure that you mean it.

In some organizations it may be considered crude to say anything so overt as "You owe me one," so gentle hints are called for. In other organizations, it would be considered naïve not to bludgeon colleagues with your expectations about their obligations, since all take it as a "fact of life" that the world works on self-interest and quid pro quo. Be sure to adapt your language to the culture. If you're still new in the culture, stay alert for phrases like these to clue you about the appropriate level of directness.

I Know You Said You Love Me, But You Never Bring Me Flowers

Even when direct discussion is sanctioned, however, there can be very different ideas about what is owed. The imprecision of exchange rates is such that even when one person says, "You owe me one," and the potential ally agrees, it is possible for genuine disagreements to arise. Sometimes, the effort put forth by one person to comply with a request is invisible to the other, so that the receiving party isn't proportionately appreciative. We have frequently seen situations in which someone responded to a request, which wasn't particularly urgent, as if the organization's future depended on it. The person who moves heaven and Earth to accommodate another may not be fully appreciated if the request was not that important to the one who made it. In that case, an attempt to call in a perceived debt could be met with, "Hey, no big deal, I was just making a suggestion. I didn't expect you to turn yourself inside-out, so don't try to lay a guilt trip on me."

Conversely, we have seen organizational members who routinely knock themselves out on behalf of others, but then downplay their efforts by saying, "It was nothing," in response to thanks. When those who have benefited are sensitive, the person who has extended himself is properly appreciated, but not every recipient of favors is sensitive. As a result, the givers come to feel that they are being taken advantage of, and the recipients go blithely forward, not realizing that resentment is stirring.

If you have made an effort for a potential ally, it requires a certain grace to point it out without sounding too crass. But hiding your light under a bushel may be a waste of a good light. The trick is to let them see you sweat a bit, without complaining, so that the effort is visible but not flaunted.

On the other hand, you don't want to be seen as overly preoccupied with the bookkeeping of obligation. The ability to deliver without calling attention to every last deposit in the obligation bank is a rare one, to be cultivated. One of the most influential organizational members the authors have ever observed regularly performed miracles for others from his "assistant to" role, but he never acted as if it were a big deal. Because his colleagues knew from their own experience how hard it was to move the bureaucracy, they appreciated what he must have been doing; and he accumulated great respect and obligation. When the opportunity to take over as director of an important new division came up, he had many supporters and was selected for the job, despite the fact that he had fewer formal credentials than other candidates.

Escalator Going Up

The way to try to collect on past debts is by gradually increasing the pressure. Unless the potential ally is deliberately determined to take advantage of you, the least possible pressure necessary to induce cooperation is appropriate. If you decide that the potential ally is unwilling, for purely selfish motives, to reciprocate, you can up the ante as far as you are willing to be seen as tough.

The first step of one form of escalation is to express explicitly the obligation as you see it and insist that the potential ally respond. The next step is to raise your voice, or "lose your temper," in an attempt to make the potential ally uncomfortable enough to comply. By so doing, you alter the exchange currencies, introducing the control of your temper as a new currency to trade: You become willing to exchange dropping your temper for (reasonable) compliance with your request.

Of course, this kind of emotional blackmail only works when the potential ally dislikes emotional confrontations; it can easily backfire when improperly applied and can cause escalated resistance. But deciding in advance that you will never use this kind of pressure can put you at a disadvantage if the one you want to influence trades in the currency of toughness. These "allies" often bank on the realization that opponents may be too inhibited to make a big fuss; in such circumstances, it is playing into the ally's hands to hold back.

Turn up the pressure just a notch by making your requests in public, in a "friendly" way at first, or with irritation if that does not work. A smiling accusation in front of colleagues to the effect that the recalcitrant potential ally hasn't learned to give and take, or only wants to take and not give, can make it very difficult for the game player to keep on refusing. Because this is no way to endear yourself to the other, it is a method to be used only when you are thoroughly convinced that the potential ally is deliberately trying to grind you down.

Ironically, there are some organizational bullies who, out of the jungle-fighter view that only the strong deserve respect, become collaborative only when they have been faced down in this way. A professor we know, for example, likes to begin conversations with an insult, just to test the mettle of his colleagues and associates. Once someone comes back at him and tells him more or less to "stuff it," he becomes perfectly amiable and amenable to influence. If you have never stood up to such a person, it can be startling to see a tiger suddenly act like a pussycat once you have established that fact that you cannot be pushed around.

Borrowing on Credit:
Deferred Payment/Collateral

If there has been no chance to build prior obligations, and either you cannot immediately command the currencies the potential ally wants or do not have time to mobilize them, then it may be necessary to request a "loan." If you have a reasonably good reputation, you can offer to repay later, either with specific goods or in an unspecified currency "to be named at a later date." Where there is prior mistrust, it is not likely that you will be able to use this approach, at least not without considerable collateral; but if the existing relationship is at least not negative, then it can be possible to obtain cooperation on the basis of a promise to pay later.

For example, Marcia Allen, a consumer goods company product manager, needed a rush order for a special-sized packaging in order to get product in the stores in time for the scheduled advertising campaign. This could cause difficulties for the pur-chasing manager whose cooperation she wanted: rushing her order would slow down other priorities, which the purchasing manager made very clear when Marcia approached him. Eager to see the important promotion succeed, Marcia made her request in return for a later payment: She offered to include the purchasing manager in future planning meetings so that fewer surprise rush orders would be needed. He would get early warnings about plans, which would allow him to make suggestions about timing and alternate materials before plans were finalized. She got her materials; and, subsequently, the purchasing manager was included in meetings where he made significant contributions to decisions about special promotions.

Similarly, in her study of successful innovators within organ-izations, Rosabeth Kanter found many examples of managers who made promises of future payback for current backing, use of re-sources, or budgetary transfers. They would offer better support services in the future, recognition when the project was a success, or other forms of payback at a later date. Sometimes, all they asked for was a pledge of resources or backing, to be paid only if others also came through. Then they would parlay the initial pledge commitments into further commitments, since they could demonstrate widespread support, and eventually could pay back the initial "investors." The backers who made early loans or pledges not only received particular goods or services they wanted, but they also gained positive reputation for being able to spot good ideas early and support them.

If the idea being pushed is suspect, or the person you want to influence does not fully trust you, it may be necessary to explore whether it is possible to put up a form of "security bond" when trying to borrow. It might be possible, for example, to offer to publicly support the potential ally *before* he or she has to deliver on what you are asking, with the understanding that the support is only a demonstration of good faith, not the repayment for the cooperation. This can be very awkward to discuss, but is prefer-able to just being turned down or stalled. It can be very freeing to a poor relationship to say something like, "I see you are not com-fortable with me, and I want to turn that around. What can I do to show good faith? Would it be helpful if I did _____?" That kind of direct acknowledgment of the problem can become a wedge to open a discussion of difficulties, or a way to make it possible to do business even when the relationship is less than desirable.

OTHER STRATEGIC CONSIDERATIONS: WHO AND WHERE?

Who's on First? Deciding with Whom to Attempt Exchanges

Many influence attempts will involve only one other person, but in complex situations there are usually multiple stakeholders, each with his or her own currencies. One of the strategic choices in these situations is whom to engage with directly, whom to just touch base with, whom to work gingerly around, and whom to avoid entirely. Influence is hard enough without trying to take on the world. But projects that involve large-scale change cannot be accomplished without judicious exchanges with multiple players.

Some of the considerations for deciding how to exchange directly with a potential ally follow.

Centrality of the Ally

□ How powerful is the other person? Power means more than hierarchial position: What needed resources does he or she command? How exclusive is the person's control of those resources? How dependent are you on that person for success? If the person gets angry at you, can he or she harm your project?

Amount of Effort/Credits Needed

□ Do you already have a relationship with the person or will you be starting from scratch? Is there any way to quickly establish a working relationship, or is the process inherently slow?

□ Is the person likely to insist on trading in currencies you do not command or cannot gain access to? How expensive will it be to you to pay in the desired currencies?

□ Would the person be satisfied as long as you at least "paid your respects" and stayed in touch, without asking anything directly?

Alternatives Available

□ Do you know anyone whose support will help gain the support of the potential ally? In other words, who can influence the ally if you are not able to directly?

□ If the person is not influenceable in the right direction, can you find a way to neutralize him or her? Can you reshape your project to take the person's opposition into account or to skirt the person's worst concerns?

In general, the important dimensions are the degree of your actual power relative to the array of potential allies, and the degree of your dependence on each. This can be represented, as in Figure 8–1, by a two-by-two table, with four resulting strategies.

When you are relatively powerful compared with your potential ally, you should plan to conduct mutual exchange discussions of the kind we have been discussing throughout this book.

If, however, you are in a relatively low-power position (even after having explored how to increase your power as described in Chapter 6) but are dependent on the ally's cooperation, then you either need to follow a submissive strategy or look for others who will help you and who *can* influence the person. Submissive strategies are those in which you are completely open and essentially put yourself at the good will of the ally. You may be able to bluff from a low-power strategy; but, when dealing within your own organization, that seldom works for long—and then you reduce the likelihood of a sympathetic hearing.

When your power is relatively high, but you aren't especially dependent on the ally's cooperation, the best strategy is to work around (isolate) the person and create relatively little need for interaction.

Figure 8–1
YOUR POWER RELATIVE TO YOUR ALLY

		Dependence on Your Ally	
		High	Low
Your Power Relative to Your Ally	High	Mutual exchange	Isolate
	Low	Plead, get help	Ignore

Finally, when you have low power but low dependence, you can ignore the potential ally, or better yet, keep a friendly manner and pass along information, but spend relatively less effort on influence. As we have stressed, there is never very good justification for being gratuitously unfriendly or nasty, since the person may become important later; but your purpose is to allocate your necessarily limited energy.

Your Place or Mine?
Choosing a Setting

Another strategic factor is the location of the actual exchange discussions. With good colleagues whom you know well, choice of location is less important. Business can be done on the fly with no loss of impact. Location may also matter very little if what you are requesting is relatively easy to give. But when you do not know the person, or there is some history of negative feelings on either side, then setting can matter a great deal.

In general, people feel most relaxed on their own turf, at their own pace. Sometimes, however, the ally's office will be a nest of constant interruptions that would make it impossible for the two of you to concentrate. In these circumstances, try to arrange to meet at a neutral conference room, or over lunch away from the office, or, if it fits the norms of your organization, after work over a drink. Any of these would be better than asking the potential ally to come to your office. Making an appointment, and specifying how much time you think the discussion will take, is another way to keep the relationship on a comfortable and relatively equal footing.

It is almost never appropriate to influence colleagues by using cheap "negotiating" tactics like trying to make the other person feel one-down in an uncomfortable chair in your office, with the sun in his or her eyes. Remember, you will probably have to work with the person again sometime.

FOUR DILEMMAS TO BE MANAGED DURING EXCHANGES

□ Openness or partial truth?
□ Stick to plan or react to the moment?
□ Positive or negative exchange arguments?
□ Stick to task or work the relationship?

Openness or Partial Truth?

The best exchanges are those from which both you and your ally get all that you both want at the lowest cost. Where each side very much wants what the other side has, and each is happy to trade, both sides make a considerable profit from the transaction. You can both go away feeling good about the deal and about the relationship.

However, the prospect of an "easy deal" immediately raises the possibility that, if you can make your ally think that your cost is higher than it actually is, the ally will think it is an even better deal, and feel more future obligation. Thus, the temptation always exists to exaggerate your own costs (and, of course, to minimize the ally's) in the interests of getting what you want at the lowest cost.

Furthermore, what if you have more to give than your ally realizes? Why reveal everything you are willing to do, especially those things that are quite costly to you, if you can gain what you want for less? That will leave more to spend on other influence attempts. On the other hand, if you hoard currencies and only dole them out when forced to, or get caught exaggerating your costs, you may reduce all chances for profitable exchange.

Concealing or altering information can have two negative effects: (1) The potential ally may not know enough about what is important to you to be creative in finding alternative ways to be helpful; or, even worse, (2) he or she may sense that you are not being wholly above board and refuse to deal with you, or feel spurred into driving a harder bargain to be sure there isn't more hidden in your treasury. Although there is potential gain from being shrewd, the act of exaggeration or concealment may elicit from your potential ally the exact behavior you do not want.

Some managers are wonderful actors and can conceal from others their true feelings, but far more managers believe in their own thespian talents than can possibly be true—since almost all managers are certain they can spot insincerity in others! Indeed, in virtually every organization we have observed, those managers who are consistently covert and unforthcoming are eventually tagged as untrustworthy and slowly frozen out of important transactions. That can be hard to believe when the nastiest person gets a promotion or has the ear of the boss; but, over time, few of these people endure in their organization. Nice guys don't always finish first, but nasty ones seldom do, at least not in situations where they can hardly get anything done without the cooperation of others. No one wants to be a sucker, yet the process of self-protection may be self-defeating.

In an particular exchange, however, the temptation to exaggerate costs will be present for both sides. Unfortunately, once one party begins to do that, the other is likely to feel the need to do it also, and mistrust grows. But if one side does it and the other does not, the exaggerator may gain an advantage, so the temptation remains.

Stick to Plan or React to the Moment?

The second dilemma arises from the dual need to, on one hand, thoroughly prepare for discussions with your ally so that you can fit your case to the ally's interests and style, and, at the same time, be ready to change course if new information emerges during the discussion. There is a real danger of missing important data about the ally during the exchange conversation if you are too focused on carrying out your plan.

Exchanges often can founder because the person wanting influence fails to do the necessary homework and then blunders past the potential ally's valued currencies or personal preferences about interaction style. But, too often, the influencer is so preoccupied with getting it right, with sticking to the predetermined game plan, that he or she misses obvious messages about what matters to the ally.

In such cases, the blindness to the signals being sent by the potential ally can be monumental. The resistant ally may say in 10 different ways what first must be done in order to obtain his or her support; but the determined influencer persists in the wrong approach because the objective is so important and the game plan said, "Stick to high lobs."

Plan to Drop Your Plan!

The challenge is to be so thoroughly prepared that you can dispense with your agenda in a flash and tune in to the hints about interests, goals, and concerns that any ally will give during conversation. This means treating objections as clues, not irritants, and staying poised to explore valuable clues whenever they appear. Planning a hike in the country but refusing to detour around giant boulders just because they were not on the map is a good way to spoil a journey. You can still reach your destination if you respond to unexpected barriers as trail markers.

Positive or Negative Exchange Arguments?

The third dilemma involves deciding whether to stick with positive arguments for cooperation or use negative arguments about potential costs—and recognizing when to switch. Never using negative exchanges can leave you vulnerable to stubbornly resistant allies, but always using them can create unnecessary enemies or give you a reputation for unpleasantness that can hamper future exchanges. It is hard to walk the line between naïvete and cynicism.

Your relative power and dependence should help shape whether you are willing to threaten the negative consequences of noncooperation. Also, the ally's honesty and responsiveness will help determine whether you need to, and effectively can, focus on negative costs, such as withholding your own cooperation in the future. While some allies need to be reminded that they work for the same organization, others would be insulted that you thought it necessary to mention it.

Stick to Task or Work the Relationship?

The fourth dilemma arises when you are dealing with a potential ally with whom you have a troubled relationship. Should you focus on the task about which you want to make an exchange, or stop and work directly on the relationship to get it to the point where the task can be more readily addressed? As we suggested in Chapter 7, this can be a difficult choice, and may call for working back and forth, through several rounds.

If you can get the cooperation you need without mentioning the relationship directly, a lot of time is saved, but often the relationship is sufficiently mistrustful to make it impossible to skip the preliminaries. This situation calls for kid gloves; too much time spent on relationship-building can make a busy colleague restless and give the impression that you are not seriously interested in work accomplishment. In general, we suggest that relationship difficulties be tackled only when they are getting in the way of direct discussion of valued currencies. Then get on with the task discussions as soon as it is feasible. Several iterations between working on the task and relationship may well be necessary to successfully complete a complex exchange.

A COMPLEX EXCHANGE PROCESS

Let's see what we can learn about exchange strategy from an organizational member's report of a reasonably complex influence attempt. Watch the way Warren Peters struggles with the dilemmas of openness and spontaneity in his dealings with Chuck Stevens, and note how he decides to avoid negative threats and discussions of the relationship with Chuck.

Warren Peters, underwriting manager in a large branch of Venerable Insurance Company, (VIC), faced a difficult problem. He was under considerable pressure to fill a newly created unit manager position in his branch; and, after interviewing several candidates, he settled on Debbie Casey, who had a good track record as a supervisor but who did not have the technical knowledge of the other five new unit managers. Debbie was willing to take the job, but her boss's boss, Chuck Stevens, was unwilling to let her go. Furthermore, although Stevens was in another division at headquarters (product management), he outranked Warren and could be a formidable opponent. Warren wanted to influence Stevens to release Debbie Casey, but he wanted to do so while preserving his relationship with Stevens for future transactions.

Background

Several months earlier, VIC had reorganized within its branches. Coordination problems between underwriting and processing had led to serious customer service problems. An extensive study by a consulting firm had resulted in the combining of these areas into units that would focus on groups of agents within each branch. Each unit would be headed by a unit manager, a position created in the reorganization.

Warren's branch had been allotted six units; the first five manager posts had been easy to fill from among branch employees, but the last position had proven more difficult. Warren conducted an exhaustive search using VIC's corporate list of promotable employees and colleagues' responses to his requests for candidate suggestions. As a result of his search, Warren first offered the job to a very good manager, who took a month to decide that he did not want to relocate to the city in which the branch was located.

Another good selection was made, but the candidate declared that he wanted his next promotion to come from the actuarial area. No one else on the company's list looked terribly promising to Warren; he knew that often people were put on the list by dissatisfied managers who hoped to "lose" them through transfer.

Scouting Report:
Good Prospect Spotted

As Warren grew desperate, and the members of the new unit became restless to know who their supervisor would be, a new assistant underwriting manager, John Maguire, suggested Debbie Casey. Although her background was neither in underwriting nor processing, she had worked for John, and he was enthusiastic about her supervisory skills and ability to learn. Warren was reluctant to go ahead, but John's enthusiasm prompted him to interview her.

Warren's first step required his getting permission to interview Casey. While he realized some people would react with surprise to his interest in her, Warren did not anticipate any major roadblocks. He contacted George Robertson, vice president of product management, who had overall responsibility for all areas of that department. (See Figure 8–2.) Robertson, who had been

Figure 8–2

PARTIAL ORGANIZATION CHART

Venerable Insurance Company

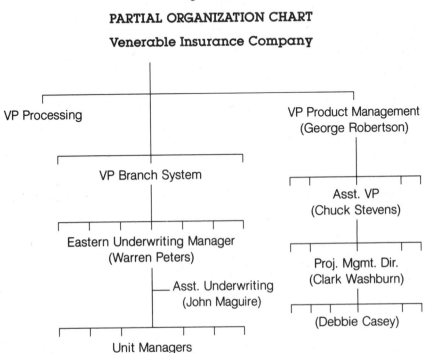

the Chairman of the original reorganization steering committee, did not object to Warren's request. He told Warren to contact Clark Washburn, a product management director, who was responsible for the area Casey worked in.

When contacted by Warren, Washburn objected vehemently to Casey being interviewed because he felt she was unqualified for the job. However, Washburn gave in when he learned that Robertson had given his blessing to the interview. At this point, Warren thought the situation was under control, and he informed Washburn he would contact Casey within the next week or two to set up the interview. He didn't bother to develop a strategy, since he assumed he was facing a straightforward decision of whether he wanted Casey.

Surprise Attack: Casey's Boss' Boss Picks up a Bat

The process turned out to be a little more difficult than Warren had anticipated, however. Chuck Stevens had been on vacation the week Warren discussed his plans with Robertson and Washburn. In the structure of the product management department, Washburn reported to Stevens, an assistant vice-president, who in turn reported to Robertson. Stevens was incensed when he discovered that Warren had gone to Robertson in an effort to pursue someone in his area. He was equally upset that Warren was looking at someone who did not have what he considered to be proper qualifications for the job. "What's it to him?" Warren wondered.

Stevens wasted no time in drawing the battle lines. He was very open and direct in venting his views to Warren on this issue. He began their initial telephone conversation by voicing his strong disapproval of Warren's going over his head to discuss a personnel issue with Robertson. Furthermore, he stated emphatically, Warren "must not have a very good understanding of the requirements of the unit manager position" if he were willing to give it to someone who possessed neither a processing nor underwriting background.

Stevens continued by reminding Warren that he had served on the original reorganization steering committee, and he personally would never consider someone without a processing or underwriting background as a candidate for the unit manager job. He advised Warren to continue to look at the list of promotable employees to find a suitable candidate for the job. That was the purpose behind the list, he told Warren, and tremendous morale problems resulted when managers chose people who were not even on it. Finally, Stevens concluded by saying there was no possible way that Casey was going to interview for the job.

Warren had not fully thought through the question of who to exchange with. Venerable Insurance Company (VIC) is a status-conscious, hierarchical organization, a fact revealed by Stevens' reaction to Warren's "going over his head," as Stevens put it, and his referral to having been on the original reorganization steering committee. Clearly, Warren was not unaware of this aspect of VIC; he had gone first to Robertson, the head of product management, trying to pave the way. Since he knew that Robertson had chaired the steering committee, he might have considered that, as a member of the committee, Stevens had a stake too. This kind of oversight can happen to anyone, so we will not be too critical of Warren, but it does reinforce the importance of doing a stakeholder diagnosis early on.

Stevens and Warren had an amicable relationship of five years with no history of problems. While there was no direct reporting relationship between the two, Stevens was responsible for product management's operations in Warren's region. Product management personnel often have to work with the branch offices to implement the price and product changes that are constantly necessary.

Thus, Warren was surprised by the barrage of objections he received. He liked to get to the heart of matters immediately and usually would readily match fire with fire. However, he contemplated a different strategy in this situation. He knew that Stevens, an assistant vice-president, had more organizational clout; by directly confronting him, Warren ran the risk of increasing Stevens' anger even further and leaving no room for negotiation.

Warren was fully aware of Stevens' reputation for being extremely stubborn. He knew from experience that fighting Stevens toe-to-toe would not be in his best interests. He had seen Stevens use high-pressure techniques in the past, and he had watched Stevens grow more stubborn as an opponent became more strident in his requests. He believed that Stevens had a psychological need to win arguments.

Furthermore, Warren couldn't see a good reason for an assistant vice president to be so caught up in a relatively minor personnel issue of this kind.

Peters Ponders:
Calm, Not Storm?

What were Warren's strategic choices at this point? He could have backed off and sought another candidate; fought back at Stevens for standing in his way; tried to line up Stevens' boss, Robertson, who had already cleared the approach to Debbie Casey; or tried to explain more to Stevens in the hope of persuading him that he had not meant to go over his head, that Casey was at the end of a long list, and she possibly could be competent for the job even if not directly experienced in some aspects of it.

Warren diagnosed Stevens as more powerful than he and likely to veto his rather urgent request; therefore, Warren needed to placate Stevens. Warren had dual objectives: obtain permission to hire Casey, but avoid all-out war with Stevens. The hiring of Casey was not worth making an enemy of Stevens; but he didn't want to have to start the search for a unit manager all over again, so he wasn't about to back off.

Warren saw Stevens as easily provoked into competitive battle. Thus he decided to keep the discussion low key no matter what Stevens did and not to be completely open about his feelings. He would not tell Stevens to "stick to issues worthy of an assistant vice president." His basic approach would be an appeal to reason, considerable deference, and quiet persistence. He would approach the situation very calmly and explain his position; he felt that if he were able to clarify Stevens' specific concerns, he had a good chance of being successful in the negotiation. He assumed that by giving Stevens more information, Stevens would come around— as if no one who understood the efforts Warren had made could come to any other conclusion. Then he would ask Stevens what options he could suggest. Warren felt that by asking Stevens how he would handle the situation, he would be able to harness Stevens' anger.

Warren carefully explained to Stevens that there was not another person in the branch who was ready to take on the responsibilities of the sixth unit manager. He recounted how they had gone to the promotables list and found a good candidate. Even though that person was interested, he eventually turned the job down. They had approached someone else, who also subsequently turned the position down. They had explored underwriting departments in branches across the country and still not come up with a suitable candidate. He finally decided to pursue Debbie Casey because she had worked for John Maguire in the past, and Maguire believed that she had the potential to be transformed into an effective unit manager.

Stevens interjected into this explanation that he felt there were several qualified people on the list of promotables. Despite the anger Warren felt building up, he remained calm and suggested they go over the work history of some of those people Stevens believed to be qualified.

Stevens eventually conceded that several of the people he had in mind had taken a number of years to attain a satisfactory work performance rating and that they were generally marginal performers. He also agreed that these people would probably need a fair amount of guidance for a period of time if they were given the position. Since he was able to get Stevens to concede on several points, Warren felt more confident. Nevertheless, Stevens became defensive; he emphatically stated that he could come up with at least eight or nine candidates, who were better for the position than Casey, from his own department.

Warren reminded Stevens that the two people who had turned the job down were both from his area. However, Warren agreed to discuss any possible candidates that Stevens came up with. He did indicate that he was a little surprised by Stevens' desire to do this, since he had contacted Stevens over a month earlier asking for any possible candidates they may have over-looked. Unfortunately, Stevens had never gotten back to him.

Stevens told Warren that he would put together a list of names for him. Before Stevens could end the conversation, Warren interjected that he would appreciate any suggestions Stevens might have for the future if the same type of situation occurred. Stevens responded that if he did not like the candidates on the promotables list, he personally would have open-posted the position through the company's job-posting program.

Warren knew that posting the job would require waiting for two precious weeks and then sifting through all the applications and interviewing all "qualified" candidates. This could be a very time-consuming process. So Warren told Stevens that although he had a lot of faith in the job-posting program, he had hoped to solve the situation more quickly; and he had feared that he would only receive applications from those people on the promotables list whom he did not want to pursue. However, Warren offered to post the job if Stevens felt that was the best avenue. Stevens replied that he would forward some names; if Warren could not find a suitable candidate from that group, he would insist that the job be open-posted.

After this conversation, Warren was frustrated. He was ag-gravated that the unit manager search was going to be further delayed and that an assistant vice president was becoming this actively involved in a personnel decision involving an employee on the supervisory level. He was also extremely frustrated that

Stevens, all of a sudden, had a list of well-qualified candidates when he hadn't even bothered to respond weeks earlier to the request for a list of this nature.

Where's the Cold Shower?
Warren Tries to Keep Cool

Warren reflected that his strategy of remaining calm and asking for advice on how to handle the situation had been relatively effective. But he was growing more frustrated. He was sorely tempted to come back hard at Stevens, hoping to embarrass him into giving way. Would being open about his anger now help or hurt his case? Was the issue big enough to fight?

Because he still didn't fully know Stevens' world, Warren found it hard not to get angry. He managed to stick to his strategy of playing it low key, but it was at some cost to his ability to be open. He did inform Stevens at one point that he was frustrated, but he told about it without allowing it to fully show. Chances are that Warren's feelings did come through his careful language, but not in so strong a way that Stevens got aroused.

Warren realized that Stevens would not back off if he thought that Warren was not taking him seriously, so Warren cooperated with the process of adding names and investigating them. He was unfailingly respectful of Stevens' views, even when they were inconvenient. By agreeing to extend the search to those on Stevens' list, he made it hard for Stevens to stick to his intransigent views about Debbie as unit manager.

In spite of all this, Warren still perceived that Stevens was in the more powerful position; so, despite the inconvenience caused by Stevens' intervention, Warren decided he would go along with the game plan proposed by Stevens. He felt that this might be his only way of getting what he wanted; if he were going to get involved in a full-scale war with an assistant vice-president, it would be over an issue of greater importance than an open unit manager position. That blocked Warren from more direct inquiry and action.

A week later, Stevens' list of possible candidates arrived. Much to Warren's surprise, the list contained only four names; and Debbie Casey was one of them. Warren was very pleased with this development. He believed it meant that Stevens recognized Debbie's potential to be unit manager, and he was relieved that he would not have to argue further in order to interview Debbie. All four people on the list were immediately contacted and offered interviews.

Three of the four candidates (including Debbie) agreed to an interview. The fourth declined the interview because his spouse had just received a promotion in another area of the company and it was not the right time for them to make a move. Within the following week, all three interviews were conducted at the branch by John Maguire and Warren Peters. Warren interviewed Debbie at the home office while there for other business. Maguire didn't interview Debbie; he was well aware of her capabilities.

Before Maguire and Warren had reached a decision, one candidate called to withdraw her name from consideration. She was a single parent, felt she would not be able to afford the increase in housing costs at the new location, and did not want to uproot her child in the middle of a school year. This left only two candidates.

Warren Goes to Bat for Casey

Warren decided that he wanted to offer Debbie Casey the position. He had been impressed by the self-confidence and maturity she displayed in her interview. While he felt that the other candidate had the required technical skills, he was concerned about her lack of supervisory experience and an apparently abrasive personality.

Warren concluded he should go directly to Stevens to inform him of his decision. While he anticipated that Stevens might balk at first, he did not expect any more roadblocks since he had followed Stevens' game plan exactly. However, Warren soon learned he had misjudged Stevens' reaction.

Stevens became furious once again. He exclaimed that there was no possible way that Warren could have chosen Debbie over the other candidates. He admitted that the only reason he included Debbie's name on the list was that he was confident Warren would decide she was unqualified when he was able to compare her with the other candidates. Stevens continued by saying there was no way he would allow a person with no underwriting or processing background to move into a position like that, especially a person like Debbie, who was extremely valuable in her current area. They could not afford to lose Debbie. The area had been hard hit by turnover, and Debbie's expertise was needed for training new individuals.

Stevens also insisted that he had to consider the repercussions from the people in his area if Debbie got the job. Many would be discouraged that a person with no processing or underwriting background could get a unit manager position in a branch office. Feelings of favoritism would arise, especially from people on the promotables list who had not even been interviewed.

Pass the Ice:
Warren Contains His Anger

At this point, Warren had four choices: He could finally get tough, claim desperation about finding a unit manager, placate further, or openly confess how hard all of this was on him and what inconvenience it was causing.

It is useful to note Stevens' currencies and the currencies Warren attempted to pay in. Stevens had an investment in the reorganization and the new position of unit manager. Although it eventually became apparent that Stevens was resistant partly because he didn't want to lose Debbie, he also did care about the quality of unit managers. He didn't want to deal with morale problems. And, by implication, we can deduce that he wanted to be taken seriously and not have his opinions ignored.

But there were two important shifts in Stevens' position, which Warren could possibly take advantage of. Stevens had inadvertently admitted that he wasn't being completely honest when he included Casey's name on the list he sent. This was a shift in the power balance, because now Warren could point out that Stevens was not playing fair, which would move Stevens some if he had any sense of honor.

Secondly, Stevens had admitted that part of his opposition arose from his need for Debbie's skills in his area, which was a far more self-interested position than Stevens had originally staked out. Although he certainly did care about the quality of unit managers, Stevens had revealed a personal motive that put his "company concern" into a shadow of self-interest. All of this provided Warren with more of an edge than he previously had felt. He could go on gently pressing Stevens, but with a bit more force. Although he was still extremely frustrated, he was able to maintain his cool.

When next the two men met, Warren had one more try at rational explanation. He calmly said that he had followed the guidelines Stevens had set up for filling the position; now that he had made a decision, Stevens was trying to prevent him from proceeding. He explained that he found this very frustrating, since the first two people who turned the job down were from product management; and, of the other three people from product management who were on the list, one didn't want to interview for the job, and one wanted her name withdrawn from consideration, which left just one person in contention with Casey. Finally, in his comparison of the two candidates, Casey was the better prospect.

Stevens quickly interrupted to ask who had actually interviewed Casey. He was under the impression that John Maguire had been the only person to conduct the interviews, and he didn't like the idea of an assistant underwriting manager being solely responsible for making a personnel decision of that size on his own. In addition, he "knew" from past experience that Maguire was an opinionated individual who tended to follow only his own ideas on certain things. Thus, he felt that Maguire might be a little blinded in his overwhelming confidence in Casey.

Warren Counter-Punches

Warren responded by telling Stevens that he understood his concerns, but that Stevens was under the wrong impression. Warren explained that he personally had interviewed all of the candidates and that he was the only one who had interviewed Debbie. Furthermore, while he liked to let people vote on certain matters, Warren advised Stevens that final decisions on important matters almost always rested with him. Thus, he personally had been impressed with Debbie and felt that she would be the best candidate for the job.

He continued to address Stevens' other concerns. While he realized the impact that Debbie's departure would have on her current unit, he reminded Stevens of the company's philosophy that no individual be held back from getting ahead due to the problems the vacancy may create. The company believes that it cannot fulfill its motto of being "First in the Field" without providing its employees with the opportunities to be the best they can.

In addition, Warren claimed he was doing a disservice to the people on the branch unit team by letting them go so long without a unit manager. They were becoming increasingly anxious about who they were going to be working for because the vacancy had gone unfilled for over two months. Warren concluded that he really did not understand Stevens' concerns, because he, Warren, was the one who had to live with the decision. He was the person who was going to pay the price if Debbie failed. However, he was confident in his decision and felt that it was in the best interest of all parties concerned.

Stevens suddenly changed his attitude. He said he had not realized that Warren had interviewed all the candidates himself. If that was the case, and Warren felt Casey was the best candidate, then the situation had his blessing. He had just been concerned that Warren might not be getting the best advice from the people who had conducted the interviews. But, now that he understood the full situation, he felt comfortable with the decision to make Casey the branch's sixth unit manager. He concluded the conversation with several "small talk" topics and questions to Warren about his wife and family. Debbie Casey was selected.

Exit Line

The turning point came when Stevens accused Warren of being too influenced by Maguire's bias, and Warren countered that he alone had interviewed Casey. This heretofore undisclosed information about the process allowed Stevens a graceful way to back off his "over my dead body" stance, since he could now claim that his only concern was to see that a competent person was picked. An important part of any exchange process is to allow exploration of common ground; Stevens could now agree that both he and Warren were trying to insure competence in a crucial new role.

When Warren realized that Stevens wanted to hold on to Casey for the sake of his own area, Warren invoked the currency of company policy, reminding Stevens that local need cannot prevent individuals from advancing. That was hard for Stevens to fight, even if his own interests were best served by keeping Debbie in her present job. By all of this, Warren demonstrated that he too wanted a good person to fill the unit manager job, which was the basis for an eventual alliance with Stevens.

Lost Opportunities

Although Warren had successfully influenced Stevens and preserved the amiability of the relationship, he had not fully responded to what he learned—or should have learned—in the exchange process. He hadn't really explored what was important to Stevens when he first found out about Stevens' resistance, which slowed the influence process by making it difficult to satisfy Stevens. When he finally discovered that Stevens was so concerned about how to replace Debbie, he could have sympathized and offered to help find a replacement. That might have strengthened the relationship rather than merely prevented it from worsening. Warren escaped without scars, but he did not build a stronger alliance for the future. Perhaps Stevens won't jump to conclusions so quickly in his next transaction with Warren, but there is no indication that Stevens came away from the exchange with greater trust for Warren.

Warren might have also shifted a bit to discussing the nature of their relationship when the going got rough; he never talked with Stevens about what it felt like to be suspected of rash decisions about personnel by someone he had always gotten along with. Done with grace, that might have earned Warren more respect for future dealings.

Instead, there is a danger that Stevens will eventually suspect that he was "had," because he may sense that Warren was not completely open with him. Warren's irritation may have come through enough that, in retrospect, Stevens will wonder just what Warren was thinking and whether he had some ulterior motive that was never revealed. This may be a minor danger; but, to win this skirmish, Warren may have unnecessarily planted a dangerous seed of later doubt. It is difficult to balance task completion with openness, and sticking to plan with flexibility, but careful attention to the tradeoffs is needed.

SHALL WE DANCE? STARTING AND STOPPING THE EXCHANGE PROCESS

Knowing when to insist on making exchanges and when to back off is an art, not a science; but it is worth exploring. Warren Peters made some decisions about not challenging Stevens based on Warren's sense of their relative power, the importance of the issue to each, their future interdependence, and his assessment of his own ability not to be suckered into competitive warfare. These are all elements rightfully taken into consideration.

It probably isn't wise to engage in heated battle with someone who is far more powerful, and whose future goodwill is important to you. When what you want is arousing strong negative feelings, you should consider just how important the ally's cooperation is and examine other possibilities. If there isn't another reasonable alternative, then going slow, working harder to understand just why the ally has such strong feelings, listening respectfully to the ally's concerns—or testing whether it's his or her feelings about *you* causing the problem rather than the particular issue—are appropriate strategies.

It is also useful to pay attention to your own hot buttons when engaged in transactions. Experienced negotiators recommend never losing your temper except when you deliberately allow yourself to do it for effect; and, although that kind of advice usually presumes a one-time opponent rather than a potential ally, it is not entirely off-target. If it is easy to get your goat, a tough ally will instinctively provoke you around sensitive issues. Thus, it is in your interest to be aware of what tends to make you angry or drives you to become nasty in a way you later regret, and to learn to recognize when you are headed for trouble. Then you can take time out to decide whether you want to go to the mat on this issue, want to raise the temperature, or calm down so that you don't do anything rash.

Although it is sometimes necessary to be very tough in making exchanges (and we will conclude this book with a chapter on hardball), it is almost never wise to be nasty or attack the other *person* instead of his or her *position* on an issue. Walk away and count to 10—or 10,000, if necessary—as soon as you feel yourself wanting to deliberately hurt a potential ally. You can be tough and honest without trying to be hurtful; pain that is a by product of honest exchange doesn't cause the same reaction as pain from a conscious attempt to maim for revenge.

The Cooling-Out Process

When Stevens realized that he had used up his arguments in favor of leaving Debbie Casey in place, and a bit sheepishly had to back off, he instinctively switched to personal small talk and "made nice." Warren Peters was smart enough not to gloat; rather, he chatted in a friendly way that saved face for Stevens and let him establish that there were no hard feelings. Each realized that it was important to follow a tough task exchange with some relationship repair.

Sociologist Erving Goffman wrote a classic analysis of the way professional con men tried to "cool out the mark," a term for giving the person who had been taken a way of thinking about the experience that would not lead to retaliation but would let the victim feel that the outcome was inevitable and not the fault of the con man. Although we are certainly not talking about cons, we refer to our earlier discussions of the problem that occurs when an organizational member has to acknowledge that a colleague was right. No one likes to feel one-down, even when he or she has brought it on himself.

Therefore, when you have survived a successful but difficult exchange negotiation like the one Warren went through with Stevens, think about how to leave your ally with some dignity. Personal chit-chat is one way; but there are others, such as letting the ally teach you something, or demonstrate superior knowledge, about another topic. As with other tools we have discussed, this need not be done cynically. In fact, unless you are a professional actor or con artist, it cannot be faked; but a dose of human kindness at the end of a complex exchange is a fitting finish.

Even when the ally has not "lost" but there has been intense exchange activity around an issue, time spent rebuilding the relationship, creating a feeling of mutual satisfaction and trust, is not at all wasted. At the very least, it will save valuable time when you engage in your next exchange.

CONCLUSIONS

Making exchanges can be very simple when trust and mutual knowledge already exist. It is almost automatic, then, to adjust requests to fit the potential ally, and each of you becomes willing to give the other considerable latitude. If you know the request will be inconvenient or very costly to the close ally, you can gracefully acknowledge it with an exaggerated statement of appreciation, such as, "I'll be in your debt forever." All that's needed is some indication that you will repay the favor, probably with interest, and that you know what a difficult request you are making.

If such prior trust does not exist, or the request is unusually costly to the ally, then it is necessary to use other exchange strategies. If what you have to offer in return is clear and desirable to the ally, it is easier just to put the offer on the table. If what you can pay is not so clear, or unknown, and not so valuable to the other, then you will need more elaborate strategies.

Similarly, the degree to which you trust the potential ally becomes an important consideration in how open you can be, and how directly you can explore what the potential ally wants for going along. It also shapes how hard-nosed to be in making demands or setting terms. Probably the best rule of thumb is to assume that your ally is trustworthy until proven otherwise, because then you will not be causing counterattacks that otherwise would not have happened.

Game theorists have found that a negotiating strategy that matches the opponent's response—trusting until you are violated, but then quick retaliation followed by a return to trust if the opponent also returns to acting in a trustworthy way—is the most successful long-run strategy. Making exchanges with colleagues in an analogous way is probably appropriate.

But, when dealing with someone who is trying to take you to the cleaners, you need to be tough and use the kinds of tactics we discussed earlier. Gradually raising your voice, going public, or calling the ally's bluff are tools you need in your repertoire, preferably so you won't have to use them. The flexibility to use such tools when absolutely needed, but to keep them in cold storage as long as possible, is vital to making successful exchanges in varied circumstances.

Finally, the kind of approach you can, or will, be willing to make will be shaped by how much you depend on that ally, and that ally only, for getting exactly what you have requested with no substitutions accepted, and on the ally's continuing goodwill. Your willingness to risk is also an important determinant of strategy, modified by the long-term versus short-term consequences you are willing to live with.

Since the likelihood of making satisfactory exchanges on reasonable terms is so greatly increased by pre-existing positive relationships, start as soon as possible to build your network of relationships. Isn't there someone you could be meeting now?

9

Lessons from a Determined Influencer: The Rise, Fall— and Eventual Resurrection— of Monica Ashley and "Project Hippocrates"

We now take a careful look at a complex situation in which there are many influence transactions over several years. After describing Monica Ashley's monumental efforts to move many people to accept an important strategic product shift at her medical equipment company, we will use the concepts introduced in previous chapters to illuminate what Monica did well and where she might have been more effective.

INFLUENCE IN IMPLEMENTING STRATEGIC CHANGE: THE MONICA ASHLEY CASE

Monica Ashley was stunned. Just as she was successfully completing a complex, two-year project that could be a major contributor to the future growth of Health Equipment and Laboratories, Inc. (HEAL-INC), she was removed as program manager by her boss, Dan Stella.

Although Dan, vice-president for design and manufacture of one of the top lines of HEAL-INC machines, asked her to stay on in his division, Monica felt that personal defeat had been snatched from the jaws of victory. The glory from her massive effort to enable HEAL-INC to adapt its hospital-oriented, technically-driven products and strategies to much wider usage would go elsewhere. It wasn't that she was hung up on glory, but it didn't seem fair to be pulled out of this incredible accomplishment just as it was finally about to overcome the ferocious opposition that had made it even more difficult than it naturally was. And,

Figure 9-1

PARTIAL ORGANIZATION CHART— HEAL-INC

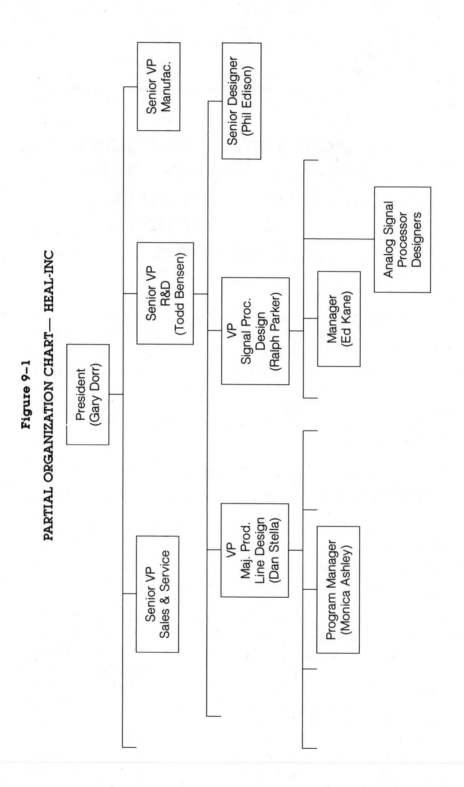

she feared—correctly as it turned out—that over a year would be lost in replacing her and getting a replacement up to speed.

HEAL-INC was a rapidly growing company making a wide range of advanced diagnostic and treatment equipment. Utilizing many complex technologies, from lasers to powerful magnets to semiconductors and signal processors, the company had thrived on the enormous latitude given its very bright employees to take initiative and pursue opportunities. Since its inception, HEAL-INC had found great success by creating equipment that appealed to the same kinds of technically sophisticated hospital researchers and technicians it employed. Early on, top management decided that creating an atmosphere of maximum freedom would be worth the waste and duplicated effort, since it would tap the creativity and energy of smart employees. The strategy had worked, and HEAL-INC's meteoric growth had been a source of pride to management and employees—and sometimes a source of puzzlement to those who had been taught to revere order and efficiency above all else.

More Tech, More Touch:
New Users and Their Needs

In recent years, however, the market had begun to shift, along with the technology in the industry. The equipment was increasingly going to be used in doctors' offices, small clinics, and storefront test labs, rather than exclusively in teaching hospitals. New users of the equipment were less technical and more patient-oriented than the hospital staffers who had been the company's original customers.

Furthermore, in order to make the equipment easier for less sophisticated personnel to use, the technology had grown more complicated; thus, far greater coordination and teamwork in design and manufacture became necessary. Many different, but interrelated, components had to be designed by teams of contributors, rather than developed for special purposes by solo "geniuses." There were pressures for some key components to shift from analog to digital electronics. And purchasers were becoming more selective, so their interests had to be taken into account at an earlier stage of product design. Finally, it was increasingly difficult for any one company, no matter how big, to custom design all the components of the equipment. The industry leaders were beginning to form strategic alliances and purchase components from outside sources.

All of this caused considerable tension at HEAL-INC and entrepreneurial companies like it. The original ways of doing things had brought huge success, and the company was young enough so that many of those who had grown with it were still entrenched. They had a big stake in their hard-won lessons about growth, decentralization, encouragement of initiative, technical orientation, and the virtues of inventing everything within the company. The voices of those arguing the urgent strategic need for greater ease of operation, more coordination of previously autonomous units, and purchasing components and subsystems elsewhere were not readily heard.

The President of HEAL-INC Recruits Monica for "Project Hippocrates"

Monica had been squarely in the middle of just such issues. She had taken on "Project Hippocrates" reluctantly, because, even though she was ready for a line job after many successful years in important staff positions, she knew there would be major opposition. Over her years at HEAL-INC, she had developed a special relationship with Gary Dorr, the current president, which began at a meeting early in her career when she caught his attention by challenging his conclusions. He liked her spirit and the hard work that had enabled her to back up her views with data when he asked why she disagreed. After that, Dorr had periodic long talks with Monica and once told her that he thought of her as his HEAL-INC daughter. So, before taking the assignment as program manager of Project Hippocrates, Monica went to see Dorr.

She explained to him her concerns, especially in relation to a key manager, Ralph Parker, the vice-president in charge of designing the key signal processor used in several lines of HEAL-INC equipment. Monica had heard through the grapevine that Parker, who was in a different division from hers, was politically aggressive and had not been helpful on another project that her boss, Dan Stella, had pioneered. A different approach to signal processing—from analog to digital—would be needed for Project Hippocrates; and, as the main designer of HEAL-INC's original analog signal processors, Parker could be a major roadblock.

So many people in her division had talked about Parker's legendary resistance to new approaches and to customer input that Monica took their views as fact and didn't bother to talk with Parker directly. She just decided that she wouldn't be another in the long line of people she knew complaining about their inability to move him; she would set out to demonstrate overwhelmingly the correctness of the need for a new signal processor design.

Dorr told Monica that he knew about the problem with Parker, and that he was working on it. He told her not to take Parker on directly, but to accept the program manager role, since she "would be protected." Before Monica could reply with her continuing concerns, Dorr ended the meeting by saying, "Monica, congratulations to the new program manager."

A Whirlwind of Activities

Monica plunged in, tackling the project with the same focused intensity that she brought to everything she did. She first interviewed the new kinds of purchasers to understand their very different needs; created a task force; recruited members from other parts of HEAL-INC; introduced to HEAL-INC for the first time to the Taguchi method, a highly disciplined product design process she had learned in Japan; and initiated a series of studies on just what would be needed to alter HEAL-INC's equipment to make it more viable for new applications. All of this activity made people uncomfortable, because the structured Taguchi process was far more rigorous than anyone was used to; and it led to something that had never been done before at HEAL-INC: a total system outline for the product revisions, including all the elements and how they would have to fit together. She created a cross-department signal-processor study group to investigate whether the existing component could handle the redesigned equipment. As Monica had intuited, the study group determined that no in-house analog product could do the job and recommended the purchase from an outside vendor of the necessary digital signal processor.

Just One More Study: Difficulties with
Outside Purchase of Signal Processors

This recommendation set off many months of problems. The decision was made, restudied, made again, restudied, and remade four times. Twice Monica gave presentations before the senior management staff, with competing presentations given by the signal-processor design group under Parker. Parker was nasty to her and made numerous accusations, including one that the technical people she had used in her study group were not competent (even though some had come from lower levels of Parker's organization, and two had been loaned by Phil Edison, the most respected technical person in the company). Parker had publicly declared that any kind of signal processor would be purchased outside only "over my dead body." And even after the senior management staff gave the go-ahead, Parker accused Monica of proceeding without permission. So, still another independent task force was created to evaluate the decision; once again, the outcome was in Monica's favor.

At the first senior management staff meeting, Gary Dorr surprised Monica by being more critical and less friendly than Monica had ever experienced. He had often complained in the past about the need at HEAL-INC to define measures that would spell out the performance of an entire diagnostic and treatment system, not just its components. Worried about the common HEAL-INC problem of components being optimized but the complete system ending up suboptimized (the whole being *less* than the sum of its parts), Monica had developed detailed, integrated plans, but Dorr seemed annoyed rather than pleased. At the meeting, he criticized Monica for the comprehensive approach.

Monica was confused, then flabbergasted at Dorr's continued critical tone. At first she couldn't say anything, she was so taken aback. Then as the meeting went on, she realized that Dan Stella, her boss, wasn't speaking up and defending the massive amount of work she had done to insure that components would not be suboptimized at the expense of the total equipment systems. Assuming that her past relationship with Dorr legitimized disagreement with him, she defended the decisions. She knew that customers used different criteria for measuring overall equipment performance than the designers of each component, and she wanted that recognized.

Parker had attended the meetings of the Project Hippocrates group, during which he challenged Monica constantly and, in her view, tried to provoke her. Because Dan Stella had advised Monica to keep cool, she avoided taking Parker's bait. Then, during one meeting at which Monica asked Parker a question, he accused her of being angry. She coolly replied, "It seems to me that you're the one who is angry." Parker exploded. Monica just let him yell, then proceeded with the meeting.

After the meeting, all who attended, including Dan, congratulated Monica for "humiliating Parker," which had not been her intent at all. She was just trying to head off a fight, as she had been advised. But the battle lines hardened further. From then on, Parker assigned one of his managers, Ed Kane, to attend Project Hippocrates task force meetings on his behalf.

At one of the subsequent meetings, Kane heatedly accused Monica of not listening and of excluding signal processor people. She was embarrassed by the attack and unhappy about being falsely accused; but, as was her custom, she handled the unjust attacks by providing more accurate information. Thinking, "If he knows the truth, he'll cool off," she told Kane the history of how the original cross-functional design team, including people from his own organization, had agreed unanimously on the need for a switch to digital signal processing, and the requisite acquisition of an outside product.

There was so much conflict at that meeting that, as it broke up, Monica's boss, Dan Stella, called a spontaneous meeting of his own managers in a nearby conference room. Because Kane was standing outside the room and he was available to attend, Stella invited him "to c'mon in and help us plan."

Once inside, an obviously outraged Kane shouted, "Who the hell do you think you are, going to an outside vendor!" and called Stella a "traitor and a renegade." Stella retorted that if anyone was a traitor it was Kane, because the signal processor department of which Kane was a member had said to go ahead, and now he was trying to subvert their decision. In Monica's eyes, the confrontation was particularly brutal ("like dinosaurs slugging it out"), especially since she knew that Stella did not particularly like conflict.

Soon after, friends of Monica began to tell her that Kane was spreading nasty personal rumors about her, including innuendoes that she was having an affair with Stella. Stunned and hurt, she decided there was nothing she could do about it. Her friends would know how absurd the rumors were, and she believed that telling others she was innocent would only help dignify the rumors. She persevered in the project.

A month later, Parker once again challenged the outside purchase decision. Monica was called to an extended senior management staff meeting where she was given one day to make a presentation of the complete program; Parker was given the next day for his rebuttal.

Twisting in the Wind: Abandoned by the President

Monica was shocked by what happened at the meeting. She had barely started her presentation when Gary Dorr began to attack her. He said that no one person was going to be in control, that Monica in particular was trying to over-control things—"like an

Imperial Chinese Emperor" was how he phrased it—and that central control was totally inappropriate for the company. Seeing Parker smirking in the background and feeling extraordinarily jittery after the attack by the president, Monica mustered her courage and told Dorr that she was only giving the complete system overview he had asked for. Every time she tried to give a detailed calculation, Dorr broke in again with criticism. Monica and her group were devastated; they were certain that Dorr had been totally prejudiced by Parker.

When Parker made his presentation the following day, Dorr was very receptive to him. In Monica's eyes, however, Parker had no solid data; and his presentation was devoid of content and filled with glib assertions and pronouncements. The main theme of his argument was, "Haven't we always met hospital needs? Just look at our original analog signal processor: It's the best in the business, and it can be adapted to any need our customers have."

As she sat there in disbelief, Monica recalled a comment Dorr had once made to her privately. He had told her that there was no way the company could do without Parker because of his signal processor contributions. After Parker finished, the people in his group were slapping each other on the back; and Kane walked over to sneer, "Ha, ha, you lose!" at Monica. She was upset that Parker and his supporters had done so much behind-closed-doors political maneuvering and it absolutely infuriated her that "politics could beat out substance" in the company. Only Dorr's earlier warning about not confronting Parker kept her from retaliating.

Sticking the knife in was not enough for Parker. He had to twist it. At the end of the meeting, Parker again brought up Monica's negotiation for the digital processor with an outside company. Dorr exploded, and yelled at Monica, "How dare you negotiate on behalf of the company?! You are a renegade and an empire-builder!"

Although, by this point, Monica was down for the count, she defended what had happened, explaining that she acted upon a decision that had been cleared by many groups. But then, when Dorr turned to Edison, the most respected technical expert, and asked him if it had gone through the review committee he headed, Edison claimed he did not remember. Monica was amazed and shocked, since the technical guru had always been friendly to her; and he certainly was present when the decision had been made by his review committee.

Dorr then said that he was going to go around the room and take a vote on going outside. He said that he personally would only vote if there were a tie. As fate would have it, there was a tie vote. Dorr turned to Monica and asked her how she would interpret the tie.

Monica had been sitting near Dorr at the meeting. After his attack, he acted conciliatory, and they even exchanged whispered comments several times, so Monica was feeling a bit restored in her relationship with him. Although she was scared of how it might be taken, she summoned up a sense of humor that she was rarely able to use when tense and deadpanned, "I would say that there was an overwhelming sentiment for going ahead with the outside negotiations." Dorr laughed and agreed. Monica was enormously relieved.

At the next senior management staff meeting, Dorr wanted one more vote on the issue of negotiating with an outside vendor. When the results were in, only one person had voted against the outside purchase: Parker. One of the executive vice-presidents then turned to Parker and said, "You will have to speak now or forever hold your peace." Parker finally retorted that the move was against his better judgment and that, when it proved to be a giant mistake, it would be on the heads of Monica and her boss, Dan Stella.

Heat in the Kitchen: Put out the Fire

Monica felt herself constantly being drawn into conflict even though she had wanted to accomplish the whole project by building consensus. In part, she had been driven by her assumptions about her relationship with Dorr. She had assumed that he still wanted her to stand up for what she believed in.

Upset, she went to talk to him about what had happened at the various meetings. He told her that she was no longer behaving appropriately; because she was acting like a "hot competitor" when she came to the senior management staff, she was disturbing the company's once-peaceful and productive environment.

In her defense, she tried to explain that it was not she who was causing the problems but Kane and Parker. She reminded Dorr that he himself had said Parker was a problem, but Dorr replied "That is none of your business." She knew that Dorr admired her for having the drive to complete her advanced studies and other complex company assignments, and that he counted on her as somebody who could carry things through, but she had overestimated the amount of support she would get from him in Project Hippocrates.

Throughout Monica's career at HEAL-INC, Dan Stella had phoned her on Sunday evenings to review the previous week and discuss what was coming up. As the infighting increased at the senior staff meetings, Stella told Monica in one of these Sunday night phone conversations that she was going too fast and causing conflict. When things got very hot, he called her into his office and tried to slow her down. She said, "Don't these people understand we have all this work to do?"

Stella replied, "Don't you understand you have to build all these relationships and deal with the politics at the top?"

Nevertheless, caught up in the need to master enormous numbers of interrelated issues, Monica pressed on. She had set a date for bringing Project Hippocrates to market, and she was determined to meet it. She knew the external competition was getting increasingly tougher, and that it would be a severe strategic blow to HEAL-INC if they missed the deadline.

Over the ensuing several months, a new team, which included many signal processor people, was formed to begin the technology transfer process and overcome all not-invented-here feelings in preparation for a contract with an outside vendor. Parker's people chose not to help specify the features of the digital signal processor. Technical experts from Stella's organization did the work, along with some people from sales and marketing. Exhaustive effort went into design and product specification documents to pave the way for a smoother-than-usual product introduction. During this period, there were vague promises from Parker's organization about modifying the existing analog signal processor to meet the new demands, but nothing tangible happened.

One More Time: Hard Decisions
About the Signal Processor

While plans to educate the salesforce went forward, Parker stirred up a great deal of tension around the decision to purchase signal processors. He used every meeting he attended to say negative things about Project Hippocrates. Several important customers even told Monica that Parker and his people had visited them to say that their analog signal processor was being enhanced to adapt to new uses, and that the digital processor that HEAL-INC was thinking of purchasing outside was "a pile of crap."

This immobilized Monica at first, because she couldn't understand how top management could allow this malicious behavior to go on. She got Stella to talk to Dorr about it, but she saw nothing happen to stop it. Eventually, it just spurred her into redoubling her efforts and pushing her project group to work harder. "I'd have gone crazy if I had paid attention to all that nasty political stuff, so I just poured more energy into the project," she reported later.

As a result of Parker's continued complaining, Dorr formed yet another committee chaired by a new engineering manager, who, because he had recently been hired away from a competitor, was assumed to be unbiased. Unbeknownst to Monica, the new manager began a series of secret meetings involving most of the same people who had been part of Monica's original task force to work on what the criteria should be for making the decision.

Within the next month, the company signed a contract with an outside vendor. Shortly thereafter, Monica learned of the secret study committee and found out it was still evaluating outside purchase. She warned that the company now had a legal obligation and could be sued if it did not go ahead with the new contract.

In spite of her troubles, Monica was proud of the negotiation and the amount of continuing vendor support that she had managed to get the vendor to include in the contract. In fact, her negotiation eventually became a model for the company to purchase components from outside.

Three months after the contract was signed, the "secret" committee announced that it was ready to hear a debate on the merits of the outside digital signal processor versus the existing HEAL-INC analog product. Kane and Monica made presentations.

Another three months went by before the committee announced its decision, which was to go ahead with the outside purchase. Meanwhile, people working on the project were completely confused; they didn't know which side to support. Monica told them to forget politics because there was work to do, but she had to keep encouraging people to get them to do what was needed.

Sudden Death:
Monica Loses Her Position

Two days before a major national meeting, which Monica had organized for HEAL-INC people from around the country to finalize the support strategy for implementing Project Hippocrates, she was called to a meeting with Dan Stella and a new personnel manager. There she was told that she would no longer be managing the program.

Crushed, Monica asked why. Stella told her that the secret committee had recommended that she be replaced by a more technical person, but that he had removed her because he thought she might have a nervous breakdown as a result of all the intensity of her involvement. He believed that she had failed to read the signals he had sent her to slow down, build relationships more, hold back her angry opinions in meetings, and, in general, learn to act "more like a top executive." To him that meant fighting battles off-line rather than in public, and learning to sit quietly through public attacks, even when they were wrong. He told her that as long as she did not understand all of that, there was no place for her in Project Hippocrates. He told her, however, he wanted to keep her on and he gave her some time to think about what her new job might be. For almost a year after that, Monica worked on minor projects as part of Stella's group.

Subsequent events made Monica feel simultaneously vindicated and regretful. Following another eight months of study, the new program manager concluded that Monica's plans were correct; and he proceeded with Project Hippocrates using the innovative strategy Monica had developed for HEAL-INC. Kane was removed from Parker's staff and was having trouble getting anyone in the company to take him on in a new position. The scope of Parker's job was eventually reduced considerably, and he lost control of the most important part of the signal processor design area. And, after a year in limbo, Monica began to acquire significant assignments again. Yet, the way in which the project had lived but the leader of it had been killed off—or at least buried alive for a year—left wounds that still ached; and Monica was determined to learn from her experiences.

Monica Reflects on Her Experiences

In retrospect, and with a year to contemplate what had happened, Monica analyzed her own problems as follows:

"I was very data-oriented in my approach to the project, which carried the day; but I didn't develop the interpersonal contacts to solidify my influence. Not being from the signal processor department, I was out of the design mainstream, yet there were many complex issues to deal with. I still haven't figured out why they allowed a female—especially one without an engineering background—to manage the project and whether they were setting me up for a big fall.

"I know I could have had Parker's support if I hadn't challenged the sacred cow of their analog signal processor product, but

I didn't see how to avoid that once we determined that the technology was too limited. When I invited the signal processor people in early in the process, they were surprised because, in their own organization, they couldn't get heard if they were not part of the original analog cult. Most of them had been trying to get the company to consider a move to digital technology for some time, but they were shot down from within their own organization.

"I had heard that Parker was an authoritarian who could not be influenced and that no one dared challenge him, and I guess I got scared. There was so much work to be done and so much market opportunity that I focused on achieving the goals without trying to directly influence Parker. He had a much higher power position in the organization and was a formidable player, so I was afraid to challenge him.

"I wanted Parker's people to recognize on their own that Project Hippocrates needed new signal processing capacity, but I see now that I should have dealt with Parker directly if I wanted to be treated as a senior executive.

"Furthermore, I have to build my confidence; I still feel like a little kid from the sticks, despite all my success. Others see me as over-confident and aggressive, but I probably act that way to overcome my own fears of somehow being 'found out.' My peers tell me that they are afraid of me and don't argue with me because they know I would bowl them over with my arguments or my intensity. They see me as angry; but I feel that I am just intense. It surprises me when they act laid back even when they have intense feelings about something; when I feel intensely, I show it.

"*I now see that the content of what I was doing—the plans, strategies, decisions—was the least important part. The most important is mobilizing support and resources. If the content is wrong, you can always change it; but if there is no support, you don't have a foundation. I was trying to work without a foundation under me.*

"Ironically, I'm getting *more* done now without having to push so hard. In the past, I thought I had to speak up and give lots of facts to prove I was credible and confident, but I no longer think that way. I don't want to be so personally exposed and vulnerable that I overreact to attacks or assume I'm being attacked when I'm not. When Dan pushed me to do some relationship building, I made excuses for why I couldn't take the time to do it. I see now that was wrong.

"I did ask Phil Edison for his help on technical issues; and as evidence of his support and confidence, he gave me two key people early on. It is easier for me to ask for help when I feel that the person is supportive. Because Edison is calm and laid back, I was too. I felt I had to stay low-key or I would lose him. I didn't see how that same approach might have worked with others. Even when Edison and I disagreed, I would try to be calm and talk slowly, which is very hard for me. I would try not to fight too hard; instead I would go away and come back to him when I had the data.

"Edison likes being "stroked," which was easy to do because his early support made me feel very positive towards him. It wasn't artificial at all. The two people he gave me were reputed to be very tough and ready to eat alive anyone who made a technical mistake. When they joined me, I went to them and told them I was not a technical expert and would need their help. They were great after that.

"Even when Edison challenged my ideas, I would never feel personally attacked. I would just want to figure out what the right answer was. When Kane attacked me, however, he would intimidate me both verbally and physically. He would even stand much too close, and when I tried to back off, he would follow me around, trying to dominate, to win, both organizationally and technically. As an engineer, Kane had no sense of how to work through a problem taking many views and business needs into account. With him it was all or nothing: if I didn't accept his position immediately, he would fight until I did. There was no sense of compromise or mutual learning. I got the impression that he would accept nothing short of complete acquiescence on my part, which I couldn't do, because the data I had simply didn't support his position. I also felt that I had to protect those people who had come to me from his organization. They appreciated my protecting them, of course; but he didn't.

"He spent lots of time building interpersonal bridges. For example, he worked hard to influence Todd Benson, my division's senior vice-president, who was a long-time supporter of mine. Although I knew what Kane was doing, I didn't bother to go talk to Todd. I figured that we had *data* on our side, so why spend time with somebody I already knew.

"In the long run, Kane's position and strategy didn't help him any more than mine helped me. He lost his job, too. We were opposite sides of the coin—he had relationships and I had data; but we both lost. Both data and relationships, together, were necessary for success.

"I never lobbied anyone, even when I knew the person that Kane had gone to. For example, an outside member of our board of directors went out of his way to congratulate me every time I made any kind of presentation on Project Hippocrates. Although, in retrospect, it is clear that he could have been a strong ally, I never followed up with him.

"I had nothing to offer Kane to get him to back off, except to voluntarily disappear into the woodwork. Although people had told me he was a bad apple and I should leave him alone, Dan Stella had said that I shouldn't get down to Kane's level of behavior, so I didn't know how exactly to respond when he attacked me in meetings.

"I suppose that I could have gone to Kane directly after his first nasty attack and warned him that if he didn't cut it out I would expose his behavior publicly. Then, when he acted up in a meeting, I could have said something like, 'You're doing it again, Kane; you're being personal about the issues instead of using data. That's just what you do when you spread rumors about me instead of dealing with the issues. Let's deal with the issues here.' If I had said it calmly, I probably wouldn't have been seen as descending to his level, and that might have stopped him.

"I wish I could learn to use humor instead of just being a fighter. But if someone like Kane says (and he did), 'You'll do this over my dead body,' should I say, 'Lay down?' I suppose if I had said something like, 'Anybody here know where I can find a gun to give Mr. Kane?' I might have broken the tension. When I am not feeling uptight and tense, I can inject humor. I see now that it works very well on senior executives here, but I haven't been able to joke when I am tense.

"I could have stayed quiet when Dorr attacked me; maybe it was immature to take him on in front of witnesses. I could have done it later in private; but I don't like seeing my people attacked, and I think it is my role to publicly defend them.

"I've seen Dorr get furious with his people, and they just seem to take it. I thought I could get away with challenging him not only because of the old relationship, but also because he expected that of me.

"Maybe when he attacked me, I could have replied quietly, 'That's not how I see it,' or, 'We have to talk; I have a different view of the facts.' That might have been a more mature way to do it.

"I forget to take the long-term view because I feel I have to win every battle. I need to learn to roll with the punches. I haven't been savvy about when to speak and when to be quiet. It looks as if laying low is more effective.

"I guess it never occurred to me that putting a senior executive in a bad light in front of others is not such a great idea. Dorr might have liked me for challenging him when I was junior, but I guess what I didn't realize was that, as you get nearer the top, you have to play by different rules.

"Dan Stella didn't support me as much as I wanted him to. He claimed that he did, but I didn't see it. And sometimes he thinks he is helpful when he is not. For example, after I complained that my ideas weren't being listened to at his management committee meetings, he would make a special point of acknowledging my contribution after I said something. But, since he didn't do that for others, it was seen as an unfair advantage. So he thought he was helping when he wasn't. Similarly, he thought that removing me from Project Hippocrates was the best thing "for my health." I needed his support, not his protection. I'm not a delicate flower. He could have handled the whole conversation much better.

"At the senior management staff meeting at which Dorr attacked me, Dan said nothing. He believes in working the tough issues in private. I know now that he was trying to work behind the scenes to back Parker and Kane off, but I would have appreciated something more visible. I got the program through for him and then got shit for it. He avoids conflict until there is a major explosion.

"I believe Dan changed as he got to the vice-president level. He used to welcome and solicit direct feedback, but now he doesn't. He tells us, 'Be senior managers; that is, be quiet and circumspect and don't engage in direct confrontation.' In the old days, there was healthy disagreement, but now it is hard to get people stirred at his meetings.

"I find Dan and I can no longer have the kind of conversations we used to have when he was more congenial and collegial. Now I have to agree wholeheartedly or disagree very gently and tentatively. When I perceived that Dan was threatened by my conversations with Dorr, I learned not to tell anybody about them. But now that Dan has his own conversations with the president, I don't think he is threatened by my closeness to Dorr.

"I guess I must have given Dan fits because, in his eyes, I became unpredictable and seemingly uncontrollable, and therefore potentially embarrassing. I guess that doesn't help him look good when he wants to win the respect of the senior managers. I don't want to embarrass him; I want to learn how to function in a better way.

"Dan has been pushing me to work more with other members of his management committee and not rely on him as my sole contact. I have been doing that, and I find that I now do feel more effective and comfortable with them.

"One of HEAL-INC's senior executives kept telling me in regards to Project Hippocrates that I didn't have to own it all. He said that the more you give away, the more will be given to you; and I'm starting to understand that. Dan tells me the same thing. Before, I was volunteering for everything. Had I volunteered for less, I would have had time for more activities, including more relationship-building.

"It's a curse to see the big picture and have a strict, self-imposed deadline, because you know how much has to be done. Dan and Dorr would tell me that they knew I was right but they couldn't handle everything I was throwing at them in the moment. When they didn't know the overall strategic plan, how could they worry about one subsidiary issue that I was pushing at them? I made people feel overwhelmed early on, which wasn't useful, nor intended. *I* felt my team was being clever and comprehensive to think of all the angles; but Dan and Dorr—most of the senior staff, in fact—just felt that I was throwing too much at them. I needed to show them an overview rather than a step-by-step plan laid out in the minutest detail.

"I guess what I really need to do is persuade myself that I am bright enough so that I can focus on what is important to others rather than on proving that I am really smart. I don't know what has to happen for me to finally accept that I am. Because I was taught to be self-critical and humble, it's been difficult for me to accept this positive view of myself; although deep down I know it's true."

Stella Looks Back

Dan Stella had his own views of what had happened, and the lessons for Monica:

"Monica took Kane's attacks on her too personally. She should have stepped back and let him hang himself. Furthermore, when he was out doing counter-marketing to the ideas of Project Hippocrates, Monica should have been selling the project; but she didn't. We're still repairing the damage.

"I agree that there was no way to deal with Parker. He does not and will not understand the needs of customers other than hospital technicians. Because he had position power, the only battle strategy to use with him was to go underground. All you can do is neutralize him, using other people. You need to practice 'octopus management': Get others to see that there's a problem, and get them to raise the issue with top management. If it comes from many sides, it can be effective eventually. But you have to be cautious how you word your concerns. The trick is to get marketing to do a full court press, since they won't be able to sell machines that are not suited to other kinds of customers.

"If Monica had been patient, others would have blocked Parker, but I couldn't back her off. She set a launch date and wouldn't budge. I kept trying to slow her down, but she wasn't having that. I was angry at Parker and Kane too, but I didn't want to add to Monica's boiling. Remember the old saying: In war, if there is no chance that you will lose your life waiting, patience wins.

"I gave Monica a card that says: 'Listen; Remove the Urgency; Trust'; but it didn't get through to her at the time. That's the hardest thing for a data-driven person to do! I know, because that's the way I am too; neither of us suffers fools gladly. We just want to pile more data on.

"She became a bulldozer, which got her in trouble with Dorr. He wasn't comfortable with a woman being so aggressive and tenacious, refusing to grovel. Although I think he learned from that experience, he was not happy at the time. That hurt me a lot. I've had a 10-year relationship as Monica's boss and sponsor, and I wanted to help, but I couldn't. She's rarely wrong about data, so it was extremely frustrating. I keep telling her, 'Give it away; it'll come back with interest.'"

CHARITY BEGINS AT HOME—AND MAY NOT BE SELFLESS

"Give it away so it can come back with interest" is not a bad theme for discussing influence and exchange. The notion of investment in others, and getting repaid with interest, is helpful to anyone wanting influence, as we have tried to show. Dan Stella was trying to coach Monica to be more influential; but, ironically, he too had a problem with influence: He couldn't get Monica to listen to his advice. Even being the boss does not guarantee the requisite influence in every case.

Give Monica Credit

Although Monica had many people and groups to influence in order to make Project Hippocrates a success, we will focus on her difficulties with four key players; Dorr, Parker, Kane, and Stella. Her ability to push the project as far as she did, through an organization that was inherently so hard to move in such a fundamentally different direction, is a tribute to her intelligence, mastery of complex data, energy, and persistence. Though being technically or strategically "right" never guarantees that you will be listened to, it is possible to go a long way when you have the data on your side. On the whole, that strategy, though incomplete, is a lot better than trying to be influential through use of interpersonal techniques when you are demonstrably wrong or unprepared. The first is all steak and no sizzle; the second, all sizzle and no steak.

As this case makes clear, attention only to getting it right is not enough to move doubters or powerful resisters. In retrospect, Monica saw that she had been too caught up in the complexities of the technical and marketing challenges to correctly assess the interests of key players, determine what she could offer them, and find ways to make satisfactory exchanges. As she put it, *"I now see that the content of what I was doing was the least important part. The most important is mobilizing support and resources. If the content is wrong, you can always change it; but if there is no support, you don't have a foundation. I was trying to work without a foundation under me."*

Indirect Influence as an Option

It is important to note that there are other, less face-to-face influence techniques that Monica could also have used. For example, Dan Stella wanted her to get other affected departments such as marketing, to take on Parker and Kane by complaining to Gary Dorr, surrounding them in an "octopus-like" attack. She could have lined up high-level supporters, such as the complimentary outside board member, to help fight the battles, or mobilized customers to more directly make their desires and demands known. All useful and sometimes necessary, these influence techniques are once-removed from the potential ally. A full influence arsenal includes weapons that do not involve making a direct "target" of the person you want to influence. Mobilizing the populace to wage war from all directions at once can help overcome superior fire power. Nevertheless, even indirect weapons involve persuading other people to help fight the battles, which comes back to *influence* as a central instrument of "war." We will continue our focus there.

Monica's Search for Potential Allies

Parker

One of the fundamental mistakes Monica made was to assume from the beginning that it was impossible to find anything in common with Parker around which to form any kind of alliance, and that Stella and Dorr would automatically be allied on everything she did. Stella, too, took it as fact that Parker was immovable ("will not understand customer needs"), which meant that he couldn't think of how to help Monica figure out what she might do, short of mobilizing others against Parker, to at least neutralize him. Although we cannot know for certain how influenceable Parker was, we can be sure that labeling him politically aggressive and impervious to customer need will lead to treating him as an enemy to be avoided, and thereby harden his opposition.

Even if a person is too negative ever to become an ally, it is worth taking a positive stance and assuming the best, because that increases the chances of at least *neutralizing* him or her. The conversion to ally may not take place, but treating the person as if it could happen might do the trick if there is any hope at all.

Position Power

It might well be that Parker was too invested in his own history with the analog signal processor to ever consider its limitations and the consequent need for going outside; but, if you were in his shoes, wouldn't you expect to be treated with *respect?* Wouldn't you want to be approached early for your views, given a chance to say how the problem could be studied, and be kept *informed* even when the data and decisions were going against you? Perhaps Parker was so irrational that no information would penetrate his negative views, and he would only use information that Monica gave him to try to sabotage her efforts; but, if she had been talking directly with him as if he were at least potentially an ally, then she would also have been free to talk to others, like Dorr, about her differences of opinion with Parker.

Since reasonable people can differ on complex technical/ strategic issues and can change their minds as data pile up, treating even a Parker as if he could become an ally, or could at least come to see that disagreement with him was not meant to be personal or undermining, would free Monica to disagree agreeably. If she then saw that Parker was attacking her publicly or behind the scenes, she could do a lot of "lobbying" without being nasty. "I've talked with Parker and he sees the world differently from the way our task force sees it, so I'd like to let you know what we're finding," is a reasonable way to make her views known without being a "hot competitor."

Kane

Kane might have been a different story, partly because he was acting as an agent for Parker, and partly because he may have been gratuitously nasty. His subsequent difficulties in getting placed at HEAL-INC suggest that others saw him as personally offensive. If indeed he was no more than a gloating competitor, he probably wasn't convertible to an ally. However, we can speculate about how he might have reacted if Monica had said to him, "You may win on this one, but don't forget that we all work for HEAL-INC and will have to deal with each other in the future. Let's keep the fight fair and forget the nasty personal stuff; you wouldn't want your behavior in regards to Project Hippocrates to haunt you, would you?" It might have made him pause long enough to accept an olive branch for future possible alliance.

An alliance doesn't require that there be any great love between the parties, only some mutual interest on one or more issues. As another high-powered female manager in a different company said to a nervous male who was ambivalent about hiring her, "Listen, you wouldn't marry someone like me, and I wouldn't choose you; but if you want someone to run your management information system really well, I'm your person."

Dorr

Monica erred in the opposite direction with Stella and Dorr. Her relationship to Dorr was a complex one. He had spotted her early in her career at HEAL-INC, spent an unusual amount of time talking with her (considering her junior status at the time), and took obvious pride in her accomplishments. Thus, Monica concluded that he would automatically understand the obstacles she was facing in Project Hippocrates and (as she assumed he had implied) protect her from Parker. What she failed to realize was that even good allies still pay attention to their own interests, and that if she crossed Dorr's interests and concerns, he wouldn't automatically deliver unconditional support.

She violated their connection in at least four ways:

1. Dorr told her *he* was dealing with Parker and not to fight with him publicly; she did, believing that it was Parker's fault and that she was not to blame;
2. She failed to recognize Parker's importance to Dorr, forcing Dorr to take sides when he did not want to;
3. She challenged Dorr in public, charming behavior when she was a junior manager, but disturbing coming from a more senior executive proposing a product revolution; and
4. In pursuit of a fully integrated project, she violated Dorr's beliefs about the virtues of decentralization and control. (As a woman, she also may have made him uncomfortable by her aggressiveness and ferocious determination, even though he may have simultaneously admired it.)

While all this was going on, she failed to spend time with Dorr, which would have allowed her to test his reactions, understand what he needed in this loaded situation, learn from him, and reaffirm the mutuality of their interests.

Stella

With Stella, Monica also had a longstanding relationship, so she assumed that he would not only defend her but do it in the public way she sorely needed. When the public support was not forthcoming, she interpreted his lack of reaction as a dislike of conflict; and therefore, she ignored the advice he gave her about slowing down. Based on her competitive analysis, she had set a date for bringing the new product to market; and she was so caught up in that arbitrary, self-imposed time bind that she couldn't hear his signals about losing the battle to win the war. Given Stella's concerns about being taken seriously as a senior executive, he couldn't be the kind of ally that Monica assumed he would be.

A part of Monica's problem with Stella and Dorr was that she was so determined to be independent and competent that she completely overlooked another key aspect of the ally/partner role: the possibility of *learning from* the ally. While many subordinates fail to be good partners because they are too dependent and can't push back, Monica was fiercely *independent,* and she failed to use the freely available knowledge of her allied bosses.

She had assumed that she was tapped for Project Hippocrates because she was expected to be aggressive, visionary, not bound by the blinders of the past, driving, and able to get things done; it never occurred to her that another aspect of this assignment was almost certainly the chance to learn more of the behavior expected of a senior executive. She didn't realize that *learning* was expected along with *performance.*

An important benefit of the partner-in-an-alliance role is the potential to give and take around the issues and to learn from the strengths of your partner. But Monica never went to Stella or Dorr to ask, "What do you expect me to learn in this assignment? What is different about this project that would help me grow in ways that you see as desirable?" She didn't see that the partner role freed her to be more of a real partner, who could both give *and* learn.

Monica had responded to the assignment like a modern-day Lancelot, charged by King Arthur (Dorr) to sally forth and slay dragons wherever she found them. She didn't see that he and Stella were offering her a partnership in which her talents could be combined with their wisdom. In an increasingly complex world, and certainly in HEAL-INC's changing world, dragonslaying requires more than one brave knight; there are too many dragons to go around! When we tried this idea out on Monica, she commented wryly, "Lots of times I did feel like a missionary; I forgot that fairly often they end up getting boiled alive in the pot!"

In general, we can conclude from Monica's experience that the beginnings of influence require the working assumption that anyone, no matter how difficult he or she is reputed to be, could be a potential ally; that assumption creates a mindset that reduces negative stereotyping and neutralizes hostility. At the same time, no alliance is permanent and unchanging; by their nature, alliances continue as long as some mutual interests are being fulfilled, but they can dissolve, despite general goodwill, if one side or the other does not continue to get its needs met. Furthermore, although it is hard to influence someone with whom there is a poor relationship, it is insufficient merely to rely on prior good feeling to preserve influence as conditions change. Alliances, like all relationships, require ongoing maintenance. Finally, the role of ally or partner has to be two-way; and partners, especially those working with their bosses, should look to learn as well as deliver.

WORLD TOUR: WHAT MONICA NEEDED TO KNOW ABOUT POTENTIAL ALLIES

Since circumstances allowed us to interview only Dan Stella directly, we will have to make inferences about the worlds of the key potential allies Monica needed; but this is no different from what Monica had to do. We benefited from the passing of time, because Monica has since gone back to Dorr and Stella to talk about what happened; but it is impossible to be sure that your diagnosis is correct until it is tested in action. Nevertheless, there is a considerable amount of data on which to base a diagnosis of the key players.

Parker

It is not terribly hard to imagine what it feels like to be a pioneer in an organization, the inventor of a key component that has been central to the company's success, recognized over the years as vital to the company's outstanding record, and then suddenly to find that a group of upstarts are claiming that your baby is inherently inadequate for the future. The currencies of *centrality* and *respect* are certainly going to be crucial to you, especially if you suspect that the president is no longer treating you as the revered dominant gatekeeper of the company's future, despite his nice words in your presence.

If you ever had any doubts about your ability to continue your technical prowess, those doubts will be sorely plucked; and you will not be likely to welcome proposals that symbolically, if not literally, mark the end of your dominant influence. Or, you may be blind to your own limits, believe with all your conviction that you have the keys to the kingdom, and be furious that people without your track record and with little ability to really understand the brilliance of your contribution are challenging you. In either event, someone in Parker's position is unlikely to have the welcome mat out for an interloper like Monica.

Nevertheless, if the above analysis is at all correct, it suggests that Monica was not without potentially viable approaches. As suggested, it might have been possible to pay Parker in the currency of *respect*, demonstrated by early and frequent consultation, ample *information* flow, and a tone of *appreciation* for his considerable technical contributions. Making clear to him that her disagreement was respectful, and based on a different reading of market opportunities rather than an indictment of his technical expertise, probably wouldn't have transformed his response; but it might have taken some of the vituperativeness out of it.

Admittedly, listening takes a lot of time. It can cause you to derail or lose your focus, and it usually creates the expectation that you will indeed respond to the potential ally's ideas and concerns. Since Monica was not going to be persuaded by Parker, nor could she win a technical debate with him—because she was not a technical expert and was only representing the work of her team members—this strategy might not have been worth the expense.

Another possibility might have been to invite Parker to meet some of the customers on whose opinions Monica and her team based their conclusions, and to manage those meetings. Direct, outside evidence (particularly from a customer group) can *sometimes* neutralize a resister in a way that filtered testimony from within the company cannot; although Parker—as narrow scientific whizzes are likely to do, and most unfortunately did in this case— could probably have claimed that the customers did not know what they really needed. In fact, when Parker did bother to seek out customers, he did it to undermine the work of Monica's project group. That isn't exactly what we might call a "customer-is-always-right" focus! Nevertheless, repeated invitations to *join her in meeting customers* "so that your expertise can be brought to bear on these massive problems" could have been a way of showing appreciation for Parker's centrality and contributions in the past.

Kane

Both Monica and Dan Stella believe that Kane is an inherently nasty and divisive person who could not be influenced. If it is true he spread the rumors about Monica and Dan that were attributed to him, that might well be so. Nevertheless, even if it is only for practice, let's see what we can glean about Kane's world and his likely currencies.

The most obvious force at work on Kane is his position as Parker's subordinate. Even if Kane had been disposed toward the team's views about signal processors, Parker's strong feelings and over-my-dead-body attitude would shape Kane's reactions. He could hardly be a good subordinate and not carry Parker's views forward.

In addition, Kane gave off cues about the combative, win-lose atmosphere in the signal processor design department, whose members behaved as if beleaguered and under assault. Indeed, since we know that Dorr, the president, saw Parker as a problem in need of a long-term solution, it is probable that others in the company had complained that the signal processor department was resistant to new approaches. Thus, the department was entrenched and under the impression it was fighting a rear guard action, which shaped the way its members interpreted any idea from another group.

In addition, Stella and his area had been on the ascendancy, struggling (and winning) on previous projects with the signal processor people, which made initiatives from one of Stella's staff even less welcome. Finally, the increasing complexity of signal processor design—both analog and digital—demanded greater collaboration. Those who had been in the business from the beginning remembered the good old "solo genius/independent cowboy" days, when one person could pull it all together and shape the fortunes of whole companies; and they may not have been comfortable with the demands from new areas and people who did not have to be listened to in the past.

Thus, even if Kane were a gentle, generous person (which admittedly he probably was not), he might have been glad to take Monica and her project on in public shootouts.

Just as Monica wanted to defend her people from attacks, Kane and Parker wanted to defend their designers—and preempt possible assaults—by attacking first. Their sense of having to fend off an attack also may have spurred them into taking the opposition to their ideas personally, and into assuming that the personal hostility or incompetence of their "enemies" had led them to disagree. Kane and Parker are prime examples of people who do not assume that dissident colleagues are potential allies; and so they stereotype in a way that may induce in their colleagues the attacking behavior they fear!

This way of viewing the pressures on Kane suggests two possible ways to pay in valued currencies. First, Monica could have tried to show *sympathy for their feelings of being beleaguered,* by saying to Kane something like, "It must be hard on you guys to have everyone coming at you about digital signal processors when you are so certain that analog equipment is flexible enough." That kind of acknowledgment and sympathy could conceivably have been an opening to dissolve the barrier of personalized nastiness that had crystallized between them.

Another, somewhat opposite, possibility assumes that Kane values the currencies of *power* and *clout* and would only respect toughness. After one of Monica's detailed presentations to the senior management staff, Kane had actually walked over to her and said, "Nice work." His compliment, delivered under pressure, may have clued Monica that Kane only respected her when he saw her toughness and competence under fire. If that were the case, she might have responded by bringing everything he was doing out into the open, countering all his ploys by making public what he was up to; or maybe just the threat of that possibility would have been sufficient to back him off. Looking back, Monica realized that it would have been worth a try, especially after attempting the more sympathetic approach first. It is certainly possible that neither Parker nor Kane could have been dealt with effectively with a direct approach, but it is hard to see how acting on the diagnosis we made here, would have made it worse.

Stella's World

Dan Stella was on the rise in HEAL-INC, and he was working hard to be an increasingly influential executive. His admission that, like Monica, he suffers fools not at all gladly, coupled with his preoccupation about not fighting in public, suggests that he was working hard to gain credibility as a top executive. Learning to "take it" when publicly attacked was for him a sign of growing maturity; but it wasn't easy when he was working on cutting-edge technologies and market opportunities that shook up established "truths" and entrenched positions. As was the case with Monica, Dan's own impatience and his need to follow the hard evidence must have put him constantly on the verge of an explosion, which, with a president like Dorr who wanted things calm and collegial, could indeed be costly.

There was a great deal at stake for Stella, then, in Project Hippocrates. It had enormous potential for the company, and in turn, Stella's division and his own position. He assigned as its leader a protege whom he liked and admired. He planned to out-last the early and strong opposition from some company curmud-geons by keeping the project moving inexorably forward in this decentralized company.

In this context, Monica's apparent inability to resist the public fights must have seemed to Stella a kind of intriguing danger. Her persistence was needed to make the project a success, but her unwillingness to tactically back off and slow down could have made the whole thing blow up. The currencies of patient *persistence* and *control*, then, were clearly very important to Stella.

Monica had to determine why she didn't respond to Stella's strong hints—and overt suggestions—about what he wanted. At the time, she felt so isolated and stretched that she failed to real-ize that he *was* giving her his own kind of support, which in-cluded coaching her about pace and self-control. She interpreted his messages as his fear of conflict and not as sage advice for a real-world strategy. Once she decided that Stella had changed for the worse and was no longer the spontaneous person he had been, Monica no longer appreciated what he offered her. The negative attribution had masked the care and wisdom he represented. In effect, she severed a valuable alliance. Had she been able at the time, as she was later, to say to herself, "Dan is smart and a friend; if he's telling me to slow down I should pay careful attention and be sure that he isn't right before I charge ahead," she could have had *more* influence with him, not less.

That doesn't mean that Stella was totally correct in his concerns; Monica didn't see herself as an unguided missile as he did, and he may have over-learned his lessons about being a calm, self-contained executive. It is possible that Stella's willingness to slow the pace would make fewer internal enemies but foul up the timing for optimum market entry, allowing a competitor to get there first. As Monica's boss and supporter, however, Stella needed to be taken seriously and enlisted by her; had she done that, she could have engaged with him on these issues, and they would have influenced each other toward more timely decisions.

Dorr's World

Diagnosing the world of a company president from several levels down, or from outside, is always problematic. In this case, however, we have Monica's contacts over the years, Stella's observations from up close, and Dorr's public reactions to Monica and Project Hippocrates to work with. Certain currencies and preoccupations are relatively evident.

Dorr had told Monica that he knew Parker was a problem, that he was working on it, and she should not engage. She interpreted that comment as license to tackle Parker and Kane head on if *they* made trouble. But if we take the problem from Dorr's point of view, it looks different. In Parker, he had a historically important, central company figure, one who had made enormous contributions, in the past. This person may have been somewhat outmoded, but he was smart and persuasive. His well-cultivated network of followers were critical to the company's continued success. As a long-time employee who had made major contributions his opinions and status were important; easing him aside *gracefully* was as important a challenge as was rushing to market with an attractive but unproven new product line.

Into this intricate minuet, which in any company would usually take two to three years to finish without causing the senior executive to lose face, whirls one of your favorite young employees. You have been nurturing her for many years, ever since the time she took you on about an issue and turned out to have done the elaborate homework to back up her controversial views. You have high hopes for her, because she has a keen intelligence and a kind of drive you have seldom been exposed to in a woman at work. But her intensity makes you nervous, because it isn't always tempered with the kind of patience that you have learned a top executive needs. Like many younger managers, she doesn't see the many hidden constituencies and issues you have to juggle from your position of overall responsibility, and she doesn't always understand why you can't just charge ahead on her behalf when she has shown you the "truth."

On the other hand, Project Hippocrates is the kind of complicated undertaking that needs her drive and energy to overcome the many factions, including Parker's, that will try to keep it from succeeding. If she can get them to agree with her plans, then you will know that Project Hippocrates is the good idea you think it is. Over the years, you have come to trust that solid innovations will eventually be supported by consensus, and that ideas which sound good but can't get support probably weren't so good after all.

This interlocking set of circumstances makes you all the more concerned about proceeding carefully. When Monica makes all hell break loose by trying to *force* many areas to work together, and sets off Parker in the process, you are furious. Now you have to publicly support Parker, and publicly condemn Monica for letting her damn-the-torpedoes-full-speed-ahead style start an all-out war in the organization. Why can't she understand that centralized control has never led to good decisions in any society and stop trying to impose her formidable, but tunnel-visioned, will on all those smart people in our organization?

If this analysis is even close to accurate, we can readily see how Monica missed the chance for support from Dorr by paying him in currencies he valued. Because she did not continue talking with him during the project, she did not fully recognize the subtle chess game that Dorr was playing with Parker; and that failure on her part repeatedly infuriated Dorr. She did too little discussing of Project Hippocrates with Dorr, which left her only the public presentations to the senior staff to get her views across, and made her vulnerable to Parker's attacks. And, she missed the more than obvious message from Dorr that signaled his discomfort with forcing the decision to buy signal processors outside. How many different studies did he have to authorize before she got the message?

Because of her blinders, Monica treated the issue as a rational decision rather than a political one that required Dorr's support. Thus, she did not do the kind of lobbying, preselling, and working the corridors that Parker and Kane did, and that Stella did on her behalf.

As Monica came to realize, she was so focused on hitting the bull's-eye that she wasn't even aiming at the broad side of the barn it was painted on. The key decision of Project Hippocrates had profound effects on many constituents, especially signal processor design, and could not be treated as mere technical challenges to be overcome by discovering statistical truth. Any important decision in an organization involves bets on the future, and therefore considerable uncertainty, which can never be completely settled by data and analysis. While analysis is an important component, it seldom reveals the whole picture. Failure to recognize that fact about important decisions, and assuming that technical homework is the only kind necessary (or legitimate), is a major reason why otherwise brilliant technical/professional employees have influence problems.

Monica Ashley's World: Priorities and Resources

Monica deserves a great deal of credit for not focusing on grabbing her own glory at the expense of Project Hippocrates. She could have easily created even more opposition if she had been perceived as in it for her own career purposes rather than the enormous market potential. At the same time, her blindness on this issue was not altogether beneficial to her nor, perhaps, the project. She may have so underplayed her own need for the kind of visibility that would have made her positions more credible that she ended up with less clout than was needed for the project.

Monica was fiercely protective of the people working with her on this complex project, which led to her strong public defenses of what had been done. These public engagements did not help her reputation with Dorr or Stella, for reasons already discussed. They made her appear combative despite her intentions to work collaboratively. Yet, when she could have been promoting the project with powerful individuals, she put her head down and continued to focus on the nitty-gritty of the project. Thus, people who would have been strong supporters were not enlisted by her, nor armed with the facts to realize all that was at stake in such decisions as the outside purchase of signal processors.

It isn't necessary to play amateur psychologist and diagnose Monica's shaky self-confidence as the reason she was reluctant to get out and mobilize support; she admitted as much herself. There is no doubt she was genuinely busy and overloaded during the project, but *she* set most of the priorities herself, and plugged away at them despite pressure from Stella to ease off and attend to interpersonal issues. Even while she demonstrated unlimited ability to undertake massive amounts of work in the toughest territory, she didn't work on building relationships. Apparently, she was reluctant to do anything that might have been seen as pushing herself forward. When threatened, she doubled her intensity, which led others to see her as supremely confident, but inside she was not sure of her own strength. In retrospect, she realized this was a challenge for her to conquer in order to continue advancing into senior executive ranks.

That doesn't mean that she should start a self-promotion campaign, which would quickly get her written off as too self-interested. Paradoxically, her willingness to argue with Dorr in the senior staff meetings probably made it appear to others that she was only too willing to step into the spotlight. Yet she held back on lobbying and working her connections in private, almost as if that wouldn't be fair.

Monica realizes she must now come to grips with the odd demands on people in her position: Put the tasks first, but don't be afraid to sell what you believe in a way that fits the culture. Some work will have to be done behind the scenes, but that doesn't make it invisible; to those who are being approached one-on-one, you have very high visibility! It is that kind of exposure with which Monica has to learn to be comfortable; she is already too good at the exposure that comes from public confrontation.

Urgency versus Success

A second choice of priorities for Monica involved the tradeoffs around the urgency of getting to market versus managing the internal political process. We have already discussed this at length, so will only note it here. For her own personal reasons, Monica chose to fix the target date and drive the project toward that; some of her difficulties were set into motion once that decision was made. With hindsight, we can see how that decision hurt Monica's effectiveness even while it helped lend a sense of urgency that probably kept things moving when they could easily have bogged down.

Some would-be influencers fail in the other direction, focusing so hard on the need to please many stakeholders that they never get the task done. They become known as "politicians," which is not a term of respect. All of their energy goes into doing no more than can be easily accepted by others, which is seen as lacking courage and integrity. Conversely, many otherwise competent organizational members make the kind of mistake that Monica did, shunning the process of selling to, and winning over, key individuals and groups in favor of more and more concentration on the task. In the worst cases, these workaholics dismiss all efforts to sell their ideas and act as if "truth" and good ideas will automatically win out—or should.

Using Her Resources

Not everyone trying to create major changes in organizations goes into the fray with as many resources as Monica did. Not only was she very smart and able to work hard, but she had an unusual number of allies. The powerful president of the company knew and liked her, and she had easy access to him. Her boss was a rising star, had long been a fan of hers, and tried to coach her and worked behind the scenes to help her. She had enjoyed positive exposure to the board of directors and knew someone there who went out of his way to be supportive. Her main opponent was someone that the president and others knew to be difficult. The company's technical guru was helpful to her and generally supportive. Monica did not exactly start from a powerless position. With all this going for her, how could she possibly have ended up as she did?

Because Monica was unschooled in the ways of influence, she mobilized these resources far less effectively than she could have. As if she couldn't quite believe that she was entitled to such good fortune, she held back from drawing on the resources. That leveled the playing field—and almost leveled her too. Instead of doing everything possible to insure that Project Hippocrates happened, and that *she* would be the manager to see it through, she tried to compensate in hard work for what she didn't bother to do in relationship-building and resource mobilization. One consequence of her misjudgment was that she never broke the project into the manageable chunks that would have let Dorr and others comprehend it. As a result, they never got behind it—or her—in the way she needed them to.

Exchange Strategy

Because Monica's relationships with each of the four key players did not lead to mutually satisfying exchanges, it is difficult to discuss specific strategies beyond what has already been described. Instead, we can look at the exchange choices of openness and flexibility again.

Monica probably couldn't dissemble if she wanted to. She has great integrity and a kind of straight-ahead style that doesn't allow for pretense. That is a considerable virtue and advantage, except insofar as it may blind her to options in dealing with tough players such as Parker and Kane. Not that it would be smart for her to get nasty and deceptive with them; we have already shown that she could have been tough without being manipulative, by starting with a sympathetic approach and then going public if necessary. Telling Kane that she would not tolerate his running her down behind her back, but doing it in a way that is in itself above board, would enhance her influence and reputation for fair dealing.

The trick is to counter dirty play with directness and an offer to settle differences face-to-face; if that does not work, talking frankly in public about "legitimate differences," and about your preference to fight openly about the issues rather than make personal attacks is more effective than underground retaliation.

In one sense, Monica's drive got in her own way when the situation called for flexibility. The most vivid example of this was when the decision to purchase digital signal processors outside kept being reopened. Instead of becoming more irritated and feeling betrayed, Monica should have asked herself why an apparently firm decision kept coming up again, and why Dorr allowed it to. If she couldn't immediately determine what was going on, she might have treated it as another puzzle to figure out, and done some exploration.

After the second senior staff meeting at which she encountered so little support, she might have gone to Dorr, for example, and said something like, "The decision to purchase outside keeps popping up and being re-evaluated. What's going on, and how do you want me to play it in relation to what I think is crucial for Project Hippocrates?" That simple question could have opened up all kinds of possibilities, not the least of which would have been a chance to find out where Dorr stood and what he wanted her to do. And asking him or Stella, or both, for advice would have demonstrated her reasonableness and willingness to bend when necessary. Without this information, she could only speculate about what was going on and attribute less than good motives to her bosses.

In the various meetings with Kane and Parker, Monica was receiving many not-very-subtle clues about what really mattered to them; but instead of taking these as data about their concerns, she concluded that they were immovable and she could do nothing but trot out the same "here's-the-rational-reasons-in-a-comprehensive-report" response that already did not work. Like the American who asks a non-English speaker for directions, and when unable to get an answer asks again—in English—s l o w l y and LOUDER, Monica became more and more determined when she was blocked; and she repeated behavior that had already proved unsuccessful. Her keen intelligence should have given her the ability to convert some of that driving energy into a sensitive receptor for the cues her opponents were sending, and change her tack if necessary.

Monica certainly made many successful exchanges with other departments, subordinates, and outside vendors. She traded in currencies of *involvement, importance/centrality, vision, challenge, respect* (for Edison and others), and her own ability to deliver to Stella and Dorr *commitment, dependable task performance,* and *persistence.* But she overrelied on using the currencies with which she was comfortable, and she wasn't flexible or varied enough.

Unrealized Exchanges

With Parker and Kane, for example, Monica could have tried to make exchanges in which she gave *respect or appreciation for past accomplishments* in return for *less nastiness and greater willingness to at least explore their differences.* She might have tried to slow down the task drive with them and work the relationship for a while. Rather than plunge ahead to prove to them with data that they were wrong, she might have gone in one-on-one and explored the sources of their strong attacks, emphasizing that she wanted either to learn from their experience and make it clear that she was not trying to embarrass them personally just because they disagreed.

With Dorr, she had a past relationship that should have made it clear that he was willing to be her confidante, mentor, or sponsor; her willingness to let him continue to advise her not only would have pleased him but also would have taught her valuable lessons. It isn't always easy for a manager who has been guided by a senior manager over a long period of time to continue in the role of eager learner. Monica had a fierce desire to establish her competence and independence, which probably pulled her away from continuing to cultivate Dorr. But he was the president, and her failure to continue close contact cost her dearly in this instance. (Most people on the executive track would kill for the presidential privileges Monica enjoyed. She threw them away unnecessarily, and, as it turned out, unwisely.)

Finally, Monica could have made a useful exchange with Stella. She might have given him the promise of *reliable, controlled behavior,* which he very much wanted from her, in return for either *more public support* or *advice* on how to get his support where it would do her the most good. He was supporting her in private, but she wasn't aware of it; and, therefore, she felt more isolated than she actually was. Even if she had known, she might have been dissatisfied without more obvious gestures from him; but her willingness to revise her own driving behavior would have made the whole subject more amenable to him.

CONCLUSIONS

The nature of any book requires complex arguments to be spelled out in linear fashion, one at a time. Each chapter introduces one set of ideas and gives many examples to illustrate them. But, of necessity, the examples are abbreviated and cannot convey the full complexity of each situation. Although many of the steps in Monica Ashley's leadership of Project Hippocrates were condensed to keep the description less than full-book length, we have tried to include enough to let the reader see how the ideas we laid out in earlier chapters work in a rich, difficult, and complex organizational setting.

If we have done our job, you can see the way the concepts interrelate and interweave with each other to create a dense, but usable, tapestry. Some of Monica Ashley's difficulties were probably unavoidable, since the stakes were large; and other observers and participants agree that Parker and Kane were about as immovable as colleagues get. Dynamite may have been too gentle a prod. The problem, of course, is that the prescriptions we have offered to Monica can no longer be tested on those identical people. But her problems were part of a pattern that affected even sympathetic former allies. Monica's intense belief that, if you have the data on your side, it isn't necessary to spend time with someone you already know, led her to misdiagnose some of the currencies important to Stella and Dorr; as a result, she couldn't hold their support.

Although there are no guarantees that following the model of potential alliances, diagnosis of your own and the ally's world, and finding currencies to exchange will work, we believe that it beats all the alternatives. In the process, you can avoid some of the mistakes that led Monica to experience the ashes of personal defeat while watching her project go on to success.

Monica's experiences illuminated the multifaceted nature of influencing both peers and bosses. All of the book's concepts are relevant to both directions. But we consistently find that after all has been said, organizational members sometimes complain, "This is all great, but my boss is *really* impossible." For those readers, we devote the next chapter to the special problems of dealing with difficult bosses.

10

Becoming a Partner with Your Boss: Influence Without Authority Raised to the Highest Level

I want you to tell me when I'm wrong,
even if it costs you your job!

Advice to a subordinate,
attributed to Samuel Goldwyn

We who are as good as you,
swear to you who are no better than we,
to accept you as our king and sovereign lord,
provided you observe all our liberties and laws;
but if not, not.

Loyalty pledge from the subjects
of the medieval kings of Aragon

A ll of the basic concepts that you need to influence anyone have been spelled out in the previous chapters. But the problems of influencing one's direct supervisor, who controls the paycheck and other valuable currencies, seem too large for many organizational members. When we train managers, for example, in the new, post-heroic leadership model developed in *Managing for Excellence*, a frequent response is, "This sounds great, but how can I be post-heroic when my boss is heroic and expects me to be?"

Even high-level managers assume that they cannot go against their bosses, either from fear or the traditional belief that he who pays the piper gets to call the tune. Yet, the rapidly changing world of work we described in Chapter 1 requires that people at all levels take initiative, really help their bosses—by getting work done and by pushing back, if necessary—and act as genuine partners.

What Do Subordinates Want?

In order to be fully effective as junior partners, the subordinates we have observed want to influence their bosses to do four things:

□ *Improve the scope of the subordinate's job,* encouraging initiative by providing more challenge, responsibility, autonomy, or discretion. "How can I get more meaningful, challenging assignments?" "Can I get my boss to leave me alone to get on with the work?"

□ *Offer higher quality supervision,* helping in the new challenges by giving better, more timely feedback and coaching, but less judgmental criticism. "I want my boss to let me know how I'm doing, not make me guess about it." "How do I get my boss to coach me, so I can improve, rather than just judge me?"

□ *Create a better work relationship,* supporting partnership by open communication, mutual influence, joint problem solving and greater trust. "Can I find a way to talk straight to my boss and have him (or her) level with me?" "I wish we could really work together on tough issues, instead of being cautious with each other." "How can I get my boss to take my opinions seriously?"

□ *Be more effective as a boss,* helping the junior partner carry out changes by obtaining needed resources, influencing upward, negotiating with peers, or planning better. "How can I help my boss obtain the resources we need for our department?" "My boss is not good at managing her boss; can I help?" "My boss is terrible at running meetings, which depresses everyone. How can I teach him those skills?"

Allies and Partners

Because your relationship with your boss is likely to be more ongoing than the sometimes fleeting alliances with peers, we will focus on the partnership aspect of alliances here. A partner is not so permanent a relationship as a relative, but chances are you will see your boss quite frequently over an extended period of time. This partnership may break up or even reverse, with your taking the role of senior partner; but it endures for some time. So how can you get your boss to provide the assignments, supervision, relationship, and skills that are crucial for carrying out the responsibilities of a partner? You will have to become proactive:

□ If you see a problem that needs urgent attention, don't wait for instructions or permission; jump in and try to solve it.

□ Bring problems to your partner's attention promptly, before they grow into bigger problems through lack of attention.

□ Fight hard to prevent your partner from making a mistake that could harm the unit, even if the partner resists listening.

□ Be honest in letting your partner know how both of you are doing.

You will need to think like a partner, not a passive, dependent subordinate:

□ Be loyal to the partnership and assume that the overall benefit of the unit should always be foremost in your considerations; join together to solve the unit's problems.

□ Value the different perspectives and talents each partner brings, even though they may lead to honest disagreements. Use the partner's different skills and experiences as a source of learning and creativity.

□ Be tolerant of your partner's foibles, since no one is perfect, and those who are in business together need to allow one another latitude as long as the unit isn't badly harmed.

□ Assume your partner's basic competence and best motives; if the partner's behavior is disturbing, regard it as merely misguided or uninformed, not stupid nor deliberately evil.

Not all partnerships function so well, as you will recall from the difficulties experienced by Ethan Burke and Brian Woods with their respective partners; but when partnerships work, the listed elements are present. The ground rules demand a lot of each partner, but they also create a powerful combination when both accept the rules and use them to complement and reinforce one another's strengths, as Ethan and Andrew and Brian and Dennis eventually did.

There are, however, a few dark spots on this rosy picture. One set of issues arises when the person who is formally designated the "superior" does not want the "subordinate" to act like a partner, not even like a junior partner. Some bosses want blind obedience, deference, and unquestioning support. They may see the subordinate who starts acting as a partner in a negative light. Challenging the boss, even when he is wrong, may be seen as insubordination. Insisting on raising problems that the boss would prefer to ignore may be seen as disloyalty. Assuming responsibility to solve urgent problems as they arise may be seen as empire-building. Sound familiar? We will address these possible responses later in this chapter.

Before you conclude that your boss is totally intransigent, however, be sure that you have made every reasonable effort to influence his or her behavior. And you need to be certain that *you* aren't causing at least some of the behavior you don't like.

ATTITUDES TOWARD AUTHORITY

Consider the possibility that *you* may be part of the problem! Sometimes the factors that can block productive partnership lie not with the boss but with subordinates. These barriers need to be removed, since they are presumably far more in your control than the attitudes your boss brings to the relationship. We have been advocating a boss–subordinate relationship that is genuinely *interdependent*. The problem is that, broadly speaking, there are three other, less productive ways that subordinates think about anyone who has authority over them: *dependence, counterdependence* and *independence*.

These three attitudes toward authority reflect the individual's experiences with a variety of authority figures, including parents, teachers, coaches, and previous bosses. The attitudes may be deeply ingrained in personality or just generalized from past work experiences, but they shape the individual's interpretations and reactions to the current boss.

Although we will talk about each as "pure" types, everyone probably has some mixture of attitudes toward authority. Because most people, however, have a dominant orientation, we will proceed with a discussion of each mode.

Dependence

Some people never get over their expectation that they will be taken care of by those who have authority over them. They want a strong figure who will know what is best, have the answers, and protect them from harm. When they find that their boss has feet of clay, or is at least human and can make mistakes, they are very disappointed. They cannot imagine themselves taking on the boss, pushing back when they disagree, or even fully sharing responsibility with the boss. "I am little and you are big," is the unspoken assumption in all their dealings with bosses.

Indeed, there are certainly bosses who, by their behavior, encourage that kind of assumption. They refuse to admit mistakes or weaknesses, hide any misgivings or uncertainty, and prefer to dominate by making all important decisions. We wrote *Managing for Excellence* in part to address these heroic assumptions that too many managers make.

However, not everyone who claims to have that kind of boss is accurately describing what the boss wants or does. The subordinate's own dependence makes him or her interpret the boss' actions as dominance-oriented, even when the boss is pleading for the subordinate to take more initiative.

For example, Tom Berger is a brilliant scientist who leads a conglomerate's high-tech division that he founded. Almost all members of his executive team have been with him since the beginning, and all are technical people who are not sure they want managerial responsibilities. They complain all the time that Tom has a big ego, wants to make all the decisions, and thinks he knows everything; and they assert that they couldn't possibly influence him once he takes a position. Despite their complaining, none of them has ever left the company; and it doesn't appear likely that any ever will.

Berger, on the other hand, is constantly upset at their collective lack of initiative. He thinks they are smart but wonders if they have lost their drive, since they so seldom push back on him. He asks for their opinions, but they offer them in such a timid or guarded way that he assumes they are not particularly invested in their views. Thus, he often finds himself making decisions that he doesn't feel especially competent to make, but they keep coming to him for the final word; and, since no one seems to want responsibility, he assumes it.

When all of this was brought to his attention, Berger vowed to push more decisions downward. He began to hold more meetings at which he told his people that, as long as they could agree with each other, he would go along with what they wanted. Jeff Jenkins, the one relative newcomer to the group, found that Berger was as good as his word: When Jenkins pushed him, Berger moved; and he never acted as if he were anything but grateful. Jenkins kept puzzling over why the others couldn't see that.

Five years later, the rest of the staff still maintained that Berger really made all the decisions, even though there was considerable evidence that he indeed had pushed a great deal downward. The group's dependence, ambivalence about really having responsibility, and its long association with a person who was smart and enterprising made it almost impossible for them to see what was right in front of their eyes.

A dependent person doesn't require a long history to learn to interpret even the smallest signs as confirmation of the boss's desires to have everything his or her way. Here is a direct quote from George Curry, a high level manager in a traditional insurance company, about his new boss, the head of administrative and information services:

"Don thinks he's participative, but I'm not sure he is. He believes in problem solving and consensus by the group, but he directs the results, which is fine with me; I like a directive style better. He's not dictatorial; he spends extra time bringing the group to his view. But after all, he's responsible. We're not used to having a say; we're waiting for direction. If people are looking for direction and don't get it, they're unsure what to do. In time, they will gain an understanding of how the boss wants it run. I can hear clearly what Don wants, even though he asks for participation. A raised eyebrow during a discussion is enough to give it away."

George's dependence leaps out at the listener; although Don may not be the perfect participative leader, George's longing to be told what to do, his assumption that everyone else wants the same directive style, and his careful scrutiny of the nonverbal signals Don might be sending suggest that Don's style is more in the eye of the beholder than the beholder could ever believe.

Counterdependence

While there are many organizational members who take a posture of dependence toward all authority figures, many others are just the opposite. Having been disappointed too often by authority figures, they automatically distrust anyone in charge, are on the alert for any move that could conceivably be interpreted as a slight, and will battle at the drop of a leader's hat. They may have learned to keep their resentment under wraps most of the time; but they are never too busy to think up reasons why their boss, and, for that matter, any higher authority in the company, is being stupid.

The willingness of counterdependents to challenge conventional wisdom (or as they might see it, conventional stupidity) can be stimulating, and it can provide needed impetus for their bosses to stay on their toes; but these organizational members can also be difficult to manage. Their first impulse is to assume that anything the boss wants to do has some ulterior, dark motive; thus, they are always on guard and quick to anger. Reaction, rather than action, is their mode. Pity the poor counterdependent's boss who hates to be challenged; the counterdependent can't help but challenge, producing a chain reaction of discomfort and fury from the boss, which thereby confirms the subordinate's worst fears about authority figures.

Put a bunch of counterdependents together and they will spend all their time railing about what assholes the bozos are who run the place. Or, they will be plotting a revolution of some kind, looking for the chance to overthrow the current leader, or, at the least, expose him for his sins. (Academics are often highly counterdependent, which may explain why the average tenure of college presidents and deans has steadily declined.)

When someone is counterdependent, even benevolent leader behavior can be subject to negative interpretation. The fear of being suckered into vulnerability overwhelms the true intent of the boss's behavior.

For example, Gregg Appel was an industrial relations manager at a large manufacturing company. Very skilled at dealing with unions, he was tough and cynical. No top manager at his company was ever good enough in his eyes. When a new general manager became Gregg's boss, Gregg as usual began to test him. The general manager (GM) decided that Gregg was valuable if he could be won over, so he made a special effort to listen to Gregg's ideas and give him extra opportunities to contribute.

A few months later, the GM asked Gregg to give up a minor assignment to take on an important new project. Others would have liked the new project, but the GM made a point of offering it to Gregg at his staff meeting so that Gregg would feel he was getting public recognition. Gregg very reluctantly accepted, then walked out of the meeting muttering to a colleague about being put on the spot and wondering what the GM had up his sleeve. It just never occurred to him that the gift horse was not of the Trojan variety; he was so counterdependent that he saw even a big favor as a trick.

Independence

The third problematic attitude toward authority is *independence*. Those focused on independence are neither hoping for a boss with all the answers nor fighting the boss to see who is bigger or smarter. They just want to be left alone to do their work, make decisions for themselves, and not worry about "politics" or pleasing the boss.

It is relatively easy to manage independents; most managers are thrilled not to have to deal with the passivity of dependents or the resistance of counterdependents, and independents are not afraid of responsibility. But the subordinate who values independence does not really collaborate and join the boss. They are self-starters, but at what they believe is important, not at what the boss or the organization says to do. On some crucial matters, such as strategizing jointly about dealing with higher-ups and others, it is hard to get independents to join.

Furthermore, their initiative usually doesn't extend easily to forming close working relationships with their colleagues. Like Monica Ashley, who had trouble with difficult peers, they would rather go about their own business, forging ahead on the tough task issues.

Although independents thrive on challenging tasks, it is hard for a manager to get them to *fully* share in departmental responsibility, since that requires a kind of joining or merging of interests that would feel too intrusive. Due to the great value they place on autonomy, their manager will not get the benefit of true collaboration—including joint problem solving, providing a sounding board, or even emotional support. But the independent doesn't want to be bothered "about all that other stuff—just let me get on with the work." That definition of work, however, usually does not include the messy interpersonal and political territory that managers must inevitably deal with.

The independent subordinate is, however, far more willing to genuinely assume responsibility than either the dependent or counterdependent subordinate. Dependents wait for instructions, like George Curry, who wanted his boss to be clearer about what he really wanted. Counterdependent subordinates complain bitterly about not having more responsibility, but aren't always so accepting of it, like Gregg Appel, who suspected that his boss had a hidden motive for assigning it. Independents like responsibility, but only reach out to take what is personally or professionally interesting. Given a challenging mandate, the right tools, and sufficient autonomy, however, they will willingly shoulder it.

In none of these three cases, however, are the attitudes of the subordinate conducive to positively influencing the boss. And, if a manager has dealt with many similarly inclined subordinates, he may not realize that it is possible—and preferable—to have a leader–subordinate relationship very different from the way he has learned to cope.

A solid boss–subordinate partnership is *interdependent* with both partners able to teach and learn from each other, take initiative, and assume responsibility. That's the goal we advocate.

When trying to alter your boss' behavior, be sure to look first at your own assumptions about authority. If you can recognize any repeated pattern in your relationships with bosses, test your feelings about your current boss against it. Could it be that your boss is not the paragon of virtue, ogre, or needy mass of emotions you think you see? Are you carrying such strong assumptions about bosses that you are misinterpreting this one's behavior? Are you uncomfortable with interdependence?

Or, at the least, is "the problem" a result of *both* your attitude *and* the boss' behavior? Some caution is in order. This is not to suggest that there aren't some bosses who could do a better job of helping you do your best, but take care not to throw stones that could just as readily be tossed back at you.

What Do Bosses Want, Anyway? And Why Are They so Afraid They Will Get It?

Of course, some managers may want dependent subordinates—or think they do—without realizing the costs of the resultant passivity. A few bosses may want the feistiness of counterdependent subordinates, and more would like the peace and quiet that come with managing independent subordinates. But how many wouldn't really like genuinely interdependent partners? Could any boss *not* want subordinate partners who own the unit's problems, carry out their responsibilities, ask for help when they need it, are loyal enough to work to prevent mistakes rather than letting them slip by as long as someone else's (usually the boss') head will roll, and make sure that important issues are raised at the right time?

Unfortunately, even though most bosses want this kind of response from subordinates, they sometimes fear the very behavior they want. They worry that subordinates who ask for help may become too dependent, weak, and unable to take appropriate initiative to accomplish work on their own. They are afraid that the person who pushes back when he or she thinks the boss is wrong will become insubordinate and refuse to do what the boss has asked, even when the boss is right. Will every request or order turn into a hassle? Will disagreement become disrespect?

Another fear is that subordinates who take initiative will go off half-cocked, without first absorbing the full context of an issue, or become empire-builders, grabbing others' responsibilities and stepping on sensitive toes. Can the subordinate turn into an unguided missile, rather like Monica Ashley did, charging ahead with all good intentions but wreaking havoc that makes the boss look bad?

Maybe most bosses want their subordinates to do the things that good partners do, but yours doesn't? If you have satisfied yourself that it is *your boss* who needs to be influenced, and not *you* who has to change behavior that results from a less than helpful attitude toward authority, then a careful diagnosis is in order. What matters most to your boss? How can you help fulfill those needs/desires/currencies in a way that will get you what you want?

We can probably safely assume that any boss will want the peace of mind that comes with knowing your work is being done well, that you can be trusted to come through and get help when that likelihood is in danger, and that you are "on his or her side," trying to achieve essentially the same goals without undermining the department or being underhanded. If you can't meet these basic requirements, the probability of being influential is undoubtedly low.

But beyond that, there still exist the problems of building a stronger relationship with your boss while exercising the kind of influence you want. Since you will continue dealing with your boss even after you make the specific influence attempt you have in mind, it is as important to strengthen the relationship as it is to win on any particular change you desire. What will it take for you to develop a good boss–partner relationship?

The combination of what subordinates and bosses want, combined with bosses' common fears about strong performance, creates an inescapable conclusion: The challenge for bosses and subordinates is somehow to find ways to *create conditions where the subordinate can be successful.* That is how both parties, and the organization, can get what they need. If the superior–subordinate relationship is working well, then subordinates can do their best work, which helps the superior as well. That just doesn't automatically happen, despite the great payoffs when it does.

No Escape: You Are Responsible for the Relationship with Your Boss

Since your boss may not feel the obligation to improve the relationship, or may not have the skills to do so, you must determine what *you* can do to improve the partnership. Good bosses are made—in part by the way in which the subordinate helps to make them! It is as much the employee's responsibility to help the boss be a good manager as it is the boss' responsibility to manage well and help his or her employees succeed.

There are several reasons why this is so. Even though bosses want subordinates to take initiative, they are naturally more risk-averse than subordinates. Subordinates tend to want challenging, stretching assignments, with considerable autonomy, while bosses are worried about getting the work out and seeing that it is correct. It is harder for the boss to worry about stretching subordinates than for subordinates to be sure they would come through if only given the chance.

Further, the nature of organizations tends to orient people to be more concerned upwards than down. Where there exist an internal hierarchy and external turmoil, each manager will be more concerned with how he or she looks to the boss, and less concerned about how he or she is seen by those below. Thus, insisting that work be done as instructed becomes more likely than giving challenge and latitude to those doing the work.

Finally, research by psychologist David Kipnis has shown that there is a natural tendency for powerful people to attribute the success of their unit to their own contributions more than to the efforts of the less powerful people they supervise. Subordinate talents get minimized, and success is seen as the result of the powerful boss's own efforts. This isn't deliberate, but apparently a natural perceptual trick of the mind. If subordinates don't find a way to prevent this, they feel underappreciated and grow resentful or less invested, which reinforces the powerful manager's beliefs about the locus of success. Therefore, for all the reasons given here, the responsibility for working on building a good partnership with your boss falls on *you*.

Responsibility for a good partnership with the boss seems to be hard for many subordinates to realize or accept. Look at the case of Morgan Brook, the chief director of plays at a university-based theater company.

Morgan was extremely concerned about the newly appointed executive director of the company. Would the new head of the organization allow Morgan more freedom to choose the plays he wanted to direct? Would Morgan be included in important policy discussion or be relegated only to directing plays?

The former executive director, Jim Burton, had been a disaster. Lacking a vision for the theater company, he would neither make decisions nor allow anyone else to. Extremely status conscious, he quickly became defensive when a subordinate made a suggestion or proposed a new idea. A cold and rejecting person, Burton played favorites. He promoted people when there was no full job for them, resulting in an odd organization that no one else could fathom.

When Burton's contract came up for renewal in January, the board split on whether to keep him. Unable to come to a clear decision, the board waffled. Instead of renewing him as director, they gave him a three-year contract as "advising consultant" to the company. He would stay on as acting director until a replacement could be found.

Over the following summer, the new executive director, Mark Nichols, was chosen. Although he would not take over until the next January, he spent a month in the late summer meeting with the board, staff, university officials, and actors. Morgan was among those who talked with Nichols.

Morgan was unsure about whether he wanted to stay on. He hadn't wanted the executive director position, but he was concerned about the company's problems and about whether Nichols could turn the place around. Morgan was especially concerned about whether he would have autonomy in selecting plays to direct. Since theater company–university relations were strained, he was afraid that Nichols would go too far in patching things by redefining the company's mission as one of "serving the university" rather than achieving the national prominence that Morgan dreamt of.

Morgan didn't know whether to tell Nichols that he had put out feelers about other jobs. He decided to use their conversation as an opportunity to sound out Nichols' position on these other concerns and get a sense of Nichols' vision for the company. Morgan found Nichols to be a much better listener than Burton had ever been, and far friendlier. When Morgan did reveal the possibility of his leaving, Nichols was not ruffled. He merely told Morgan that several years earlier he had thought of leaving his previous job, adding, "But I decided that it was better to leave on the upswing, and I hope you consider that too."

Other staff found Nichols to be personable, although they thought he was playing his cards close to his vest. Also, the disturbing rumor began to circulate that Nichols had agreed to Burton's request for office and staff support. Resources were tight and staff resented the idea of Burton capturing precious budget and space. Everyone worried whether Nichols could "stand up to Burton."

Morgan met again with Nichols in the early fall to review plans for plays in the upcoming year. These choices reflected the directions in which Morgan wanted the company to go, and he was relieved that Nichols gave him permission to move ahead without grilling Morgan on all the details as Burton had. Although he was reassured, Morgan still wondered how much autonomy he would actually have. Could he really choose the kinds of challenging plays and guest actors that would build the company's reputation?

Morgan also worried about whether he would be restricted to choosing and staging plays, as was the case under Burton, or whether he would be given a chance to influence broader policy as a member of Nichols' staff. Would Nichols be open to influence, or did he have his own unwavering vision that would dictate direction?

By December, when Nichols arrived, Morgan was leaning toward staying on and seeing what Nichols would do. He wanted to talk to him one more time, but he admitted to a colleague that: "I don't know how direct to be with Mark. I'm afraid that if my view is different from his, it will only antagonize him. I think I'll try to carve out a lot of independence for my area and then see what Mark does in the coming year."

Morgan's oscillation between wanting autonomy and wanting influence have led him to a preoccupation about where Nichols stands that leaves Nichols' needs completely out of the picture, and ignores any responsibility Morgan might have for making the relationship a good one.

Morgan is so worried about *everything* that it never occurs to him that Nichols might be wondering whether he can get support from Burton's former subordinates; whether there is anyone he can count on; whether people will level with him; whether they are going to be reasonably influenceable or locked in to rigid positions before they have even discussed where they might go; and, perhaps, whether he can fill Burton's shoes. At best, Nichols is still trying to figure out the organization and the players; and he needs allies, colleagues, people who will level with him. A golden opportunity is staring at Morgan, but (with apologies to Pirandello and Shakespeare) Morgan and his colleagues are "several characters in search of a boss"; and they can't see that even a boss bleeds sometimes.

Nichols has, in fact, sent some strong signals that he can be talked to directly and welcomes a more collegial relationship with staffers. But Morgan is still responding to Nichols as if he were

Burton; he doesn't quite believe what he sees. He can't conceive of the possibility of *mutual* influence, of dealing with a boss who could have a vision and still be influenced about objectives and ways to achieve them. Since his first message to Nichols was a threat to leave coupled with a desire for autonomy and distance rather than interdependence, Morgan may have caused Nichols to be more cautious than he would otherwise be. If it is not too melodramatic to ask, could this be an "American tragedy" in the making?

By now, it should be clear that we believe that much of the responsibility for getting what you want from your boss rests with you, the partner/subordinate. You must help create the conditions that allow you to be more productive. In that context, the remainder of this chapter will look at what you might do in the four key areas in which subordinates often want improvements in the way they are managed: improved job scope; quality of supervision; improved work relationships; and the boss doing his or her job better. For each of these areas, we will show how to use the new "partnership with your boss" role and the components of exchange to deal with the problems and dilemmas they raise.

Improved Job Scope: Challenge, Autonomy, and So On

In Chapter 9 we described in detail the way in which Monica Ashley fell from grace while heading Project Hippocrates. For some time thereafter, she was frustrated because she no longer got the kinds of central, massively challenging assignments she had been given before. In part, she had to wait long enough to allow the dust to settle; but, to a great extent, her future was in her own hands. She needed to make her boss, Dan Stella, believe that she had learned the lessons he cared about (if indeed she had) and show that she could now do what she had been unable to before: exercise patience along with her persistence and keep disputes from turning into public shoot-outs. She had to demonstrate to him that she was ready for the kind of high-level, high-visibility assignment that she thrived on and wanted.

Utilizing Partnership to Gain Responsibility

The implication of partnership in altering job scope is that the subordinate wants to be able to share in the responsibility for the success of the unit and take on new tasks to help that happen. That requires having challenging and meaningful tasks; even more, it suggests that the subordinate be a partner in deciding how tasks will be allocated. Because the subordinate knows his or her own capacities and interests—and knows what would be a reasonable stretch versus what would pull him or her apart—it is reasonable for the subordinate to participate in the decision process. Asking for a part in the decision is not a request to displace the boss but a means to include in the process the person who has important data that can lead to a more informed decision.

However, as in the case of Monica, the boss may not agree with your assessment of your capacities and readiness, especially if, in his eyes, you have messed up a previous assignment. What do you do then? How can you convince your boss to let you handle more? You will need to learn enough about the boss' concerns to be able to determine exchanges that will address them.

Utilizing Exchange

The key is to initiate some kind of discussion with your boss in which you can listen very hard to his or her concerns about letting you have the kind of responsibility you desire. As long as you keep in mind that the purpose of the conversation is to find out how you can improve your performance, an outcome in which your boss has an interest, too, you need not appear pushy or demanding. Often, if you come across as really wanting help to improve performance and deliver what the boss needs, there is a double benefit: You learn the boss' concerns and therefore the currencies you will have to deliver in, and you relieve the boss of worrying about whether you can take it if he tells you the negative stuff that he has been sitting on all along.

Exploring what you need to know in order to show you are capable of more may be possible by any of the following means:

- □ Saying directly that you would like to change the nature of your assignments
- □ Waiting for a time when the boss is giving you feedback anyway and then raising the issue
- □ Asking the boss for some comments on your strengths and weaknesses as a way in
- □ Initiating a conversation by stating your own views of what you are good at and what you want to work on for improvement, then inviting comment.

Unfortunately, too often in these situations, the subordinate only listens to the boss' concerns, whether stated directly or hinted at, just long enough to begin to argue the boss out of his or her "erroneous" view. The boss says that the subordinate didn't do his homework before a big presentation and, without thinking about it, the subordinate jumps in to say, "Oh, I can explain that . . ." Or, the boss broadly hints at the subordinate's need to control her temper, and the subordinate angrily demands to know, "Who accused me of that? That's ridiculous!" Or, the boss says that it takes a long time to develop the kind of judgment required to perform task X successfully and the subordinate starts reciting a list of what she has accomplished in only a few short months or years—never stopping to first inquire about the areas of complexity, the nature of the judgment needed, the right intermediate assignments, or where current tasks could help.

In the very process of discussing the subordinate's capabilities, the subordinate often proves the boss' worst fears to be true. The lesson here, as in all other organizational situations, is not to ask the question unless you want to hear the answer, and listen even if it makes you uncomfortable.

What could Monica Ashley have done to earn her way back into Dan Stella's confidence? Aside from continuing to do excellent work on the assignments she still had, she could have asked him to explain more fully what he meant when he kept telling her to slow down; or how he viewed the tradeoff between slowing down to avoid arousing public opposition versus possibly missing market opportunities; or why he had concluded that it was never productive to fight in public; or what signals she sent that made him think she was on the verge of a breakdown; and so on. Because they had a good relationship of 10 years' standing, she might even have asked him what he did with his anger and impatience when the old guard made unreasonable and irrational accusations, or how he had changed as he moved up, and what he was doing to make himself a more effective executive.

None of this inquiry would be helpful if she were not ready to listen to the answers; but, by making a genuine effort, she would demonstrate that she is not so emotional that she cannot listen; that she has the interest to learn how to do what he had hinted she should do; that she takes seriously the need to keep learning as she advances; and that she recognizes that the game changes some as one gets nearer the top.

Furthermore, if Monica could admit to Dan that she had been caught up in the heat of the project, as she did to herself in her reflections a year later, that in itself would be a sign of growing maturity that would reassure him. In fact, something like that *has* happened, and Monica is out of the penalty box and once again being asked to take on mainstream, vital projects. Not a bad comeback for someone who had plummeted so far and so visibly!

As in Monica's case, it also can be helpful, once you know your boss' concerns, to propose a small-scale test of the responsibilities that you want, rather than trying to get everything all at once. If you have an idea of how your boss can limit his or her exposure while letting you have more latitude than usual, you have a better chance to get the opportunity to prove yourself.

Changing the Quality of Supervision Your Boss Provides

Using Partnership on the Boss-Subordinate Contract

If your boss is not giving you the kind of helpful supervision you want—doesn't give timely feedback, seldom coaches you in a supportive way, offers no career advice, or points out every error without acknowledging what you've done exceptionally well— the partner–boss concept can be useful. Partnership assumes that each partner needs the other for complementary strengths and knowledge, not that each has to go it alone. Therefore, if one partner is not getting something desired from the other (in this case senior) partner, it is the obligation of the one who wants more feedback or support to work to create the conditions to get it. It is not only the boss who can initiate in this area.

Say, for example, that your boss harshly judges your performance—or never comments on it—when you merely want a bit of coaching. You don't want to be told everything to do, but after a meeting you'd love to get her comments on how you could have better dealt with the cost accountant who seemed so petty, or his reasons for exploding at Sally but ignoring an equally weak contribution from Nora.

If you think of yourself as a partner, you can take the initiative to ask something like this, "Ricardo, I'd like some help on my ability to deal with people who are giving me a hard time. You seem to be good at that, and I'd like to learn from you. Would you be willing to talk about my encounter with Ulrich? I don't feel good about how I responded; I didn't defend the department the way I wanted to. Any thoughts on what I might have done?" As with Monica Ashley and Dan Stella, taking the initiative to admit you want help, asking for something specific that is reasonably fresh, and responding with interest rather than defensiveness, all smooth the way for your boss to give you what you want.

If your boss evades the issue, you don't have to give up. You can ask if the subject makes him uncomfortable, or if there is a better way to capture her insights. You can stress how much better you think you can do for the department if you learn to be more effective at the particular skill in question. You can offer to make an appointment to discuss it if that would be more convenient. One rebuff does not have to end the incipient partnership.

All these steps comprise an attempt to redefine the nature of the traditional boss–subordinate contract. Where the exchange used to be "I'll do what you say if you'll take care of me," it becomes something more like, "I want to perform well, which will be helpful to you, but to do it we both have to take responsibility for helping me learn. I'm willing to do my share; now, will you join me?"

Subordinates thinking about such a direct request for help have two concerns that hold them back: Will I look weak to my boss; or, once I start getting help, will I be able to stop the boss from giving far more than I wanted? Let's look at each of these worries.

But My Boss Hates 90-Pound Weaklings: The Tension Between Admitting the Need to Learn and Wanting to Look Good

What stops many people from trying this method of altering relationships with their bosses is the fear that the bosses will see them as weak, ineffective, confused, or lacking in leadership ability—lacking in the right stuff. Perhaps the boss has said outright that no one should ever admit he has anything to learn; or maybe the subordinate has merely inferred this from the boss' behavior, but the subordinate believes it as gospel. While many bosses still make heroic assumptions that get them into trouble, many subordinates assume that their bosses are so entangled in heroic assumptions that any sign of the subordinate's being merely mortal is the kiss of death.

Certainly there are managers who would react that way. Although the percentage is probably far smaller than cautious subordinates believe and has been steadily decreasing in this era of dwindling emphasis on machismo, there undoubtedly remain managers who still operate on the General Patton/Vince Lombardi-type assumptions that you are never too hurt to play; and you must never show any signs of weakness because that would console your enemies.

Even with such a tough-as-nails boss, it may be possible to ask for help in a way that is in itself strong. You can *demand* to know how you can be an outstanding performer, making your request from a posture of being strong enough to expect tough standards. "I need to know in order to deliver" is not the plea of a wimp. This approach can appeal even to a macho boss and change an attribution of weakness to an impression of strength.

You could also point out to your boss that he or she is *assuming* your request comes from weakness instead of a positive motivation to be more effective. Or, if you can't break the boss' attributions of flaws, you could try to reframe your request in terms of the gritty stuff you want to learn in order to reach your peak capacity. Remind the tough boss that even great athletes need continuous coaching and learning.

With such true believers, however, it may be necessary to keep a stiff upper lip and try to stay in their good graces by anticipating what they want rather than trying to change the relationship. Some bosses are remarkably determined to act against their own self-interests.

Nevertheless, acting as if you already know what your boss wants may lead to worse consequences than risking that your assumption is wrong and testing it. Consider the classic example of "Bob Knowlton," immortalized by social psychologist Alex Bavelas in a disguised business school case study that still grips employees at all levels of organizations.

Bob was a relatively new project head at a high-tech company doing aerospace work. He had worked very successfully on a research project; and he was grateful to his boss, Dr. Jerrold, for appointing him as leader of the special team research project that arose from Bob's discoveries. There were some problems in the project, however, that were getting in the way.

At the end of one day, a brilliant stranger, sent by Jerrold, appeared in Bob's lab. Bob detected how bright the stranger was, but he felt instinctively uncomfortable in his presence. When Bob was informed the next day by Jerrold that the stranger, Simon, was a new and special acquisition, and might be available to work in Bob's group as a "way of getting started," Bob agreed, despite his discomfort, to accept Simon. Jerrold seemed pleased when Bob acknowledged how bright Simon appeared to be, and Bob didn't want to admit that he felt threatened by Simon. Instead, against his judgment, he responded to Jerrold, "I hope he stays; we'd be glad to have him." Jerrold was a nice person, but he was very focused on success; one of his favorite lines was, "The sky is the limit for a man who can produce!" Bob made the assumption that he could not tell Jerrold his true feelings, for fear that Jerrold would think less of him.

When Simon made significant contributions to the team and was publicly recognized for them, Bob felt increasingly uneasy. Instead of asking Jerrold about his plans for Simon, Bob quietly started to make inquiries about other jobs. He hastily accepted a lateral move, notifying Jerrold by letter that he was leaving because of "family health problems," rather than openly admitting his concerns. He didn't stay long enough to learn that Simon was about to be assigned to a new project team; and that Simon was never perceived as a rival to Bob, just an exceptional resource that might be used to help various projects.

For his part, Jerrold was stunned and disturbed to lose Bob, and to lose him without even a face-to-face explanation or farewell. In fact, he was sufficiently upset to ask a professor in an executive program Jerrold was attending what the professor made of this puzzling resignation letter, and the facts were subsequently gathered.

Bob Knowlton's unnecessary departure, we propose, is only one dramatic example of the price paid by subordinates who assume that their bosses will react negatively if the subordinates acknowledge that they do not already know everything there is to know, or have worries about their performance. It is not that there aren't some bosses whose first reaction to such "revelations" would be scornful or punitive, but few could resist a subordinate who insists that better performance is the motive for asking for help, coaching, or development. That is an exchange that offers direct and considerable benefit to both parties.

As we near a new century, most managers surely must realize that continuous learning will become a way of life in organizations; the subordinates who recognize this first and request help to grow are the most likely to be favorably received. They will also achieve the most. General acceptance of the need for growth does not guarantee that your boss isn't a lonely exception, but the risk of failure to try to alter the relationship is, in our view, at least as great as the risk of continuing to try to outguess your boss and thereby stay out of trouble.

"Help Me, but Don't Help the Hell Out of Me"

Sometimes the opposite problem is encountered: The boss is only too ready to help and gets too involved. What could be a valuable resource, since any boss probably knows a thing or two, becomes an enormous burden. Even a gold coin to hang on your neck can become a millstone if it is too large. How can you capture the best of what such a boss has to offer without being obligated to take all the advice and "guidance" that comes your way?

The key, once again, is to show such a boss that too much "help" hurts his or her own interests. Being swamped with more advice than you wanted will reduce the challenge in your job and thus reduce your ownership of the problems and your responsibility for solving them. If your boss rides the bike for you instead of just giving you instructions, support, and a gentle push, you'll soon have to call her every time you want to get anywhere.

Even worse, if you feel stifled by this experience, you might not ask for help the next time you need it, to preserve your latitude. Ask your boss, "Do you mean to push me into avoiding asking for help? If not, if you still want me to use my judgment about when to get you involved in tough issues, then you need to give me breathing room. You don't want me to be tempted to cut you out, do you?"

The same general approach might be used to show your boss that his or her overinvolvement is tempting you to pull back, "I want to be a responsible partner to you; but when you try to take over for me, I start to back away. I don't want to go passive and let you do everything, and I can't believe that's what you want. Do you?" At the least, these kinds of questions ought to prompt a good discussion about what the boss does want, and what you require to be as useful as possible.

Improving the Superior–Subordinate Work Relationship

In the past, when there were problems in the relationship between superiors and subordinates—lack of trust, openness, and mutual ability to work well together—it was assumed that the subordinates would have to modify their style to fit the superior's preferences. That was just the way it was. Further, it was not considered to be legitimate to try to influence the boss; that would be political or presumptuous. Finally, problems in the relationship were not open for discussion; that would be touchy-feely and unbusinesslike. "Grin and bear it" was the rule.

The partnership role needed in current organizations, however, requires more give and take between boss and subordinate, although the subordinate or more junior partner probably still has to adapt more than the superior or senior partner. But the acceptance of direct discussion about problems makes it more possible to find creative win-win solutions instead of the old method in which the winner gloats and the loser licks his wounds—until the next confrontation.

Good relationships work when there is mutual adaptation, since the senior partner can't get the kind of openness and commitment needed in complex and changing organizations without taking into account the needs and wishes of the junior partner. Winning an argument is hardly a victory if the loser starts to withhold vital information, passively accepts everything that the boss says without taking initiative or using judgment, or just goes through the motions on making and carrying out tough decisions. Bosses need the full commitment of subordinates—followed by action—in order to make the unit function properly.

Furthermore, as organizations become more diverse to encompass the range of specialties and talents needed to cope with rapid change and increased complexity, bosses and subordinates must have the capacity to complement each other. In the day of the knowledgable workforce, when no single individual has a monopoly on talent and answers, good subordinateship cannot consist only of constant agreement with the boss. Bosses cannot afford to send in the clones; they must create, value, and work with strong individuals who have the knowledge the boss does not; and both must learn to blend views rather than always fight to win or compromise away strength.

Thus, there are powerful forces pushing everyone in supervisory positions to seek partnerlike responses from those they supervise. Bosses need to be able to say, for example, "I am good at seeing the big picture but not good at attending to crucial detail; thank heavens for Junior Partner's conscientious attention to the little things that mean a lot," rather than look at such a difference and proclaim, "I can't be bothered with that midget-mind who can't see the forest for the trees."

Nevertheless, not all bosses are interested in having the kind of work relationship with subordinates that includes openness, full trust, and expression of all feelings, or collaborative problem solving. What can you do if your boss is not ready for the kind of partnership you want?

Cost-Benefit Analysis

In Chapter 7, we explored the tensions around directly discussing relationship problems. Clearly, some bosses are too uncomfortable to ever do it, as was Rob Farr, the CFO who Maria Cuore found unwilling to discuss relationships. But there are ways to sneak up on a discussion that have a better chance of working, much as Maria learned to do. The operating principle is to use language that is more businesslike than relationshiplike, expressing your views in a less "personal" way.

One set of business concepts involves cost-benefit analysis. Usually used to assess investment or other big decisions, it can be applied to your relationship with your boss. Your analysis could go something like this:

> Boss, can we examine how the way we communicate and make decisions affects our performance? There are many benefits of our current style. You inform me on a "need-to-know" basis; that saves time and lets you preserve important confidences. You ask my opinion when you think I have a contribution to make; that method is efficient and it lets you control communication from the people who work for you. And you can ignore what I say when you don't agree, which saves hassles for you. It also lets me spend more time on my job.
>
> But we should look at the costs, as well. Things are moving so fast you aren't always aware of what I need to know, so sometimes I find myself going in the wrong direction because I don't have the right data. Other times I know things that could help you, since my training and assignments give me different kinds of data; but if you haven't first talked with me, you sail into mined waters with one eye blindfolded. As a result, it's hard for me to be fully invested in our departmental decisions; I could have helped navigate around unnecessary blow-ups, but I was never given the chance.
>
> Are the benefits worth the costs? Would we be more "cost effective" if you and I found a better way to pass information back and forth?

Notice that relationship-oriented phrases, such as "share feelings," "trust," and "openness" are omitted from this approach. Rather, the language is businesslike and hard-headed about the nature of information exchange, which is at least part of what trust and openness are about. There's no guarantee that this way will work, but at least it doesn't wave red flags in the face of a bull-headed boss or one who is made uncomfortable by discussions of relationship issues.

Another approach is to discuss with the boss what it would require to make him or her include you in decisions earlier on, or let you know more about what's going on. By acknowledging that you will have to do something different to get included, you keep the burden on you, which may at least make it easier for the boss to set conditions on you and, in turn, places a burden on him or her to reciprocate if you "shape up."

Stylistic differences and disagreements with your boss can be handled in similar ways. We stand by our assertion that you can tell anyone, even your boss, anything if you speak to his or her interests and concerns and show how he or she will gain from what you propose. "We see the world differently on this one, I know; but you want this decision to be successful/correct/accepted/implemented so I wanted you to have the best data and richest perspective. Let's explore how our combined views could get us to a better decision."

Disagreeing Without Being Insubordinate

It's not so easy, you say? You're right. There are some managers who are highly resistant to any kind of disagreement from subordinates. Even though it is a very costly position to them, since it cuts off news they need to hear, there are some diehards who are still imagining themselves to be ruling by divine right—and to be speaking *ex cathedra* when they take a stand. At least some of these managers are impermeable; but, if you use the kind of approach we advocate, you may be more likely to influence such a tyrant than you ever assumed.

Let's look at an example in which a manager is facing a difficult, and apparently unapproachable, boss. Malcolm Miller, a controller in a large scientific organization, is concerned about how to deal with his new boss. The boss had been a high-ranking military officer before joining the organization. In several early meetings with Malcolm, "the general" had suddenly interrupted Malcolm's attempts to argue a point based on his knowledge of the organization by saying sharply:, "Wait a minute, let's get this straight; I'm the boss and you're the subordinate! I don't want to hear any more about this."

Malcolm was extremely frustrated, but he believed he could not do anything to counter such a hierarchical attitude. We suggested utilizing currencies the boss would value, in language that fits his style. The "pushing back" would need to be done in a manner that established respect for the power of the boss' office, and would need to utilize language that fit the general's experiences, but at the same time demonstrate that it was possible to be respectful while disagreeing. Malcolm's "script" might look something like this:

> Well, General, I would never want to question that you are the boss; and I fully respect your position. I'm a very loyal person, and I want to be sure that you make the right decision. Part of my job as your subordinate is to protect you from snipers, and in this case I think you are about to walk into a trap. Here's why I'm resisting backing off on this one. . . . Of course, if you order me

to stop, I will, since you're in command; but I'm really concerned about making sure you don't get ambushed on this issue.

Indeed, Malcolm later learned that another colleague—one on Malcolm's level—had refused to back down from the General. The peer insisted on taking the matter to the General's boss and the risk paid off. He won the issue and established a more peer-like relationship with the General as well. So the apparently invulnerable lion had already been bearded in his den, and the challenger had survived to fight another day. Malcolm had overestimated his boss' unassailability.

Malcolm has plenty of company in the world. Many people assume the worst about bosses they think they can't influence, and they never find out that more than they imagined was possible. They posit that the boss is a negative, impossible person, and they decrease interaction just when it is most important to stay in touch. After all, not only does staying in touch make it easier to gather information about just what currencies matter to your boss, it also allows you to demonstrate that you are on the boss' side, that you are a true partner who will do everything you can to prevent the boss from making a mistake that would go against his or her own objectives.

It is by no means easy to get that kind of message across, but when you do you can make a friend for life. Strong bosses who prevent anyone from disagreeing with them are their own worst enemies; they try to dominate everyone, but, when they are successful at it, they suffer by cutting themselves off from the kind of information they need. Saving bosses from their own strength is a risky but potentially very rewarding business; the rewards increase when everyone else who deals with that boss is too afraid to test the possibilities.

Helping Your Boss Be More Effective in the Job

One of the areas in which it is most desirable to influence managers is their ability to do their own jobs better so that, ultimately, you can better perform yours. Many people have good relationships with their bosses, are satisfied with the challenge and autonomy they are granted, and receive the supervision they want; but they find they could improve performance if they could influence the way their bosses function in their roles. Nothing is more frustrating than to watch your boss do something poorly that you could help with but not know how to assist in a way that won't be resented.

True Grit: Being a Worthy Partner

As you boss' partner, you have an obligation to be forthcoming when you have needed information. On many issues, you automatically have information that can be useful; for example, you know what impact the boss is having on you and, often, on your peers. You may also know how the boss is seen further down in the organization, in other units, and possibly by some of his or her colleagues and superiors. In addition, you may have some skills that your boss does not, like the organization member mentioned in an earlier chapter who was good at writing memos while his boss was not. Knowledge in any of these areas can be invaluable to a manager.

For example, Catherine Weiler, a personnel manager in a manufacturing division of a high-tech company, knew that her boss, the division general manager, was frustrated about the lack of initiative from his direct reports. Yet he was blind to his own part in creating their passivity. At the meetings he ran, his frequent oscillation between *laissez-faire* openness and impatiently taking charge had led subordinates to believe that he would inevitably do things his way, no matter how many times he requested their ideas. Catherine believed that, if she could get him to see how his own behavior was sending the wrong messages to his people, he would be far more effective and tap the considerable talent of his team.

For Catherine, it was not hard to see interpersonal patterns, because she had considerable experience in observing and facilitating group dynamics. Her boss, who had been trained as an engineer, sensed that he wasn't effective; but he had no idea what to do. When frustrated, he'd jump in and make a decision, which only led to more of the passivity that made him frustrated in the first place.

Catherine, however, held back, because she was concerned about his pride and whether he could take a suggestion about leadership style from a subordinate. They got along well, but she wasn't sure he would welcome feedback on his way of running meetings. After all, he had been doing it for a long time.

Ultimately, Catherine decided that, as his loyal supporter, she should try to be helpful. She knew that her boss was an impatient person, which was part of his problem. A quick thinker, he would get irritated at how long it was taking his team to come to grips with an issue; and he would jump in with a solution. So Catherine decided to approach him in terms of a currency he valued: time.

She asked him if he were satisfied with the way the meetings were going, and he confirmed that he was not. Then she said that she thought she knew a way to speed up decision making, and she would be glad to help do that if she could. She caught his attention. He began to discuss the issues with her, which made it easier for her to say that she thought he inadvertently made the problem worse.

Although he never became an outstanding meeting leader, he did work at breaking his self-defeating pattern, and at encouraging his people to initiate by making clear requests of them, with deadlines, and then waiting for them to take hold. Most important to Catherine, he was grateful to her; and he became willing to plan with her and then review results after meetings. When other team members saw that the general manager was trying, they invested more effort, and the team became somewhat more effective.

Part of what keeps people from doing what Catherine did are the kinds of attitudes toward authority explored earlier. Overdependence leads to the belief that the manager will know everything without needing help from below and a reluctance to risk offending the manager by presuming to offer help. It may also lead to disappointment when the manager turns out to have feet of clay, as will inevitably be the case.

Counterdependence, on the other hand, also does not lead to offers of help, except in a sarcastic or punitive way that is hard for any boss to accept. And the independent subordinates figure that the problem is the boss' and needs no attention from them. Only a subordinate who accepts the idea of genuine interdependence, of full partnership, will be willing to look for supportive ways to help the manager be more effective.

Here's another example of someone who was willing to address the problem of trying to develop her boss without making him feel threatened.

Hilda Scheller's boss, Mel Bender, was a person who just couldn't say no. Remarkably amiable, he didn't want to hurt anyone's feelings, so he would say yes to all requests; then he would not do much to follow up. If he received any opposition from his boss or peers, he would not fight for what he had promised; but, rather, he would come back and sheepishly report that he had lost on that issue.

Hilda was unhappy about this, not only for herself but for the department. She felt that, if she could get Mel to take more responsibility for his commitments and push them at higher levels, she would be making a real contribution to the entire group.

At her next planning meeting with Mel, she laid out a series of suggested action steps; and he, as usual, nodded agreement to everything. Each time, she would say to him, "Do you really feel comfortable fully backing this?" After the fifth time she asked the same question, Mel asked her what this meant.

Hilda replied, "I just want to be sure that I can count on your support, because I've found that you tend not to fight for things you have previously agreed to. For example . . ." (and she proceeded to list several specifics). Mel was surprised, partly because he didn't quite think of himself that way, and partly because he was a bit amazed that Hilda had noticed a tendency that he vaguely worried about.

They discussed the general problem, then worked out specifically what he could support. She scheduled a follow-up meeting to hear how it had gone and to reinforce his commitment. As a result, they began to strategize before other meetings on how Mel could sell his ideas, and he became more effective.

Often, it seems that only great courage would allow you to tell your boss that there is something he or she could do more effectively, or offer to be helpful; if your motive is genuine help and not punishment, if you really care about the effectiveness of your boss, and you do it in the spirit of partnership, then many bosses will be more grateful than resentful. Part of why it is "lonely at the top" is because so few subordinates see that bosses need to learn and grow, too. Good bosses appreciate the person who is willing to be helpful. The exchange of information about performance (or advice on how to improve it), in return for appreciation from the boss (and, with luck, better ability to do your job), is a beneficial exchange that is too seldom executed.

CONCLUSIONS

Without a partnerlike approach, it will be difficult to influence most bosses. If the boss doesn't think you are on his or her side, all the techniques in the world are unlikely to work. You can push much harder—and with better results—when you really are doing it to be helpful and not just to punish the boss for past transgressions and injustices. It isn't the words, "I'm on your side," that matter; it is the inner conviction that you want influence because it will help the boss and the organization, not just you.

It helps not to store your feelings too long before approaching the boss about what you want, since your belief that the boss is making a mistake—of opinion or behavior—tend to build and multiply, then explode at inopportune times and in inappropriate ways. It is exceedingly difficult to focus on the boss' needs, interests, and concerns when you are angry and would like to behead the wearer of the crown.

Influence begins with a clear understanding of the other person's currencies. If your own attitudes toward authority blind you to what your boss values, you will have a hard time figuring out what to exchange for the influence you crave. If you make authority figures into gods who are always right; or devils who can't be; or remote icons who are too removed to be relevant; you are unlikely to notice that they are also struggling to find their own influence. It is in their humanness that the clues to influencing them reside. Unfortunately, despite great skill and good intentions, there are some bosses—and peers, too—who just won't budge. For those difficult people we have reserved our most potent arsenal, and we offer a concluding chapter on playing hardball when nothing else works.

11

When You Can No Longer Catch Flies with Honey: Hardball Strategies for Influence

There is a classic joke about the optimistic young child who is offered only a room filled with horse manure to play in; undaunted, the child enthusiastically digs in, exclaiming, "With all this horse manure, there must be a pony in here somewhere." In general, we have argued that influence is most likely to occur when you make optimistic assumptions about the possibility of finding valued goods to exchange. But, sometimes, circumstances make it impossible to work the positive side of the exchange equation; only negative exchanges—those that raise, or threaten to raise, costs by direct action or withholding of something desirable—have any chance to move the deeply resistant potential ally. The hoped-for pony turns out to be a stubborn, or mean-tempered, mule.

What are the circumstances that require a tougher, less mutually rewarding influence strategy? Sometimes there is just not a match between any positive currency the ally wants and those you can deliver, so that you can't create sufficient obligations. Occasionally, because your efforts on behalf of a potential ally are not perceived as any more than doing your job, the ally doesn't acknowledge that anything is owed to you. At other times, the potential ally is determined not to give in at any price you can readily afford, either because cooperation would be very costly for the ally, or because of the relationship.

It is also possible to find yourself in a position in which you believe your own personal survival in the organization is at stake, and that makes you prepared to sacrifice a great deal even though the potential ally is not making it easy for you. And, finally, every so often you will encounter a genuinely nasty person, boss, or peer, who is playing it dirty and wants to hurt you.

Monica Ashley may have been dealing with just such a person in Ed Kane, who not only ridiculed her task efforts, but also apparently spread false personal rumors in an attempt to discredit her. When that kind of thing happens, it is hard to think about any mutually satisfactory way of responding; self-protection takes over.

It is naïve to think that being nice will always work as a way of influencing someone who wants to harm you; some measure of toughness is required if you want to have a full repertoire of influence strategies. Nevertheless, it is needlessly cynical to believe that unmitigated nastiness and revenge is the only effective response to another's negative behavior.

For our concluding chapter, we offer some ways of being tough while preserving the possibility of eventual collaboration or alliance. You may at some time in your career encounter a person who will force you into retaliatory viciousness, but that is a kind of guerrilla warfare we leave to those who still think that killing for peace is the only way to settle disputes. Instead, we will show you how you can be resolute in pursuing your legitimate interests without turning transactions with difficult people into win–lose contests. There is little point in initiating exchanges in ways that guarantee the creation of a permanent enemy.

ACCENTUATE THE NEGATIVE: RAISE YOUR ALLY'S COSTS

In all of these cases, when you desperately want something from a highly resistant person—because you are convinced that it is needed for the good of the organization, or to insure that you will be around to do your best for the organization—it becomes necessary to find ways to raise the ally's costs unless he or she complies or stops being impossible. Stressing the negative— "here's what will happen/not happen if you don't go along"— has its dangers, which we will explore soon; but it also can have a depersonalized quality that takes some of the sting out of the extra pressure. In effect, you are saying that it would be too bad if the ally missed out on the benefits from compliance, putting the emphasis on the nature of the transaction and not on the person. It isn't the same as saying, "You're a jerk for refusing, and I hate you for it"; rather, it is an attempt to show the recalcitrant ally that there are hidden benefits, even if they result from your *not* taking negative action.

One Step at a Time:
Gradual Cost Escalation

This raise-the-costs strategy requires considerable finesse in its execution and should be used with caution. The basic ground rule is to raise costs, or indicate your intent to raise them, a little at a time. Gradual escalation is the way to minimize negative responses, allow yourself the most room for preserving the relationship, and increase the number of options you have. In the examples that follow, the people who are working hard to acquire influence move doggedly from step to step; we will identify the variety of increasingly intense measures they have devised for upping the ante for their difficult allies.

We will begin with Albert "Sonny" Day, a commercial insurance salesman who was very aware of the process of gradually increasing the costs of noncompliance with the requests he made on behalf of his customers. The nature of Sonny's work involved long-term relationships with his clients. Preserving their business, however, required special services, necessitating the cooperation of many other departments in the company. Sonny constantly had to ask for unusual attention—estimates, reports, calculations, expedited payments—from colleagues in line and staff jobs; but, in a highly compartmentalized company, he didn't always get what was needed to keep large accounts satisfied:

"Often the departments had too narrow a view; they only thought about the convenience of their own area. So, one of my functions was to provide them with the larger perspective of customer need: In the long run, we were all dependent on the clients.

"My initial strategy was to do a lot of asking and requesting; but I always made sure that I followed up. Sometimes it was just a note to that person, or a letter or call to his superior. That was crucial.

"I started soft and then moved hard. If my requests didn't get anywhere, I upped the ante as far as I had to, until I was really playing hardball. For example, I'd say to someone who wasn't giving any help, 'Your lack of response is pissing off my client, and if we don't get a satisfactory answer by tomorrow noon, I will tell the regional manager that *you* are the reason we lost this account!' I hated doing this; there was always a knot in my stomach, but I did what I had to.

"Then, for really tough cases, I used the principle that everyone has an enemy, and I tried to find that person's enemy. I didn't have to raise my voice or make nasty threats; I'd only have to say something like, 'I'm having trouble getting anywhere, so I guess it will be necessary to talk to the insurance association.' But I would only do that kind of thing as a last resort, when my survival was at stake."

Sonny was in a rigidly segmented company that focused less on customer need than on departmental autonomy, which made it hard for him to get reasonable consideration of his requests. In companies more attuned to pleasing customers, any request from a salesperson on behalf of a client would automatically receive a swift response, but Sonny started with a disadvantage. Thus, he was forced into seeking more leverage than he personally preferred, and he eventually changed his employer. But, while he was with this organization, he learned to push harder and harder, as needed.

Notice that, despite his desperation and his willingness to raise costs in stages, Sonny always tried to keep customer need and company benefit at the forefront. He wasn't using tough tactics just for personal gain, although he had a lot to lose in commission income if he couldn't serve his customers. He wasn't asking for anything that was improper or against company interests, however, and he always gave fair warning before doing anything that would make someone look bad.

Increasing costs to a colleague doesn't always involve the direct threat of using customers or higher-ups to gain their cooperation. Even without such measures, it is possible to be tough-minded in order to get what you need. Let's look next at someone on the other side of the service relationship and her interactions with a high-status professional who can't seem to follow established procedures.

Lisa Chan was the director of the word-processing center at a major accounting firm. She supervised all the dictation, typing, and reproduction services for the headquarters office, juggling secretaries, typists, expensive equipment, deadlines, and accounting professionals with efficiency and good humor. One of her greatest challenges was convincing the professional staff to give her sufficient lead time on their work. The nature of the practice meant that there would always be a certain amount of rush work for clients, but much of the work was sufficiently predictable to make planning possible. Her operation was relatively lean, as mandated by the managing partner, and she could not operate efficiently if staff continuously made everything "top priority."

Lisa tried hard to accommodate special requests. She went out of her way for the accountants who were friendly and appreciative when she rushed their work; but there remained those who failed to respond to her repeated requests, reinforced by the managing partner, to observe minimum lead times on work that could be scheduled in advance.

One staff accountant who gave Lisa fits was Hollis Leffing-well. A major user of word-processing services, Hollis never failed to be charming and appreciative when he missed deadlines, which he inevitably did. Lisa had tried a number of ways to get him to plan his work, but his good intentions never translated into compliance with her department's guidelines. If she could get him to do what he was supposed to, it would be far easier to schedule her people, less necessary to put others off, and, by curbing the worst offender, set a good example for other users.

Sure enough, when the next monthly reports were due, Hollis once again missed the deadline. A few hours before the work had to be delivered to the management committee, Hollis appeared with a sheepish grin and said, "Gee, Lisa, I'm sorry I'm late, but I've been working at revising this report to get it right. I'd hate to give lousy information to J.C. and his group. Can you possibly find a way to squeeze this in? I'd really appreciate it."

Lisa seized her chance to provide more resistance to Hollis than she had in the past and increase the costs of his behavior without destroying their relationship. She reached out for the report but did not take it. Instead, she said, "You know, Hollis, this really upsets our priority schedule. We're close to tax season and the rush is on."

Hollis replied, even more sheepishly, "I'm really sorry—I know it would be rough."

Lisa continued, looking at him intensely without returning his smile, "I can accept this now on the condition that your reports and other regular work can be in *on time* from now on. It upsets our schedule too much this way."

Hollis saw that he was defeated. Acquiescing with a chuckle, he said, "You've got me; I'll do it."

Resisting the chance to rub it in, Lisa responded, "Thanks, that will make everyone's life easier." Her impression of Hollis was that he was not the type to pull rank and insist that, as a senior partner, he get special treatment; but, because even milder partners had tried worse, she was careful to preserve her position. She was prepared to fall back on the rules if he began to bully her: She would just put his work in the queue, which would mean it would not get done in time, but she didn't want to resort to this bureaucratically "correct" tactic unless forced to it.

The next time Hollis delivered this kind of work, he was several days ahead of the deadline. She instinctively knew what to do to cement the improvement. With exaggerated gestures, she exclaimed, "Oh, my heart, this is too much of a shock! Hollis on time? I don't think my ticker can take this." As she thought he would, Hollis laughed hard. There were plenty of partners whom she would never have joked with in this way, but Hollis's good-natured style allowed her to reinforce his new behavior in a matching style. He has been conscientiously getting his work in on time ever since.

Going Up? When the Recalcitrant
Colleague Is Your Boss

Lisa escalated costs for Hollis by making it clear she would no longer do favors if he did not make the effort to get routine work in on time; but she had the advantage of being in a service-providing position, giving her a potent cost to invoke. Not always are difficult allies in such a disadvantageous position. When the person who is really difficult to influence is your boss, and he or she is stuck in negative behavior, you have to work hard to find unprovocative ways to escalate the costs.

Consider the experiences of an engineering manager we will call Don Offenbach. Don found on a new job assignment that his boss was inappropriately hounding one of Don's subordinates, and Don was struggling to find a way to get his boss to back off.

"In March, I was approached by Fred Wilson, director of engineering of the eastern division of our parent company, about a job assignment that he hoped would interest me. Fred and I had never worked together, but each knew of the other's characteristics and accomplishments. Everyone with whom I spoke knew Fred as brash, impersonal, demanding, and short-tempered. During our prejob negotiations, Fred (who had been drafted for this division about one year ago) confided to me that corporate had given him approval to do whatever was necessary to turn his division into a productive and efficient organization. He also explained that, when he delved into the personnel statistics, he found that the group (with a few exceptions) had been formed with lower-quartile people. In order to upgrade the group, he immediately acquired a few key upper-quartile employees. Fred was offering me a new position reporting directly to him. His ultimate goal was to return to the northwest division with me as his replacement in the east.

"On my first workday, Fred informed me that there were three "dumb ass" engineering managers working for me that he wanted replaced as soon as possible. Because of my recent arrival, I begged off for 30 days so that I might become familiar with the division. Initially I assumed that Fred was correct in the assessment of the three managers; but as time progressed, one of the three (Ray) appeared to differ from the other two. Ray responded instantly to requests made of him, accepted any task that was put forth, and worked diligently to get good, justifiable solutions. My concerns for the job and the people influenced me to apply more than normal amounts of time observing their work habits and performance. At meetings and in discussions with other organizations it became apparent that Ray had the respect and confidence of everyone on the program with the exception of Fred.

"During lunch with Fred one day, I asked him to explain his reasons for wanting to replace the three. His concerns regarding the other two were understandable, but I pursued his opinions on Ray. Fred considered Ray worthless and felt that all of the problems seemed to originate from Ray's area. His releases were usually late and/or incomplete, he lacked the answers to important questions, and he was continually asking for more people even though the manpower curve for the division was in the reducing mode.

"After expressing himself very vividly, Fred tensely questioned my concerns about Ray. Listening to my observations, Fred became very upset. He ordered me to quit wasting time with Ray and to speed up the process of his replacement.

"My next move was to check on Ray's background. Assessment of Ray's personnel folder revealed no negative statements. Actually it was just the reverse. In his last 14 years of employment in our company he had had a variety of engineering and management assignments. In every case, Ray's capabilities in design, management, and cooperation had been praised. This was later verified when I spoke to his previous supervisors.

"Being thoroughly confused at this point, I decided to confront Ray. In the two-hour discussion that followed, Ray stated that Fred had informed him personally, prior to my arrival, that he was going to be fired. I asked Ray to explain his perception of Fred's reasoning. His story concurred with Fred's. His releases were late, even though he was working 40–50 percent overtime. He repeatedly requested additional personnel, and his area was the major origin of problems. He also had difficulty answering some of Fred's questions related to the early parts of the program. But Ray also pointed out that he had been assigned his area of responsibility only six months prior to Fred's arrival. Since the program was over four years old, the design problems had been created by managers that Ray had replaced. However, each time that he had used this reasoning, Fred had become more and more irate. Ray also expressed the feeling that his workload was considerably greater than in other areas. I closed the discussions with the promise that I would continue to work on the problem and that in my opinion the harassment was unjustified. I informed Ray that I appreciated the fine job that he was doing and requested that he continue his good performance.

"Next I studied the workload in all areas and found evidence confirming Ray's analysis. I then shuffled available manpower so that the capability was more evenly distributed. I explained to Fred that I had no plans to replace Ray and, in fact, thought that he was doing a creditable job. Fred became furious and made it quite clear that Ray's performance could reflect on me.

"In the months that followed, Ray continued to do his tasks well. His group started meeting schedules and eventually eliminated the need for overtime. However, Fred continued his relentless badgering. In meetings and in the group, he continued to try to embarrass Ray, especially when I was present. To my amazement Fred didn't apply the harassment to me. In fact he seemed to give me more and more freedom and responsibility as time went on."

Breathing Room Options

Is there anything Don can do to get Fred to leave Ray alone? He has already tried a rational approach, collecting data from Fred about the problems with Ray, following up with his own investigation, explaining the history of the problems, reorganizing work to improve Ray's performance, then going back to Fred with evidence that Ray really was a solid performer. Since none of this has worked, further escalation will be necessary.

Don has already shown that he has faith in Ray's ability to deliver, since he has continued to support him after Fred pointed out that Don's performance rating could suffer from Ray's efforts. This is a step in the right direction; the willingness to guarantee your own performance to your boss if the boss will let you do it your way is usually enough of a desirable exchange to create the desired latitude. As a next step in raising costs, Don might make this even more explicit than he has, adding that, if Fred continues to harass Ray, Don can no longer guarantee that his unit will deliver the right level of performance.

Part of what Don has to decide is whether Fred can be confronted more directly. Will Fred respect Don for being tough, or will he explode and nail Don in an undesirable way? Don could make alternative attributions: Fred's a bully; Fred can only deal with a subordinate who says yes to everything; or, Fred is impatient and doesn't believe in coddling people, so Don's patience with Ray bugs him. Based on what had transpired so far, Don concluded that Fred was able to take direct pushing back. Fred had subtly communicated his respect for Don despite Don's refusal to follow his directions in regard to Ray. That suggested to Don that Fred's style is probably to keep pushing until he meets a tough response. Toughness is one of Fred's currencies. And Fred wants Don to succeed so that he can return to the Northwest and leave the eastern division in good hands, making confidence in Don's judgment another important currency. These currencies were apparently more important to Fred than data about Ray's performance.

Finally, Don chose to escalate, with words to the effect of, "Look Fred, you had enough faith in me to bring me on board to help you accomplish the turnaround. I've been getting results, and I want to continue doing that, but you're making it hard for me. We've talked about Ray lots of times. I don't think I can convince you to appreciate him. But, dammit, he works for me and I'm responsible for him. I am absolutely convinced that he can do the job, and he's doing it. If you won't get off his back, it could really screw things up. From now on, if you don't like what he does, talk to me, not him! If you don't agree to lay off him, I can't guarantee that I'll be able to continue our successes. If you want to run my area your way, that's okay, but then don't expect me to be able to deliver. So what do you want, to keep harassing Ray, or to let me do the job well, using my best judgment?" Fred sputtered, then agreed.

This kind of pushing back used several forms of negative currencies to create the space that Don wanted. It stressed performance as the most important outcome, and made it clear to Fred that his behavior would prevent the performance he definitely wanted. It acknowledged Fred as the boss, but reminded him that, in a hierarchy, Don has the legitimate "right" to manage and judge his direct reports; continuously violating this would undermine Don's ability to manage successfully. If Fred continues to interfere, he will be responsible for results that may be poorer than those he was already getting. And, by referencing his successful track record and the confidence that Fred had shown in him on other matters, Don implicitly threatened the loss of something valuable. There were, thus, several negative costs Fred could avoid if he would back off Ray, and he did. Furthermore, Don used a tough style of interaction that reflected Fred's own behavior, adding valuable currency that reinforced Don's position in the exchange.

The Ultimate Escalation: Betting Your Job

Don never got to the point of threatening to quit if Fred refused to stop harassing Ray, but that would have been the ultimate weapon if Fred hadn't come around. The only thing worse would have been to go back to the northwest division and disparage Fred, but that would not have altered Fred's behavior and would be a form of gratuitous revenge that we don't condone. The person who cuts a fellow employee down behind his back risks ruining his own reputation more than the reputation of the person targeted for revenge.

There are times, however, when all other attempts to influence an important ally, especially your boss, leave no choice but to put your job on the line. Certain issues are too important to allow to die, either because you are convinced that the boss is about to make a giant mistake, you feel unjustly treated, or you have decided that the job is not worth having if your boss continues certain behaviors.

If all else fails, and you consider the issue important enough to take considerable risk, then the last resort is to make an offer, based on your sound diagnosis of the boss' situation, (you hope) your boss "cannot refuse." You do this, of course, only when the possibility of being fired as a result is no more painful than continuing as is. Chris Hammond, for example, discussed in Chapter 5, used this strategy in dealing with the boss who did not want to give her credit for her sales efforts. She pulled out all the stops, threatening to leave and take with her sales that her boss needed to make his quota, and burying them so that he would miss his goals. This is not an everyday exchange strategy and could easily backfire, but it is occasionally useful. It is an attempt to preserve a partnership that would otherwise explode, and preservation may be preferred by the boss who realizes the alternative.

In another documented situation, Donna Dubinsky of Apple Computer decided to throw down the gauntlet to her boss' boss, Bill Campbell (and in turn to President John Sculley), when she was sick of having to defend her department's distribution strategy. Donna felt under siege from other areas that had proposed (with the support of company founder Steven Jobs) a change to a just-in-time inventory system that she was certain was inappropriate for Apple's business. Finally deciding that she would resign if she were not allowed to examine her department's strategy without the interference of a task force, she told Campbell that, if he didn't agree to her terms, she would leave Apple. Since she had been doing an excellent job and was considered extremely promising, Campbell and Sculley agreed.

Again, this was a high-risk act on Donna's part. She genuinely was not sure that her ultimatum would work, but she had tried everything else she knew to do. That does not mean that she had no other strategic choices—indeed, she was in that uncomfortable position because she had not reacted positively or actively to questions raised earlier about inventory—but the ultimatum had its intended effect. It showed that she was very serious about finally being ready to do the requisite analysis, and willing to put her job on the line for her beliefs.

Donna's strong track record made the outcome a fairly safe bet, and the relative openness of the Apple culture helped, but she did not know at the time what her chances were. The level of her desperation was such that she had openly challenged Sculley about other issues at an off-site training meeting the weekend before, but she did not realize that her outburst at him had impressed him with her integrity. Publicly challenging your company president is not usually a preferred strategy, as Monica Ashley discovered, but it is not always automatic suicide either.

Let's look next at the experience of Edward High, head of the strategic planning office at WWM Corporation, a large, progressive company.

High had moved into the strategic job from a line job three years previously and was increasingly frustrated at his lack of impact on the CEO, Martin Wagner, and in turn, his difficulties in getting the company to take help from the planning office. He finally decided that he would go for broke. He wrote an angry memo to Wagner in preparation for an upcoming meeting, appealing to Wagner's pride in his leadership skills and desire to be effective. But High was frustrated enough that he was prepared to be fired. As you read the memo (Figure 11–1), make an assessment of the likely response from Wagner, the CEO.

Figure 11-1

HIGH TO WAGNER MEMO

WWM CORP.   INTERNAL MEMO   (Personal & Confidential)

To: Martin Wagner
From: Edward High, Strategic Planning Office
August 15, 19XX

Martin, three years ago my boss told me I was crazy to
accept this job, that I would give up in frustration
within two years. My only chance for success, he said,
was to somehow get you to spend time thinking
strategically.

Another piece of advice I received was that, to stay in
a strategic planning job more than four years meant you
had been co-opted by the chief executive. After a time
you lose your objectivity; a fresh approach is
periodically required. Conversely, if you maintain
your objectivity, you run the risk of being so prickly
that the chief executive wants you out.

I have been in my job three years. I am frustrated. I am
now so prickly that after you read this you will
probably throw me out.

I perceive WWM Corp. to be adrift—the base gradually
eroding and senior management lacking a sense of
urgency to fix it. The single driving principle
necessary is lost in a large gray area. I felt I needed
to more precisely define the problem I perceived.

I will attempt to write down for you what I believe our
problem to be. The problem has two parts: style and
substance.

Problem: WWM has no credible plan to be successful over
         the long term.

There are problems of "substance" and "style." I will
discuss "substance" with you and Jim when we have our
next strategy session on September 8th. The "style,"
since it is sensitive, emotional, and subjective, I
will write privately to you here, rather than discuss
in a more public forum.

Figure 11-1 *(Continued)*

The problems with "substance" are:

    The base business
    The growth business
    The nonstrategic, non-end user business
    Results

As I mentioned, we will discuss these problems, and what the strategic planning office thinks you should do about them, on September 8.
"Style" problems include:

    Leadership
    The leader
    Organization
    People
    Central theme

I believe "The leader" and "Leadership" to be the most important problems and the ones that trouble me the most, so I'll focus on those two issues.

Leadership

The Executive Committee (EC) doesn't "do" work. They identify a problem and delegate it down. They seem to take responsibility for very little. Their job is done if they delegate. The EC doesn't use our Total Excellence (TE) techniques. When was the last time it used the problem-solving technique? The last EC meeting was a disaster. This style becomes known throughout the building. It puts TE in danger of becoming something the top tells the middle to do to the bottom. If you, as a group, don't find it useful, kill it. Don't spend large sums on something that isn't useful. If it is useful, use it and publicize its use.

The EC doesn't focus on the major issues in the business. The strategic planning office did an analysis some months ago that attempted to correlate the EC's agenda with the strategic issues in the business. There was not a high degree of correlation.

The EC fosters submission of unrealistic plans. I don't believe that any member of the EC has the least bit of confidence in the 1985 revenue plan submission. Yet you

Figure 11-1 *(Continued)*

accept it. There was no <u>strong</u> direction to redo the
plan, and take action to <u>bring</u> expenses in line with
likely real revenue growth. No one believes the C
subsidiary submission. Yet you accept it—and worry
about the results later. The risk/reward equation is
out of balance in WWM. C subsidiary and F subsidiary are
major embarrassments. No one has lost their job, been
demoted, etc. That example repeats over and over. The
EC does not have a broad business background. There is
no technical expertise on the EC. It is widely accepted
that the failure of the Northern Lights project was a
marketing failure. Where is the marketing voice on the
EC? Which brings me to

Leader

We are in many of the world's most competitive
businesses. I believe that you understand, very
clearly, that the business is in trouble. I perceive
that you are "frozen at the switch," however. You
understand the very tough actions that need to be taken,
yet you're not "combat tough" enough to take them.

You have delegated too much to the vice-chairman and
SBUs; yet you can't, or won't, take back the reins. You
seem to have delegated the responsibility for strategic
decisions to the heads of worldwide manufacturing and
the SBUs, even if those decisions cross SBUs and
sectors. The session you had with your major staff heads
they found exhilarating, until the end when you said, in
effect, "At the end of the day you staff people can go
home and forget about it; the SBU head is charged with
resolving those issues." They were devastated. What
about you and the vice-chairman? You know that I don't
believe in decentralization in time of crisis, but there
is a difference between decentralization and
abdication.

If you are wedded to decentralization, I'll give you my
thoughts on the role of the CEO in a decentralized
company and I'll grade your performance.

Role	Grade
1. Resolve cross-SBU issues	Below average
2. Validate SBU strategies	Very poor

Figure 11-1 *(Continued)*

3. New initiatives   Below average
4. Social responsibility   Outstanding
5. Human resource development: Average
   source, selection, development,
   motivation

In the past, when you have taken charge, you've made things happen. For example, Affirmative Action. You took personal charge—drove the issue—progress was swift. Again in Total Excellence, you drove it, put your credibility behind it—it moved forward rapidly.

You should be doing the same with our business problems. For example, the Products X & Y. You should be spending time in Minneapolis and Boston understanding the strategies, the direction, the competitive edge, pushing resolutions. You're getting too far from the business. I was dismayed when you asked at the EC meeting, when the name "Mykonos" was referenced, "Who is Mykonos?" The fact that Mykonos was formed by two of our research department's most respected people, that they have capitalized on one of our more significant strategic errors, should have been enough to fix them in your mind very clearly, had you been as close to the strategic issues of the business as I believe you should be. Whether SBU strategies make sense should be a key concern of yours, not merely delegated to manufacturing and SBUs.

The staff at corporate headquarters has a difficult time helping you. In addition to demonstrating your antipathy to staff, I don't believe you know how to use staff. Properly used, they can help serve as senior management's eyes and ears. Given your management style, they are caught in a cycle that is increasingly destructive to their proper functioning, to wit: Staff attempts to get the information it needs to keep informed and offer insight to management; the line complains: We are usurping their prerogatives; We are meddling; We are prying; to you, in turn, We are shut out; We don't provide the help we are capable of providing; We are regarded as overhead and not very effective. End result: Staff is frustrated and management is less effective and less informed than it should be.

Figure 11-1 *(Continued)*

It seems to be against your nature to spend a lot of time on strategic issues. You are very good at it when you do it. You don't spend enough time with the EC—on-site, off-site, wherever—on the things that will be important to us in the future. If you do, you certainly don't involve the officer for strategic planning. We worked hard on the environment questions that will be important in the future. They received polite attention and no further interest. The same was true of 1993. We got a lot more interest from middle management than from the EC.

Finally, I believe you would be more effective, and of more value to WWM Corp., if you concentrated more time on WWM problems, and less on outside activities. Our next few years are crucial—if not to our survival, certainly to our success. WWM needs 100 percent of your time on its problems.

People

Our talent base is eroding, our infrastructure diminishing. (During one particularly dull meeting last week, I wrote down the names of 20 people in the mid- and upper-middle management ranks who recently left us and who I regard as losses. It was not a very comprehensive list.) Our senior ranks are thin, e.g., the replacements for almost all of us are a problem. Jack Welch (General Electric) once mentioned that he spent 70 percent of his time on people development. How much do you spend?

The morale and pride of the employees currently at WWM is an issue and you are certainly familiar with that. The effort we are mounting to counteract the issue is not clear.

Finally, under People, I will discuss my own role. I feel less a part of senior management than I have in years. The OSP's advice seems no longer to be sought. You recently said that you value my experience in the business, yet you almost never take advantage of it. In over a year now, the President has not asked for my advice. I have no problems with him. He is bright, ethical, and competent. He just seems secure enough in his own strategic instincts that he doesn't perceive a need for me. Get me out of here?

Figure 11-1 (Continued)

I have attempted to describe half of our problem: the
management style that contributes to our lack of a
credible plan for success.

I have gone on long enough. Obviously, I am available to
discuss these issues with you. I regard them as vital to
our, in your words, "becoming the kind of company we
need to be."

Also, we'll see you on September 8 to review the
"Substance" problems.

Ed

When High arrived at Wagner's office, he was half expecting
to be thrown out. Instead, Wagner said, "This memo really made
me angry. You know why? Because it's at least half true . . . Let's
talk about it." At the end of the conversation, Wagner offered
High a promotion to one of the top jobs in the company, which
High accepted.

Several years later, at High's retirement dinner, Wagner said,
"Ed wrote me the toughest letter I've ever gotten. I sure hope it's
the toughest he's ever written! But he has since told me that he
admires me, because I've made a lot of changes in how I do things
as a result. At WWM, we need to be able to shoot straight with
each other, and we'll miss Ed's willingness to do that. Thanks, Ed."

Was High a genius or a kamikaze pilot? He obviously had
some sense that Wagner could be confronted, or he might have
censored his attack a bit. The anger that comes through in his
memo may have unnecessarily increased the risk that Wagner
would miss the content and only get mad. Although High got an
important promotion as a result, he did not get chosen to be president before he retired. Yet, whatever else Wagner felt, he appreciated that someone who worked for him was unafraid enough to
push him hard on things he cared about. The curse of the powerful is that many do not talk straight to them, so the one who does
may vault to the forefront—or be shot for delivering the message.

It isn't always necessary to take extreme measures to push
back on your boss, and sometimes the inability to achieve influence may reflect either that you have a bad idea or are using
inappropriate influence techniques. For example: The *Boston
Business Journal* reported in January 1989, the sad tale of Larry
Tseung, who worked for Digital Equipment as a software services
consultant. He was ordered three times to give up an idea for

computers-in-conference that he insisted on pursuing. After the fourth time, he was forced to resign. When Tseung started his own company using the idea, Digital claimed that the concept was restricted by their employment contract and threatened to sue. Tseung, following an ancient Chinese tradition developed to assure that the Emperor would read your appeal, sent Ken Olsen, Digital's president, a letter written with Tseung's *own blood*, in which he appealed for permission to proceed with an idea that Digital hadn't wanted anyway. There is a good chance that this may not have been a currency that Olsen valued.

How much risk to take depends on your own capacity to live with the worst consequences, and how long term a view you want to adopt. It is undeniably true that in the long run we are all dead, so ignoring the short term is foolish; but it is equally true that acting only in the short term while pretending that there is no long run is a good way to get bumped off. Judgment is needed.

INTO EVERY LIFE SOME RAIN MUST FALL: ROTTEN APPLES AND HARDBALL

In most of the examples in this book, the potential allies or partners have been difficult but not malevolent. Although it is far less likely to happen than most people assume, every so often you will encounter a genuinely rotten colleague. This calls for a different set of escalation tactics for self-protection, assuming that you are certain that the problem is totally in the other person, and not a result of something you have done, or are perceived to have done. Monica Ashley may have bumped up against such a person in Ed Kane.

We will take as an example the sad experience of Rudy Martinez. A young lawyer aspiring to become a partner in the corporate law department of a major law firm, he was innocently chatting at lunch one day with Walt Oliver, a more recent member of the department. Walt began to complain about their boss, Herb Lewis, the department head and one of three senior partners in the group. Herb had been a star in his earlier years, with a reputation for creative thinking. But Walt was unhappy with the *laissez-faire* leadership style Herb had adopted. He complained, "We are like a ship stopped dead in the water. There's no direction. Not only that, but he blocks anybody else from taking initiative."

Rudy realized that Walt was reacting to a staff meeting a few days earlier of all 10 members in the corporate department. Walt had been asked to study the feasibility of the department's having a more focused thrust, and, as a result, he had strongly recommended that the department should specialize in mergers and acquisitions. When Walt finished, Herb leaned back in his chair and said, "Well, I don't know . . . I believe in adhocracy, letting a thousand flowers bloom. I think each of us should do our own thing." That seemed to kill the interest of the group; all the energy went out of the room.

Rudy agreed with Walt's evaluation of Herb: a nice guy but a black hole for ideas. Not only didn't he provide any direction, but, if anybody else took initiative, Herb seemed to sabotage it.

Normally Rudy wouldn't make waves, but he was startled at how strongly Walt felt about this issue. Walt had reason to be upset, but Rudy had always perceived Walt as too much of a politician to take on the boss openly. Because Rudy was pleased to learn that Walt had feelings similar to his, he agreed that Herb's style was hurting the department.

"Let's all three of us go out to lunch," Walt suggested, "and confront Herb on all this." Rudy hesitated, but Walt seemed determined, and said he would make the arrangements.

When Rudy arrived for the lunch meeting, Walt and Herb were already there. After they ordered, Herb opened by saying, "Rudy, Walt has been telling me that you have trouble with my leadership style. What's your problem?"

Stunned, Rudy mumbled that there must have been some kind of misunderstanding, praised Herb's brilliance, quickly thought of a tiny issue that he could mention so that he wouldn't appear to be lying, then made small talk through lunch and left as soon as he could. He subsequently learned that Walt was not above similar tactics with all his colleagues, and had frequently tried to sabotage other peers with Herb.

What could Rudy have done, at the time or afterwards? It is easy to say that Rudy should have somehow known about Walt's reputation, but, even with inquiry, he might not have found out. And it is likely that, at some time in anyone's career, a dirty player may spring a nasty surprise. Therefore, it is not realistic to suggest that Rudy could have avoided all possibilities. No one can guarantee a total lack of unpleasant surprises, and it is tiring to live in an organization always on its guard, so let's accept that some such events—hopefully infrequent—are part of life.

The Sunshine Law

One of the best tactics for dealing with anyone who tries to sabotage is to get as much as possible out in the open. Dirty players count on being able to work behind the scenes and under cover, relying on others' reluctance to be explicit when burned. But, since most nastiness makes the initiator look shabby when it is seen in broad daylight, efforts to get everything out in the open are important.

Had Rudy been less stunned, or less afraid of unpleasantness, he might have looked right at Herb and said, "I am really shocked that Walt has told you that I'm the one with concerns. When we talked, he expressed a lot of opinions, too. I don't see how we can go further until we get this cleared up. Walt, are you going to be open about what we discussed? I thought we were going to be helpful to Herb; if this is an attempt to make me look like a troublemaker, I won't play. I want us to have a strong division, not make each other look bad."

Of course, we have the benefit of time and distance; but, since what we suggest Rudy should have said is merely what he was thinking all along, more or less, it is not completely the result of hindsight.

Instead of being embarrassed in front of his boss, Rudy could have used the opportunity to show his desire to be helpful even while making Walt's game visible. Although it is hard to formulate a perfect comeback when someone unexpectedly zings you, it isn't necessary to get it just right. The simple principle is, if you genuinely were trying to act for the organization's good, say so; and be open about your reaction to the surprise attack (insofar as it isn't just pure desire to jump up and wring the colleague's neck).

Maybe all Rudy could have mustered would have been an exclamation, "I'm shocked!! I thought we were in this together. What's going on, Walt?" That would have been enough to get started in a way that didn't leave Rudy totally exposed. If Walt then denied everything, Rudy could explain to Herb that he was misled, but that he wants to help the boss be most effective; and, if necessary, he'll do that alone.

None of this works if Rudy was trying to do someone else in, or nail his boss, but if he *were* genuinely concerned with the future of the division (which indeed he was), then saying so need not be excruciating. The Walts of the world are so busy conniving that it never occurs to them someone else might actually want to do the right thing, which is their blind, vulnerable spot. They don't realize how slimy they would look if their victim were to speak up and talk straight. It is even possible that Walt doesn't see himself as nasty, but rather has another explanation for what he did. The effect of his behavior could be very different from his intentions; raising the question forthrightly and without attacking allows the apparently malicious person to reveal different intentions, should there have been any, and learn the consequences of how he or she acted.

Saving All My Love for You: The Calculated Confrontation

Another approach is to take an early exit, as Rudy did, collect yourself so that you are sure of what you want to do, then strongly confront the colleague. This can be done with cool anger in front of witnesses, or a controlled explosion in private. As experienced negotiators will advise, it is probably a mistake to *really* lose your temper in an organization, but allowing yourself to express anger you genuinely feel (*not* faking it!) can be a useful tactic if saved for such situations. Controlled anger that is focused with laserlike intensity, or a bit of screaming, can make it harder for the manipulator to be sure of what you will do in the future, which then serves as a buffer against future surprise attacks.

One of the authors found that this worked with a colleague who was, as usual, trying to manipulate and bully him (in this case about office space), by looking right at the colleague and saying in a loud voice, "Don't mess with me, Harry, I teach negotiations!" Harry backed off, and was much nicer from then on.

Spread a Little Sunshine

Finally, if direct confrontation is not possible, perhaps all you can do is spread the tale around the organization so that others are warned about the person. As we have noted, however, this has its own dangers. The nasty person probably won't be thrilled with you when word gets back, and may be inspired to try for greater damage in return. Since you probably don't have the full revenge and bad temper arsenal he or she has, it's not a great idea to get into a contest of escalating swinishness. (You were nice enough to buy this book, which gives you the benefit of the doubt as to your inherent good nature.)

Secondly, when neutral organization members see you retaliating by talking about the person, they may see only your retaliation and assume that you are the dirty player, talking behind the other's back. Like the basketball player who gets a foul called for swinging back after his opponent unobtrusively elbowed him, there may never be a chance for true justice; and you don't even get the benefit of instant replay. Nevertheless, since reputation is so important in organizational life (as we argued in detail in previous chapters), as a last resort you can try to be certain that the person who has nailed you gets the headlines he or she so richly deserves. Just don't abuse the tactic, and remember that some weapons are only for defense.

In general, all tough tactics such as those we have described are far more potent when you only *threaten* to use them. Once launched, the results may be unpredictable and uncontrollable. It is thus better to warn the Walts of the world of what you will do if they keep on playing dirty pool, in a convincing way, than to actually retaliate. Just be sure you are prepared to act on your threat if forced to.

No Bullet-Proof Vests: The Risks of Escalation

We have already hinted at some of the personal dangers of using hard-nosed strategies that escalate the costs to your potential—or unworthy—ally. Your reputation can suffer, causing others to view you as an initiating Walt, not a wronged Rudy. You may be viewed as concerned about self rather than organizational effectiveness. Or, in some settings, your complaints may be perceived as "crying wolf" about what people in your organization see as the natural rough-and-tumble of dedicated people with different views of what would be good for the organization.

A further danger is that a focus on how to escalate costs for those you want to influence will make it too easy to stereotype any resistance, and lure you into attributing negative motives just when you should be thinking about understanding the currencies of a potential ally. The alliance orientation should be preserved as long as possible, until the occasional villain forces you to abandon it, rather than dumped as soon as the potential ally *appears* to be playing rough. There is greater danger in failing to search for the goals and interests of allies than from failing to keep your guard up.

Yes, there are rotten apples, but we have seen plenty of situations where each side was certain that their own motives were pure while the other's were poisonous, and neither could get past these biases. For example, a group of hospital administrators we consulted with behaved viciously to each other for years, each convinced that "everyone else but me" was willing to trample his own mother to harm the others. Yet each one, without exception, told us that he hated the way they treated one another, but felt he had to strike first because the others were so ready to attack. When this was revealed, they breathed a collective sigh of relief and began to discover more virtues in one another than any had dreamt of! Think of their experience before leaping to negative conclusions about someone who won't behave as you'd like.

When an escalation strategy does prove necessary, however, another risk is that you will find it highly stressful. If you do not like conflict and tension, it can put an ever-tightening knot in your stomach, as it did for Sonny Day, the insurance agent who felt trapped into raising the stakes for associates to get their cooperation.

The reverse is also true, however. Some people can't bring themselves to carry out what they know they should do, and they suffer from the bottled anger. A group of manufacturing managers at a high tech company talked about how badly they were treated by others in the organization, and how frustrating it was constantly to bend themselves out of shape because their organization pounded them with the notion of being "good team players." As one of them put it, "I've got a wall full of plaques for being a good guy; just once I'd like to throw one when I'm being taken advantage of but implored to 'do it for the glory of the company.'" This manager is a candidate for an ulcer.

I Have Seen the Future and It Could Be Bleak: Organizational Dangers of Using Exchange Strategies

Self-Interest Runs Riot

Creating an organizational climate in which members are skilled users of tough-minded exchange strategies raises a number of risks for the organization as well. Done without real concern for creating mutual advantage, and without commitment to the overall good of the organization, setting everyone loose to wheel and deal can create a monster of self-interest. Where everyone thinks only of his or her own success, and doesn't work to find and satisfy the interests of other members, cynicism and mistrust grow, making it increasingly difficult for anyone to take initiative on behalf of the organization and ever gain cooperation.

Instead of increasing numbers of close, trusting relationships where considerable latitude is extended to colleagues and everyone can be generous in helping one another before they know what's in it for them, relationships are fraught with mistrust and everyone demands cash on the barrel head. Some readers may operate in such organizations; they are neither effective nor pleasant places to work.

An equally unattractive risk variation arises when members are focused only on the acquisition of personal power, to accumulate favors and resources only to be able to lord it over the less fortunate, rather than building credit so that they can be more effective in accomplishing organizational ends. Recent descriptions of bureaucrats in the Soviet Union and other eastern European countries reveal enormous resistance to needed economic reforms because personal privileges would be challenged. Dare we suggest that in the corridors of power in Washington—and in some companies that allegedly follow the profit motive—similar preoccupation with personal advantage rears its head?

There is a big difference between organizations in which people are only interested in "what's in it for me," and those in which that question is only asked in the context of numerous opportunities to help others accomplish organizational ends. And remember, we have shown that self-interest can include currencies such as doing what's right, creating excellence, realizing the organization's vision, doing challenging work, and so on. Pure personal self-interest is not enough to forge a successful organization, any more than would be the assumption that everyone will work hard just for the glory of good old Profit, Inc.

Power Acquisition for Its Own Sake

Recall the engineering manager, mentioned in a previous chapter, who became so enamored of the exchange process that he irritated his close colleagues with his constant deal making. Organizations that encourage turning even routine transactions into negotiations for their own sake run the risk of turning participants off. It is hard to sustain respect for inveterate wheeler and dealers, because they seem to revel more in making a deal than in its merits.

Lyndon Johnson, for example, who was a master trader of obligations, lost respect and gained many opponents who resented the way he gloated at his victories and seemed to pursue winning for its own sake. An organization that focuses too hard on the *means* rather than the *ends* of influence can produce needless cynicism and resentment. These tactics *reduce* power, since mistrust blocks willingness to cooperate when it isn't absolutely necessary.

The Potential of the High-Initiative, High-Influence Organization

Nevertheless, the dramatic forces of organizational change we described in Chapter 1 won't go away any time soon; and the needs for organizational members at all levels to take initiative, seek responsibility, and find ways to gain the cooperation of colleagues and managers can only increase. When everyone is skilled in the forming of alliances and in creating exchanges where they can acquire influence by helping others achieve their goals, organizations can be fast, flexible, focused, and fit to their environments. They can manage to be agile despite their size, because the talented people in them know how to do what is needed to create results:

- □ Pay attention to what is really important to other members.
- □ See even those with different interests and expertise as potential allies rather than as adversaries.
- □ Go out of their way to help one another, because that builds the credits to trade in.
- □ Diagnose the needs of, and take initiative towards, people who won't cooperate, rather than see them as enemies and write them off.
- □ Create win-win results, which lead to a cooperative, trusting environment in which it is easier to make the exchanges needed to get work done through ongoing mutual influence.

Organizations with these characteristics will have the ability to compete in the tougher environment all will face, and will be exciting places to work. Everyone will be able to take initiative and mobilize action; sell their ideas and respond in kind to the good ideas of colleagues; have their justified organizational needs met while meeting others' needs.

You can do your share to make your organization effective, and in the process help yourself, if you accept that there is no escaping exchange, and put your energy into doing it well on behalf of your department and overall organization. You can help replace the crutch of authority with the engine of influence.

It should be abundantly clear by now that we believe in giving your associates the benefit of the doubt, in acting honorably, and in keeping your actions aimed at helping the organization succeed. In the long run, not only is that strategy ethical and satisfying, but it also happens to be the most effective. You don't have to be a naïve sucker who gives away the store by knuckling under to those who won't give you an even break; but cynical, preemptive attempts to compete at the expense of your allies is poor strategy. It hurts you and the organization.

As the wonderful president of Versatec, Renn Zaphiro-polous, says to his new employees, "May you get just what you deserve." We wish you abundant alliances, rewarding reciprocity, ever-profitable exchanges—and increasing influence.

Notes

Chapter 1   Influence and the New World of Work

Page

1   Every enterprise is composed . . .
Peter Drucker has been a remarkable predictor of management
trends for many years; this quote is from "Management and the
World's Work," *Harvard Business Review*, Sept.-Oct., 1988.

Rosabeth Moss Kanter's work has been a central influence on
our thinking. She looks at broad issues in illuminating ways;
much of our book brings a close-up lens to her research. The
quote is from her latest book, *When Giants Learn to Dance: Mastering the Challenges of Strategy, Management, and Careers in the
1990s*, Simon & Schuster, New York, 1989.

2   Following are several "snapshots" . . .
Because the nature of influence as a subject is sensitive, and effective influencers do not always want to reveal their approaches
to colleagues, we have had to disguise most individual and company names throughout the book. Often we have also disguised
the industry, attempting to preserve the essential characteristics
while concealing identity. Many of the issues discussed are so universal that readers may be certain they know who we are talking
about when there is no actual connection. Any overlap with names
of real people or companies, except where there is no disguise, is
inadvertent and accidental.

7   Jack Welch . . .
Quote from *General Electric Annual Report*, 1988. See also "Inside
The Mind Of Jack Welch," Stratford P. Sherman, *Fortune*, March 27,
1989, for more on Welch's concerns about the "white knuckle
decade" ahead.

The impact of technological change . . .
Some of the sources for the realization that speed is vital are:
"How Managers Can Succeed Through SPEED," Brian Dumaine,
Fortune, Feb. 13, 1989; "The Winning Organization," Jeremy Main,
Fortune, Sept. 26, 1988; "Is Your Company TOO BIG?" *Business-*

Week, March 27, 1989; Tom Peters, "Tomorrow's Companies: New Products, New Markets, New Competition, New Thinking," *The Economist*, March 4, 1989.

8   In response to these . . .
The information on Hewlett-Packard's goals for product development speed-up comes from *Fortune*, Feb. 13, 1989.

At Northrup . . .
The information on the B-2 and the quote about early involvement of manufacturing people by Jeffrey Mirisch, Manager of CAD/CAM development, is from "Smart Factories: America's Turn," *BusinessWeek*, May 8, 1989.

9   As management consultant . . .
Barry Stein is President of Goodmeasure, Inc., a Boston-based consulting firm. He wrote about the mean time between surprises in a Goodmeasure client newsletter in 1984.

10   recent *Fortune* survey . . .
The survey of CEOs was reported in "And You Thought You Had It Tough," Carrie Gottlieb, *Fortune*, April 25, 1988.
The forces of change . . . Rosabeth Moss Kanter, in *When Giants Learn to Dance*, uses four F's to summarize organizational requirements, but she uses "friendly" instead of "fit." We also believe that organizations need to be friendly to their customers, but given the focus of our book, "fit" was a better fit.

11   As we demonstrated . . .
Managing for Excellence: The Guide to Developing High Performance in Contemporary Organizations, David L. Bradford and Allan R. Cohen, Wiley, New York, 1984.

IBM, for example, . . .
"IBM's Customers Know About Problems Akers Is Dealing With in Reorganization," Michael W. Miller, *The Wall Street Journal*, Feb. 1, 1988. "Akers's Drive to Mend IBM Is Shaking Up Its Vaunted Traditions," Michael W. Miller and Paul B. Carroll, *The Wall Street Journal*, Nov. 11, 1988.

12   Even apparently traditionally . . .
One of the first people to identify this phenomenon was Raymond E. Miles. See his recent article, "Adapting to Technology and Competition: A New Industrial Relations System for the 21st Century, *California Management Review*, Winter, 1989. See also Robert Eccles and Dwight Crane, "Managing through Networks in Investment Banking, *California Management Review*, Fall, 1987, and "The Ad-hocracy," by Henry Mintzberg, in James Brian Quinn, et al., (eds.) *The Strategy Process*, Prentice-Hall, Englewood Cliffs, NJ, 1988.

The Power of Information . . .
See Lynda M. Applegate, James I. Cash, Jr., and D. Quinn Mills, "Information Technology and Tomorrow's Manager," *Harvard Business Review*, Nov.-Dec., 1988.

with direct access to . . .
From a speech at Babson College Founder's Day, April 11, 1989, by Patrick McGovern, Chairman, International Data Group.

13   Tougher Customers . . .
See for example, "Consumers: A Tough Sell," Christopher Knowlton, *Fortune*, Sept. 26, 1988.

The Shrinking Middle . . .
For example, Miles (see previous note) reports 600,000 mid and upper managers lost jobs from 1984 to 1986.

17   Strategic Alliances . . .
There has been a wave of attention to alliances as a way to multiply resources and flexibility. For example, "Strategic Alliances," *Fortune*, Oct. 3, 1988; Car makers have agreed to nearly 300 joint deals, in *Newsweek*, "Driving Toward a World Car?" May 1, 1989.

alliances growing 20 percent per year . . .
Jeremy Main, "The Winning Organization," *Fortune*, Sept. 26, 1988.

According to a study . . .
Gary Hamel, Yves Doz, and C.K. Prahalad, "Collaborate with Your Competitors—And Win," *Harvard Business Review*, Jan.–Feb., 1989.

19   Although there are no guarantees . . .
Alliances break apart when either or both parties decide that they no longer have sufficient mutual interests to sustain the relationship. See, for recent examples: "Divorce, Wall Street Style," Alison Leigh Cowan, *New York Times*, Jan. 22, 1989 (buyout firm breaks up because partners clash); "Shearson Drops Myerson & Kuhn In Dispute Over Billing Practices," Laurie P. Cohen, *The Wall Street Journal*, April 12, 1989 (abused retainer relationship); and, "Ego Clash: Calvin Klein vs. Bob Taylor," Francine Schwadel, *The Wall Street Journal*, April 12, 1989 (Chairman of Minnetonka wants to start over without Klein, whose cosmetics company was purchased in 1980).

Your Boss as a Partner . . .
A report on some companies' desires to avoid using terms that imply inferiority appeared in "When Are Employees Not Employees? When They're Associates, Stakeholders . . . " by Jolie Solomon, *The Wall Street Journal*, Nov. 9, 1988.

22   Give and Take: The Process of Exchange . . .
The concept of exchange is central to this book, and will be
given detailed treatment in subsequent chapters. Some of the
literature on which we draw: George C. Homans, "Social Behavior
as Exchange," *American Journal of Sociology,* 1958, p. 63; Peter M.
Blau, *Exchange and Power in Social Life,* Wiley, 1964; Peter M. Blau,
Bureaucracy in Modern Society, Random House, New York, 1956;
Peter M. Blau, *The Dynamics of Bureaucracy* (2nd ed.), University
of Chicago Press, 1963.

23   Making Alliances Work . . .
In her doctoral research at Harvard University, "Cooperative
Alliances: A Study of Entrepreneurship," 1988, Andrea Larson
looked at successful alliances between smaller companies and
found that they functioned much like well-developed interpersonal
relationships. As trust developed, companies (not just a few individuals) became more open with each other, sharing information in
anticipation of problems, rather than only communicating what the
contract called for.

Chapter 2   The Law of Reciprocity

26   I have done enough . . .
This inscription from a statue called Mantiklos Apollo was cited
by Janet Tassel in "Mighty Midgets," *Harvard Magazine,* May–June,
1989.

28   The Problem: Ignore the Law of Reciprocity . . .
The article on reciprocity is by Alvin Gouldner, "The Norm
of Reciprocity: A Preliminary Statement," *American Sociological Review,* 25, 1960.

29   A classic study of prison guards . . .
The study is by Gresham M. Sykes, *Society of Captives: A Study
of a Maximum Security Prison,* Atheneum, New York, 1969.

Exchanges . . .
See notes for Chapter 1. Also, a former doctoral student at the
University of New Hampshire, Paul Samuels, got interested in ex-
change and wrote a thoughtful qualifying paper in economics
that was useful to us: "Economics and Equity in Social Exchange,"
Dec. 1979.

31   Compensation for costs . . .
While we were working on the development of our ideas on exchange, Berlew published an excellent piece called "What you can
do when persuasion doesn't work," in *NTL Connections* (A newsletter for alumni of NTL Institute Workshops), April 1986, 3, 1. His
ideas parallel ours and were helpful in clarifying our thinking.

Chapter 3   The Power of Mutual Exchange

60   Persuasion . . .
An excellent summary on the research about persuasiveness can be found in Chapter 8 of Roy J. Lewicki and Joseph A. Litterer, *Negotiation*, Irwin, Homewood, IL, 1985. This is also an excellent source for much of the research on formal negotiations.

62   They are nice to others . . .
Thanks to members of the Babson College Spring '89 MBA Negotiations class for their useful comments on the negative reactions to insincere favors deposited in the "favor bank" in anticipation of creating obligations.

63   The strategy is complicated . . .
This research is reported in J. K. Chadwick-Jones, *Social Exchange Theory: Its Structure and Influence in Social Psychology*, Academic Press, New York, 1976.

Chapter 4   Goods and Services

74   A useful way of conceptualizing . . .
An excellent discussion of the need for managers to establish far-reaching exchange relationships in all directions was written by Robert E. Kaplan, "Trade Routes: The Manager's Network of Relationships," *Organizational Dynamics*, Spring, 1984.

75   The ability to say "yes" . . .
One of the best discussions of power in organizations can be found in Rosabeth Moss Kanter's, *Men and Women of the Corporation,* Basic Books, New York, 1977.

82   As Tracy Kidder . . .
His wonderful book about the designing of a computer at Data General is *Soul of a New Machine*, Little-Brown, Boston, 1981.

88   Contacts . . .
In addition to Kaplan's article on trade routes, another research report on the value of widespread contacts is John Kotter's, *The General Managers*, The Free Press, New York, 1982.

90   For example, in a classic study . . .
Peter Blau's wonderful book on how exchange worked in a large organization is *The Dynamics of Bureaucracy* (2nd ed.), University of Chicago Press, 1963.

91   Rosabeth Moss Kanter discovered . . .
Rosabeth Moss Kanter's book on how innovators actually accomplish change within organizations is a major source of ideas for our work. Just one of her many interesting discoveries was that

some managers innovated against the grain of their companies, even when they knew they might be punished for it. *The Change Masters,* Simon & Schuster, New York, 1983.

Chapter 5   Knowing What They Want

104   Dan Stein . . .
The issues involving young engineers desiring influence are contained in a teaching case, "Growth at Stein, Bodello & Associates, Inc.," written under the supervision of Allan R. Cohen, copyright © Babson College, 1983, and reproduced in Cohen, et al., *Effective Behavior in Organizations* (4th ed.), Irwin, Homewood, IL, 1988.

109   Dorothy and Hank . . .
The situation described is from a role play based on a video case that we made with Wilson Learning, Inc. for the training package to accompany *Managing for Excellence.*

112   The Negative Attribution Cycle . . .
We will use our version of attribution theory throughout the book. The theory was reported in H. H. Kelley, *Attribution in Social Interaction,* General Learning Press, Morristown, NJ, 1971, and F. Heider, *The Psychology of Interpersonal Relations,* Wiley, New York, 1958.

113   People interact more with those they like . . .
For an elegant summary of the research in many settings that supports this idea, see George C. Homans, *The Human Group,* 1950, and *Social Behavior: Its Elementary Forms,* 1961, both published by Harcourt Brace Jovanovich, New York.

117   Self-perceptions do not reflect negativity . . .
See Carl Rogers, *On Becoming a Person,* Houghton Mifflin, Boston, 1961.

118   Donald Chiofaro . . .
Quoted in *The Boston Globe,* Oct. 23, 1988, "Has he heard of FAX Machines?"

Chapter 6   You Are More Powerful Than You Think

136   Rosabeth Moss Kanter . . .
See *The Change Masters.*

146   Claude Bebear . . .
Example is taken from "A Clash of Egos Strains a French Marriage," by Thomas Kamm, *The Wall Street Journal,* Nov. 29, 1988.

147   Chris Hammond . . .
Excerpted from a teaching case, Chris Hammond (A) in Allan R. Cohen, et al., *Effective Behavior in Organizations.*

150   Tom Owens . . .
Excerpted with permission from research notes on "Medco," by
the consulting firm Goodmeasure, Inc., 1982. The research was
directed by Rosabeth Moss Kanter for *The Change Masters*.

Chapter 7   Building Effective Relationships

158   Or, as many social scientists have . . .
For a review of the work that led to this counter-intuitive finding, see Peter Warr, "Attitudes, Actions and Motives," (Chapter 11)
in *Psychology at Work*, edited by Peter Warr, Penguin, New York,
1978.

Chapter 8   Exchange Strategies

184   J. Douglas Phillips . . .
Cited in "Companies Try Measuring Cost Savings From New
Types Of Corporate Benefits," by Jolie Solomon, *The Wall Street
Journal*, Dec. 29, 1988.

188   Robert Moses . . .
A fascinating book documenting a myriad of ways that Moses
used his position and skills to achieve influence unethically,
Robert A. Caro's is *The Power Broker*, Knopf, New York, 1974.

       Dale Carnegie . . .
The granddaddy of influence books is *How to Win Friends and
Influence People*, originally published by Simon & Schuster, New
York, 1936. Some of Carnegie's ideas are useful, but implicitly
assume that hearty good cheer can cover up phony interest in
what is important to the other.

193   Rosabeth Moss Kanter . . .
Again, the research referred to is from *The Change Masters*.

211   Experienced negotiators . . .
Although tricky tactics can easily backfire, there are many ne-
gotiators who advise their use in certain situations. See, for
example, *You Can Negotiate Anything*, by Herb Cohen (no relation),
Stuart, New York, 1980, or *Give and Take*, by Chester Karrass,
Crowell, New York, 1974, or any of Gerald Nierenberg's writings.
The strongest advice about being principled can be found in Roger
Fisher and William Ury, *Getting to Yes*, Houghton-Mifflin, Boston,
1981. As mentioned earlier, an excellent resource on negotiations is
the text by Roy Lewicki and Joseph Litterer, *Negotiation*.

212   Erving Goffman . . .
This highly original article by Goffman is, "On Cooling the
Mark Out: Some Aspects of Adapting to Failure," published in
Psychiatry, 1952.

213   Game theorists . . .
This research is reported in Robert Axelrod, *The Evolution of Cooperation*, Basic Books, New York, 1984.

Chapter 10   Becoming a Partner with Your Boss

251   Loyalty pledge . . .
This wonderfully contingent promise to obey when convenient was quoted in *The Economist*, March 11, 1989. Modern employees implicitly pledge just about the same loyalty to their bosses.

261   David Kipnis . . .
His research on the way powerful people take more than their share of credit for success is in *The Powerholders*, University of Chicago Press, 1976.

269   Bob Knowlton case . . .
This evergreen case was written by Alex Bavelas at MIT, and has been reproduced in countless management texts, including Cohen, et al., *Effective Behavior in Organizations*.

Chapter 11   When You Can No Longer Catch Flies with Honey

285   Don Offenbach . . .
This is a case entitled "The Misbranded Goat," written under the supervision of David Bradford, reprinted from *Stanford Business Cases 1983*, with the permission of Stanford University Graduate school of Business. Copyright © 1983 by the Board of Trustees of Leland Stanford Junior University.

289   Donna Dubinsky . . .
The documented instance referred to is in a teaching case series, "Donna Dubinsky and Apple Computer, Inc., (A) and (B)," written by Mary Gentile under the supervision of Todd Jick, Harvard Business School, 1986.

296   *Boston Business Journal* . . .
The sad case of Larry Tseung was reported in an article January 23, 1989.

303   Lyndon Johnson . . .
Johnson's tactics have been widely reported. See especially Robert Caro's book, *The Path to Power: The Years of Lyndon Johnson*, Vol. 1, Knopf, New York, 1982.

305   Renn Zaphiropolous . . .
The quote is taken from a Harvard Business School videotape of a "typical" workday at Versatec; Renn closes a welcoming speech to new employees with it.

Index